IMAGES
of America

KINGSBURY AND HUDSON FALLS

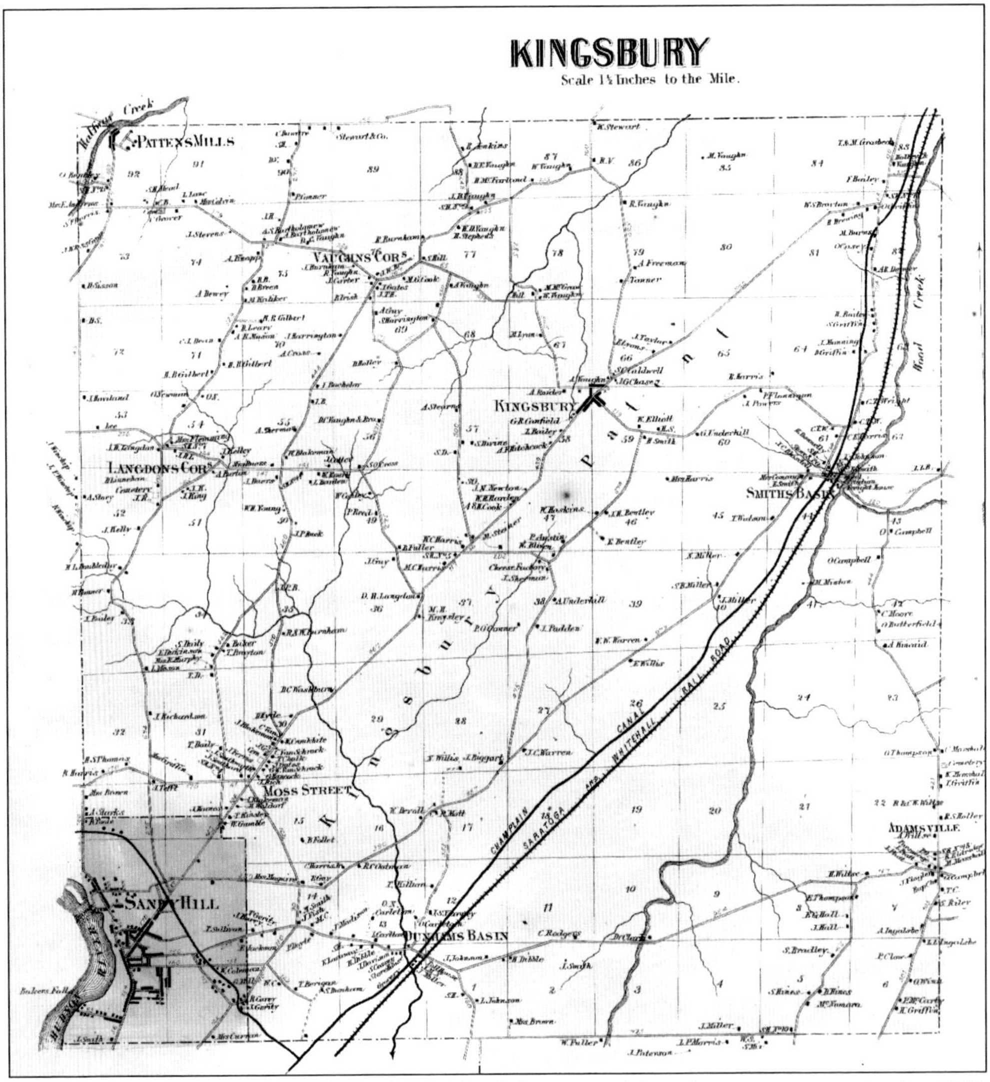

This map of the town of Kingsbury shows all of the original lots that were set out in the 1762 survey of the town. The map is from the *1866 Atlas of Washington County*.

IMAGES
of America

KINGSBURY AND HUDSON FALLS

Paul R. Loding

ARCADIA
PUBLISHING

ISBN 978-0-7385-0534-3

Published by Arcadia Publishing
Charleston, South Carolina

Printed in the United States of America

Library of Congress Catalog Card Number: 2001088818

For all general information contact Arcadia Publishing at:
Telephone 843-853-2070
Fax 843-853-0044
E-mail sales@arcadiapublishing.com
For customer service and orders:
Toll-Free 1-888-313-2665

Visit us on the Internet at www.arcadiapublishing.com

Contents

ACKNOWLEDGMENTS

Kingsbury and Hudson Falls, 200 years in pictures, would not have been possible without the help of many individuals. The people who allowed me to use one or more of their photographs are too numerous to list in the book, but I thank them all. Three individuals, however, each contributed a large number of pictures and offered important information: Mary Brown of Glens Falls offered the Griffin family photographs and some early paintings; Michael LaCross made his collection available and provided information that he had received from the late James Cronkhite; Washington County Historian Joseph Cutshall King allowed the use of early 1870s photographs from Sandy Hill, many of which have never before been seen by the public. The assistance of Kingsbury and Hudson Falls officials was also of great help, in particular that of Town Clerk Holly Mabb and her deputy Sylvia Weaver. In addition, Fort Edward Historian R. Paul McCarty came up with requested information at a moment's notice, and officials at the Feeder Canal Alliance and the New York State Canal Corporation were always helpful.

Finally, there are two men from my past without whom I would not have had the interest or inclination to write this book. One is my high school senior history teacher, who always made a point of stressing to his students how important history is today. The other is my uncle, who told me stories of the history in our backyards, developing my interest at a young age. Therefore, I would like to dedicate this work to my teacher Edward Kelly and my uncle George LaMere.

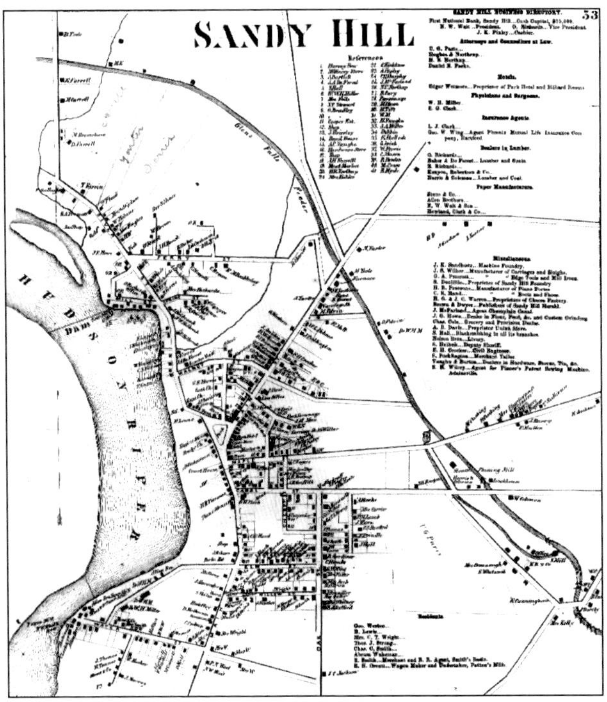

This 1866 map shows the village of Sandy Hill.

INTRODUCTION

In most cases the birth of a community has some important event associated with it. In the case of the town of Kingsbury, it was the start of the last of the French and Indian Wars, in 1755. In early September of that year, a British officer ordered that a road be cut between the Hudson River and Lake George. It was this road that made it possible for speculators to visit here during the next five years.

In 1761, a group of speculators approached the royal government of New York to purchase a township on the upper Hudson. The best location was at the bend of the river where it turns south, where there was a large falls, the largest on the whole river. Under the authority of King George III, a charter was granted for the township of Kingsbury on May 11, 1762. The name of the township came from a small parish on the western outskirts of London, which still exists as a station on the London Underground.

The town of Kingsbury was first surveyed in the autumn of 1762. The first settler, Thomas Bradshaw, arrived in 1763 and built his home in the north central part of the town. He was followed the next year by Albert Baker, who settled near the large falls and built the first mill in town, at the falls. Baker built a small wing dam at the top of the falls to run his sawmill. Today, these falls bear his name, Bakers Falls.

Shortly after Baker arrived in Kingsbury, a second miller settled here. His name was John Jones, and he built his sawmill in the northwestern corner of the town along Halfway Brook. The area around the Jones mill became known as Jones Mill Place. The first reported death of a Kingsbury settler was that of Jones. He died in 1772, leaving his widow and seven sons to run the mill operation.

The community became sharply divided after the outbreak of the Revolutionary War, in 1775. Many inhabitants were Loyalists, including all of the Jones brothers. At one point the Loyalists forced the Whigs to extinguish a celebratory bonfire, lighted to commemorate the Battles of Lexington and Concord. After a year or so, the Loyalists were forced to flee to Canada, leaving their homes, farms, and mills to the ravages of time.

Two major military events took place in Kingsbury during the Revolution. The first was the 1777 invasion by the army of Lt. Gen. John Burgoyne, en route to Saratoga. The second was the October 11, 1780 raid by a small army of 800 British and Loyalists. Led by Maj. Christopher Carleton, the raid of the upper Hudson region was aimed at destroying the bountiful fall harvest. In the process, all of the buildings in town except three owned by Loyalists were burned to the ground.

Following the Revolution the town was rebuilt. Albert Baker and Thomas Bradshaw put up new homes and a new mill. Edward Patten purchased the foreclosed John Jones land, built his first mill, and renamed the settlement Pattens Mills, which it is still called today.

In spring of the 1781, the town of Kingsbury was annexed by the state of Vermont and remained so until the end of the year, when the Vermont General Assembly gave up its claim. In 1782, the state of New York officially organized the town. The first official town meeting was held, and the minutes of that meeting are still in the town records.

The area of town near Bakers Falls was incorporated as the village of Sandy Hill in 1810 by New York State. The name Sandy Hill had been used to identify that section since 1792. In the 1840s, Sandy Hill was enlarged to include everything within the current boundaries of Hudson Falls. In 1910, the village name was changed to Hudson Falls.

Since the founding of Kingsbury in the 1760s, the business of the community has changed a great deal. During the first 20 years, the town had a few small mills, but the main occupation was subsistence farming. During the next 100 years, larger farms and more mills were developed, and logging and several types of mining were added.

Two principle types of mines were developed in Kingsbury: limestone and bluestone. Near the hamlet of Smiths Basin, there was a large lime-producing operation. At a limestone quarry located east of the canal, there were 10 limekilns until about 50 years ago. On the western border of the town next to Warren County, there is a huge bluestone quarry. This quarry yields the building material that is called Kingsbury bluestone or Kingsbury dolomite. This building material was used in the construction of the Saratoga Battle Monument, the Bennington Battle Monument, and part of the Brooklyn Bridge.

Two developments opened Kingsbury up to commerce with the outside world, bringing new growth and prosperity. The Champlain Canal went into operation in 1823, followed 10 years later by the Glens Falls Feeder Canal. Later in the century, the railroad arrived. Both the canal system and the railroad made it possible for local manufacturers to inexpensively bring in raw material and ship out the finished product.

In the 20th century, one major change affecting the community involved schools. In the early 1900s, children attended small one- or two-room schoolhouses, located within a couple of miles walking distance from home. By the 1950s, schools had become centralized and most children took the bus to a large school in or near the village.

The village changed, too, mostly as a result of fire. More than anything else, major fires have altered the way the village looks. Today, along Main Street, eight empty lots remain, the former sites of century-old buildings that were swept away in flames. Most of the structures on the east side of the village park and the west side of Main Street north of the park were built as replacements after fires destroyed the original buildings.

As the 21st century proceeds, the community stands ready for great changes that the future will surely bring. For now the past two centuries are in sight, as *Kingsbury and Hudson Falls*—200 years in pictures—unfolds.

One

Important People and the Falls

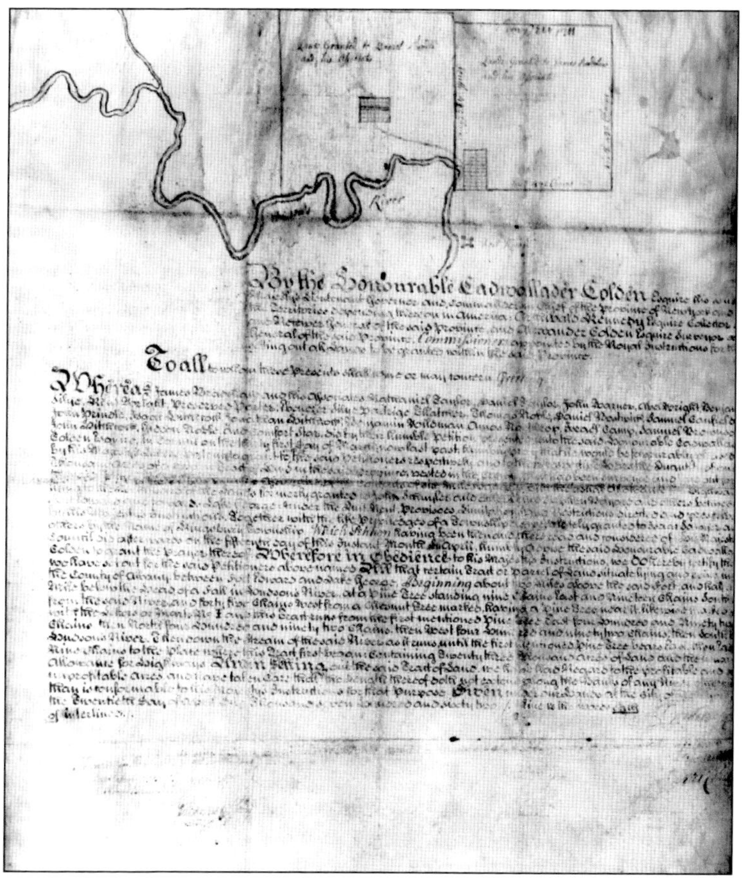

The oldest and most important document owned by the town of Kingsbury is this 1762 deed for the township. It sets out all of the boundaries of the new township. At the top is a map showing Kingsbury, the town of Queensbury, and a very fine drawing of the Hudson River.

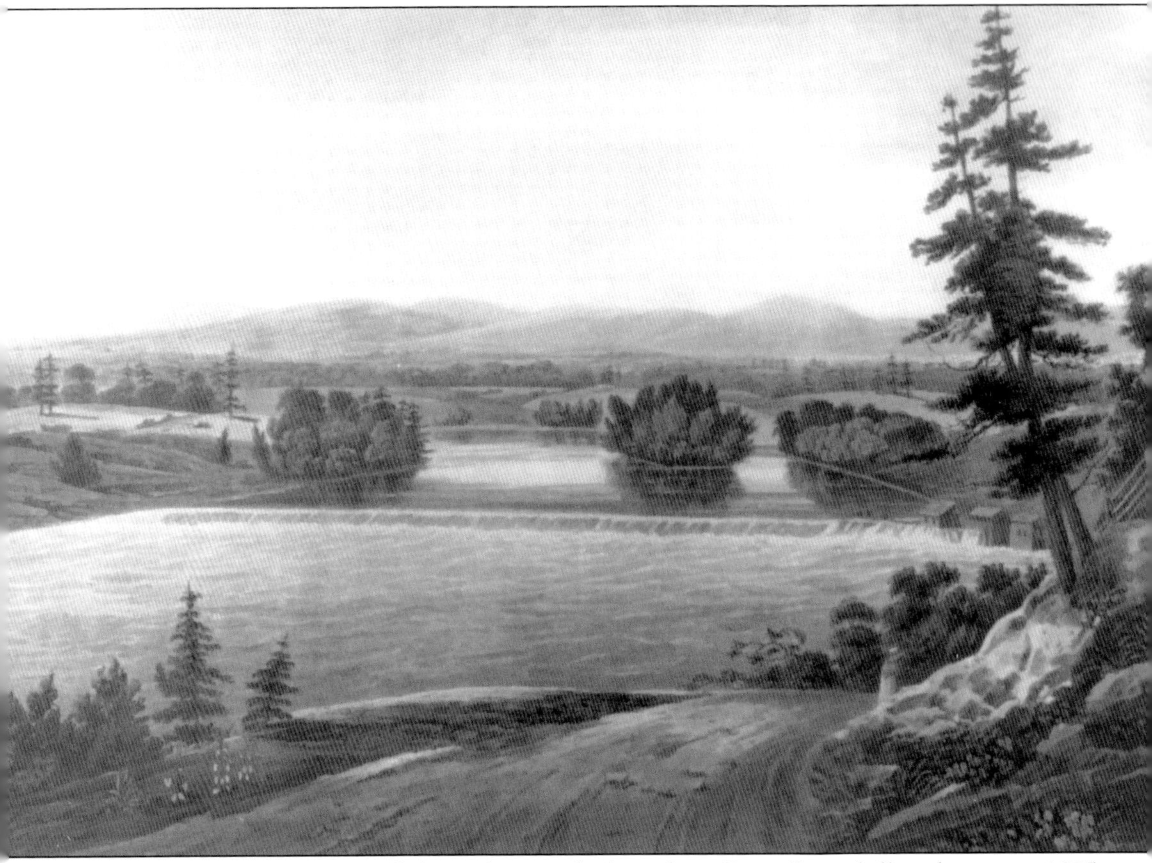

This painting by W.G. Wall shows the view looking down River Street hill to the west c. 1825. Except that there were no buildings then, the scene looks much the same today.

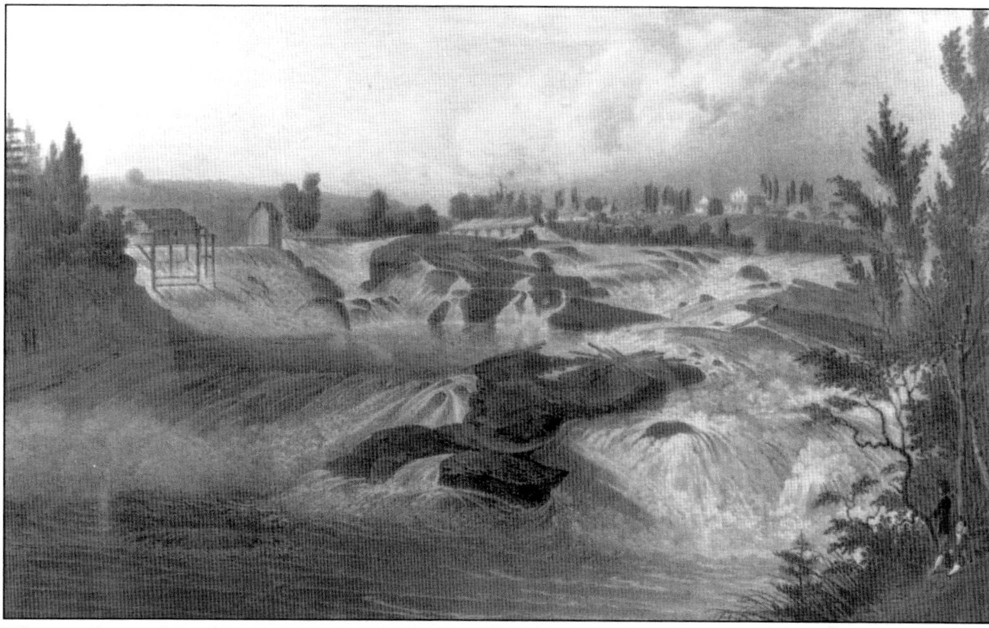

This is the earliest known view of Bakers Falls, dating from c. 1828. Painted by Milbert, it is part of his *Picturesque Views of the Hudson River* series. It shows the first bridge across the Hudson, two mills on the west shore of the river, and a few buildings on top of the hill around the green.

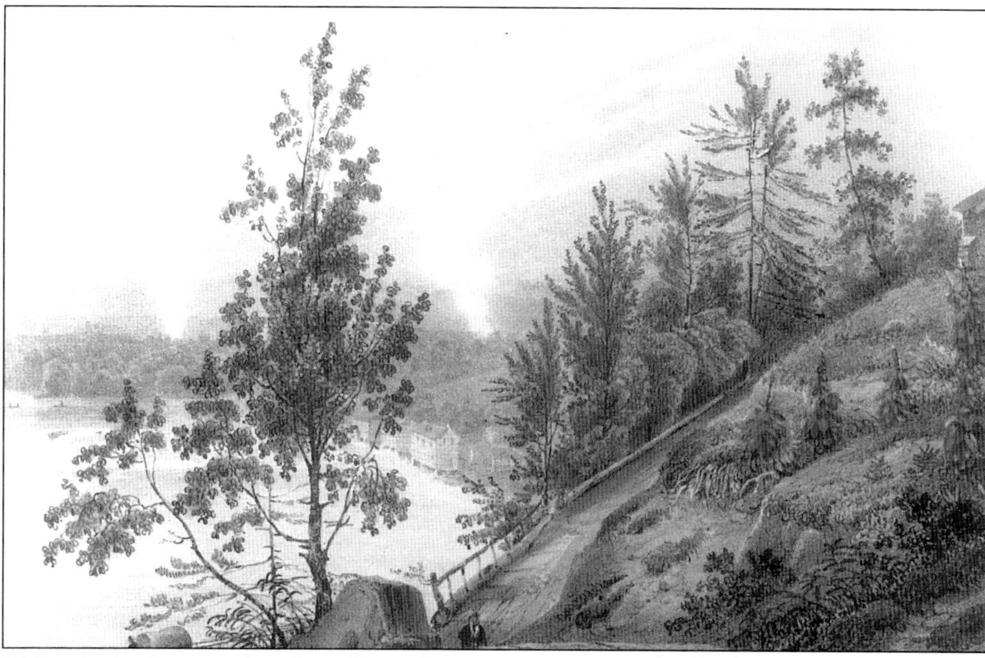

This painting is not a view down River Street, as it appears to be. Rather, it is a view of a road behind the buildings on the west side of the village park. For a short time, the road was used to cross the river on the first bridge, which was built in 1813 by Solomon Parks, who resided on the Saratoga County side of the river. The partially covered bridge stood until a flood destroyed it in 1835. The painting is also one of the Milbert Hudson River series.

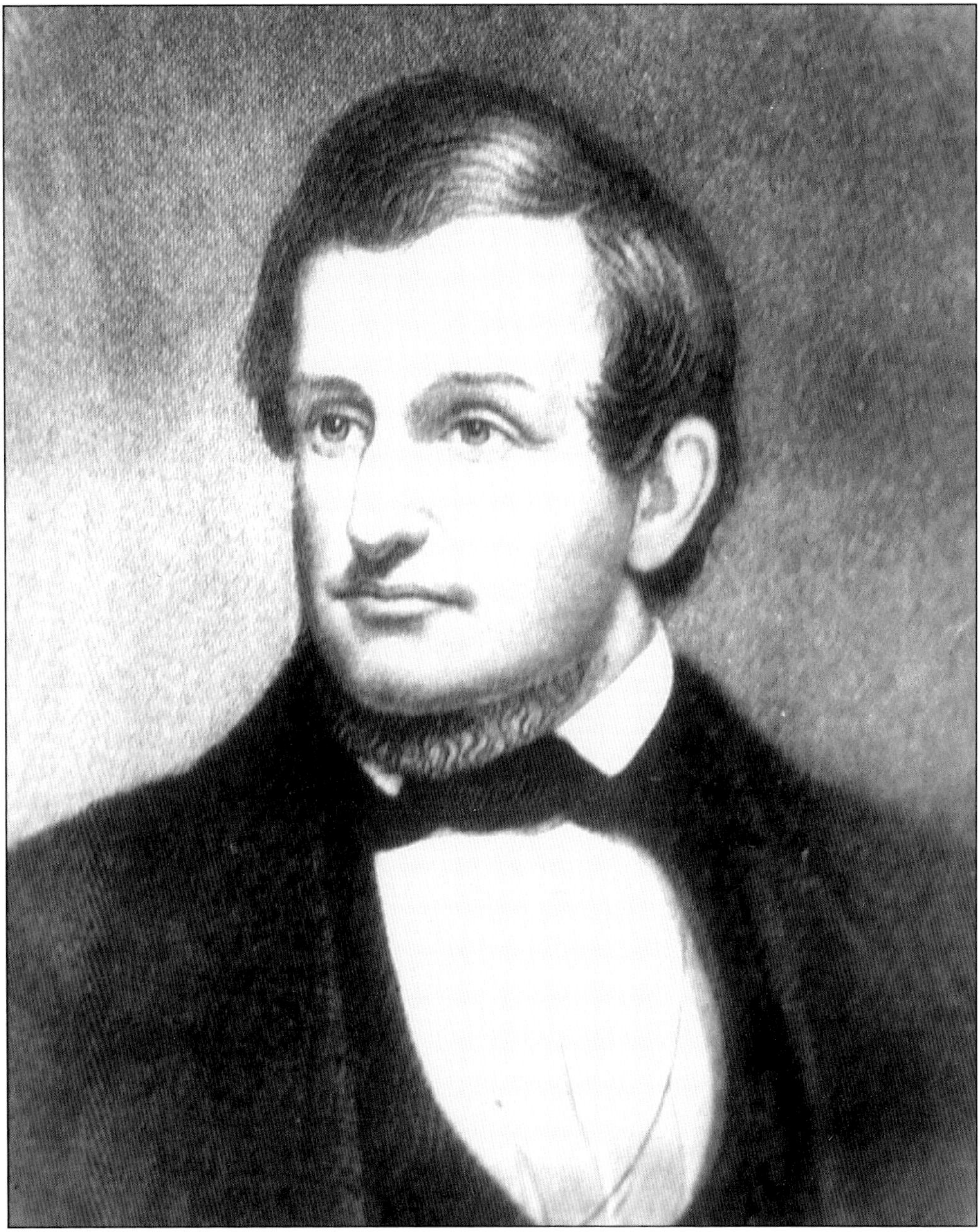

Gov. Nathaniel Pitcher was born in 1777, the year Lt. Gen. John Burgoyne and his army passed through Kingsbury. Pitcher's parents had resided in Kingsbury for several years prior to his birth. As a boy, Pitcher never had any formal education but learned to read, write, and do sums at home and with other children in the neighborhood. As an adult, he read the law and became a lawyer. As such, he soon became politically active. He served as Kingsbury town supervisor, was one of the first members of the Sandy Hill Village Board, and was elected a state assemblyman, senator, and member of Congress for three terms. In the War of 1812, he served as a major general of militia. In 1826, Pitcher was elected lieutenant governor of the state with Dewitt Clinton, whom he succeeded upon the governor's death in January 1828. No person from Kingsbury has ever equaled Pitcher in the number of elective held.

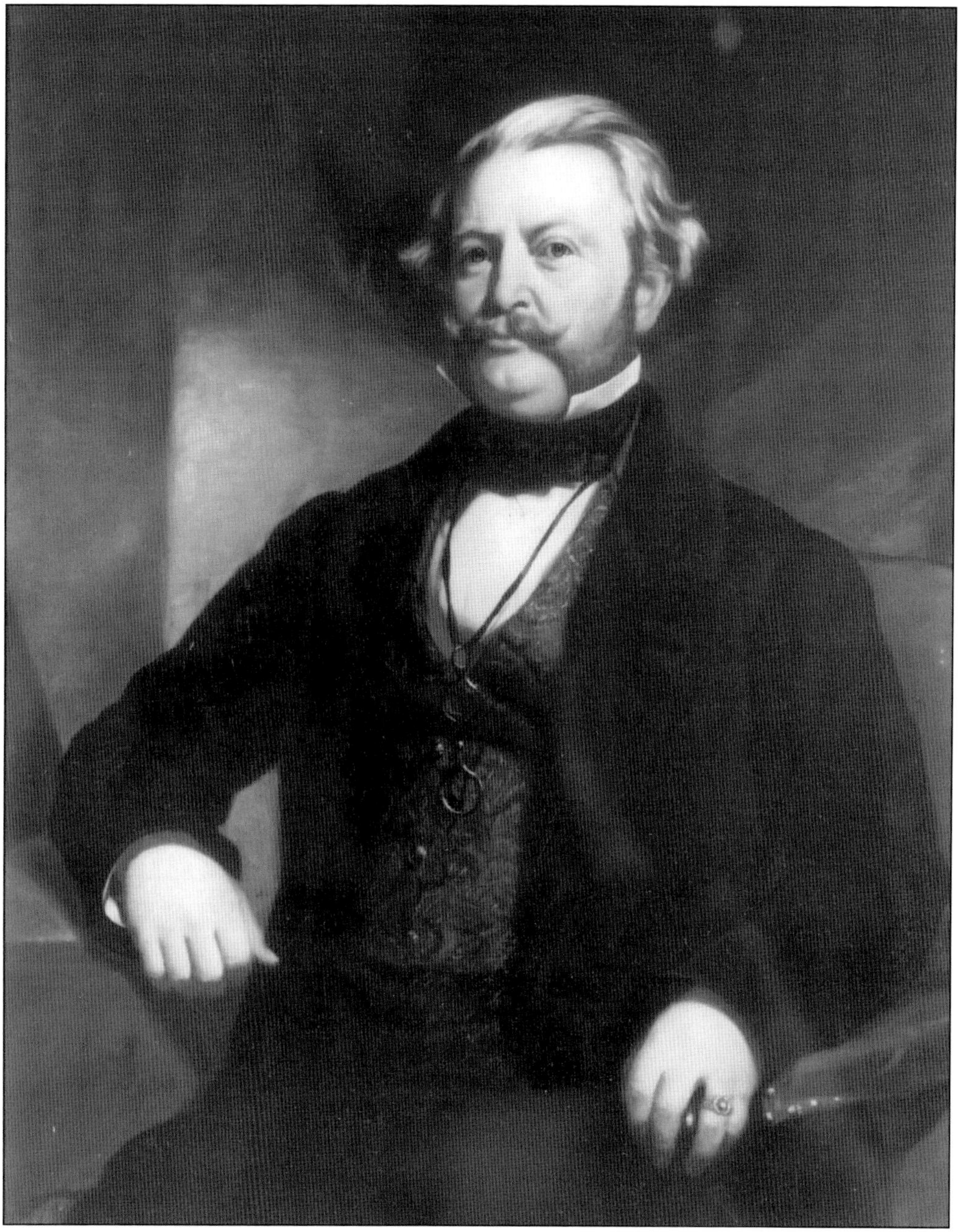

The Honorable Townsend Harris was born in 1803 in a small hat shop on the east side of Main Street, across from the village park. He attended some of the informal neighborhood schools until he reached his mid-teens. Then, his parents sent him to a brother's place in New York City to get a more formal education. Upon graduation from college, he went into the Asian trade business. Due to Harris's experience in Asian matters, Pres. James Buchannan appointed the Kingsbury man first consul general to the Empire of Japan in the mid-1850s. Most historians credit Commo. Matthew Perry for opening trade with Japan. However, all Perry did was to deliver Harris, who then spent years negotiating the first trade agreement, of any nation, with Japan. Harris served until 1863.

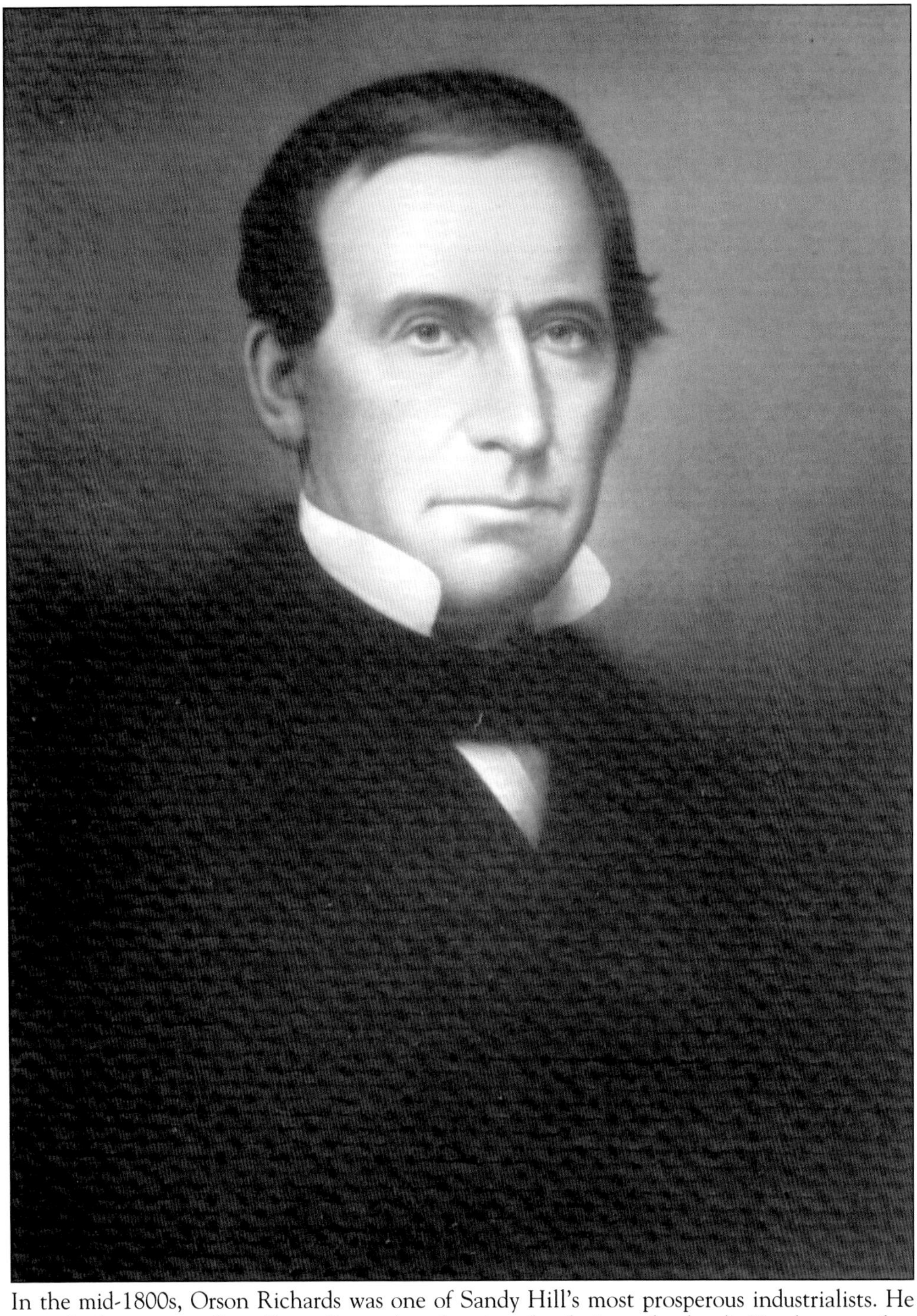

In the mid-1800s, Orson Richards was one of Sandy Hill's most prosperous industrialists. He owned a huge sawmill on River Street (on the site of today's trash plant). He also served as town supervisor from 1862 to 1864. He built a narrow-gauge railway that connected his mill to the Glens Falls Feeder Canal on the top of Melbourne Avenue hill. During the winter months, you can still see evidence of the rail line on the side of the hill in the woods.

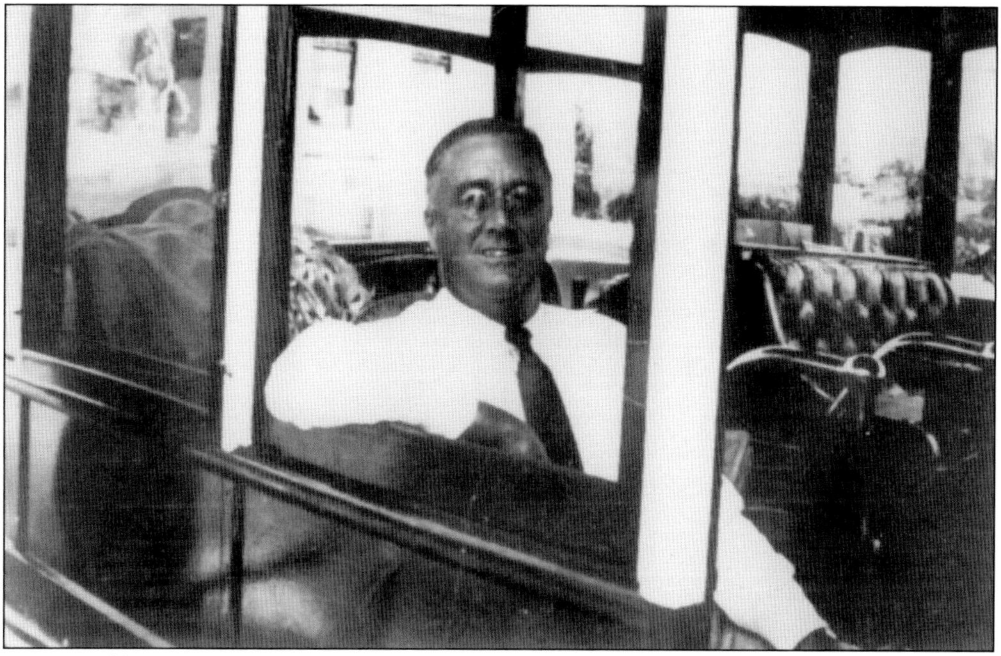

Gov. Franklin D. Roosevelt sits in the governor's yacht at Lock No. 9 in Smiths Basin. He looks young, tanned, and healthy, but in the back of the yacht are his crutches. Photographer Ernie Yasko took this picture in the early 1930s.

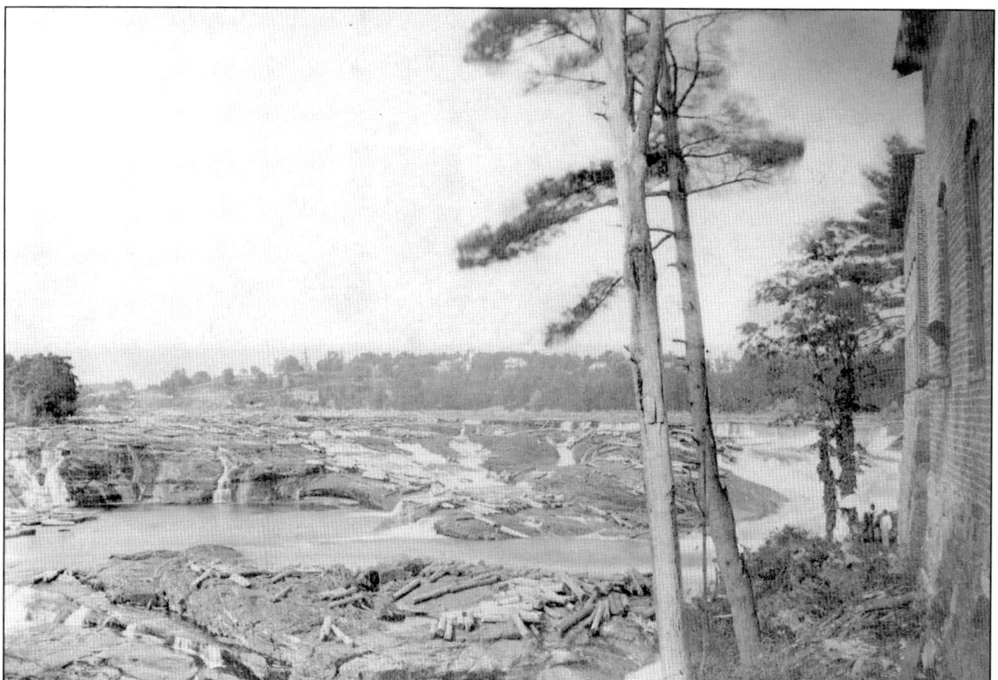

This is one of the earliest photographs (the very earliest that the author has seen) of Bakers Falls. It was taken *c.* 1870, from the area of the mills. Visible in the background are the steeples of the First Baptist Church, on the left, and of the first St. Mary's Church.

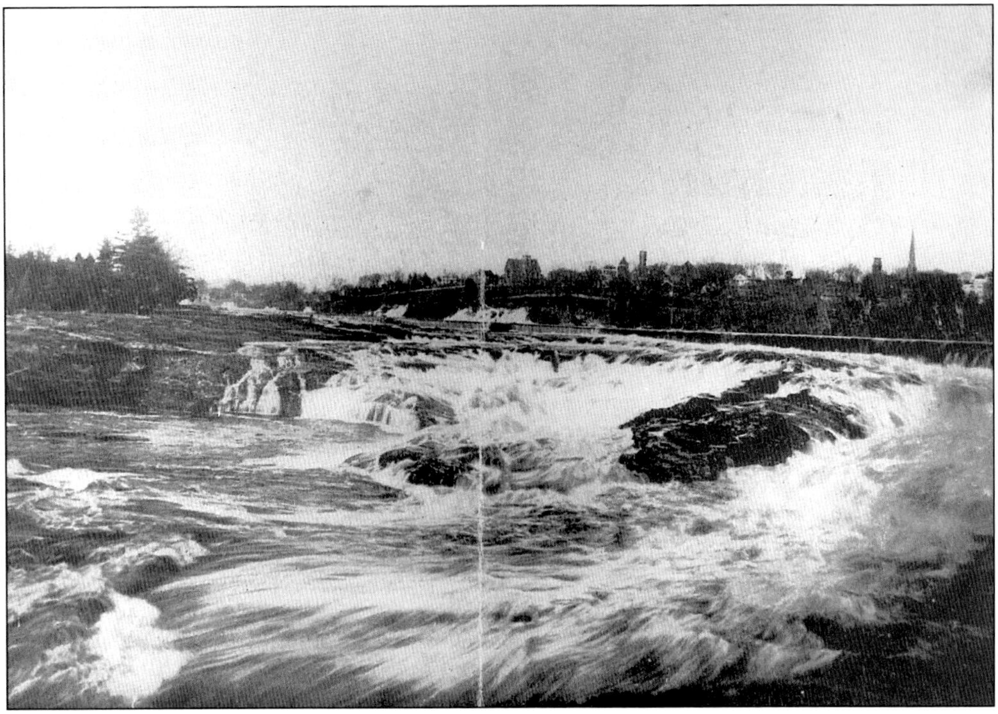

This spectacular photograph of Bakers Falls gives a good indication of how fast the waterfall was. It also shows St. Paul's French Catholic Church—just before the steeple was erected—in the middle, and the steeple of the new First Baptist Church, on the right.

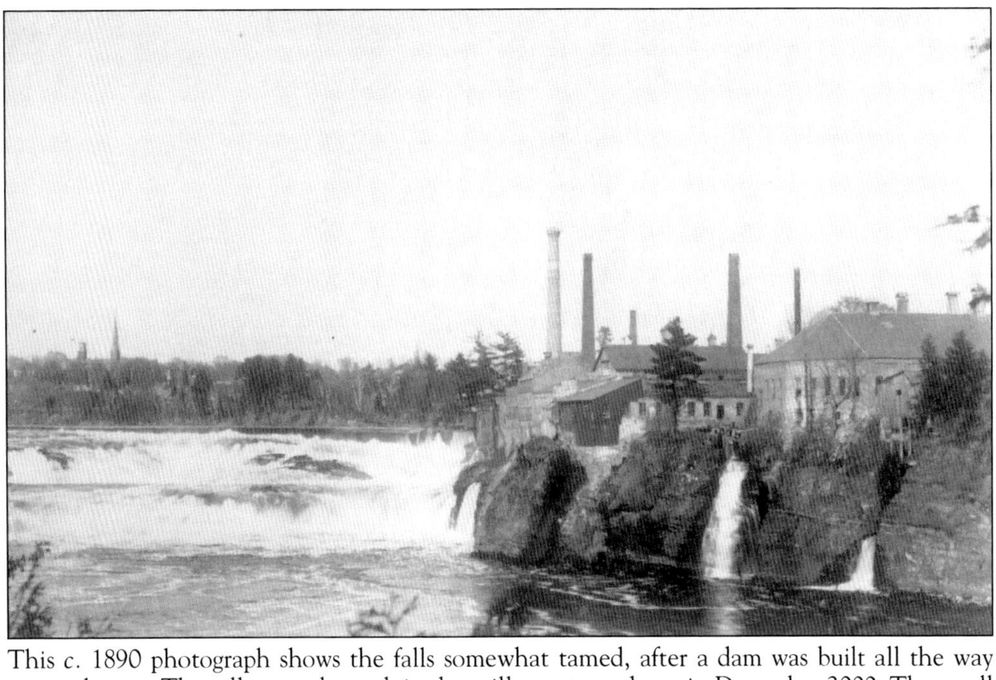

This *c.* 1890 photograph shows the falls somewhat tamed, after a dam was built all the way across the top. The tallest smokestack in the mills was torn down in December 2000. The small tower to the left of the steeple is on the front of the Washington County Courthouse.

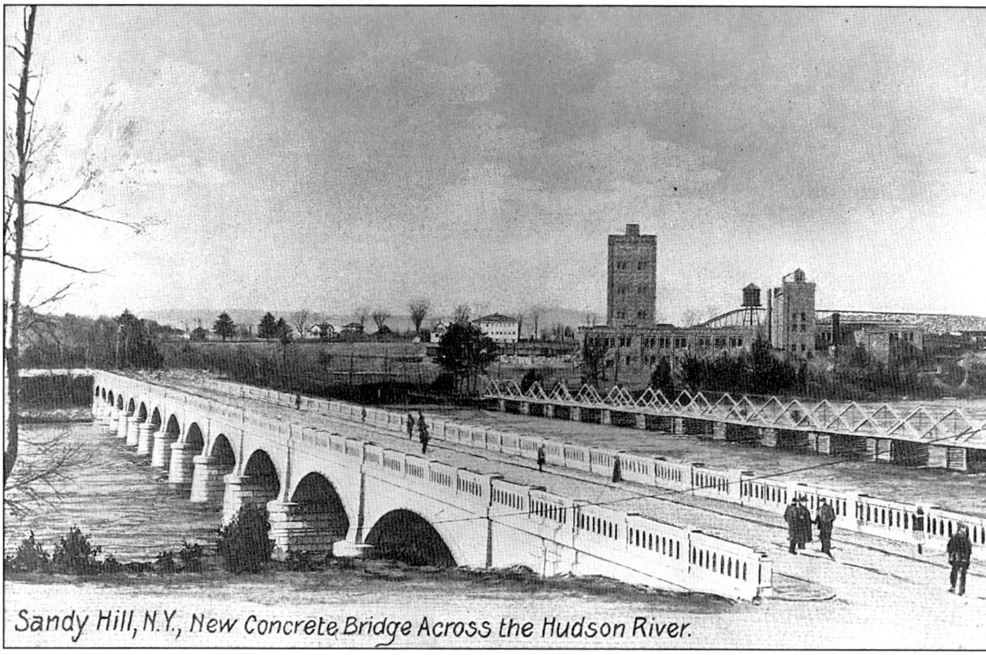

This view was taken looking west across the river in 1905. The large mill is one of the paper mills owned by Union Bag. That company first built the wooden bridge and then paid the entire cost of having the cement Fenimore Bridge constructed. At the time it was finished, the Fenimore Bridge was the largest cement structure in the world.

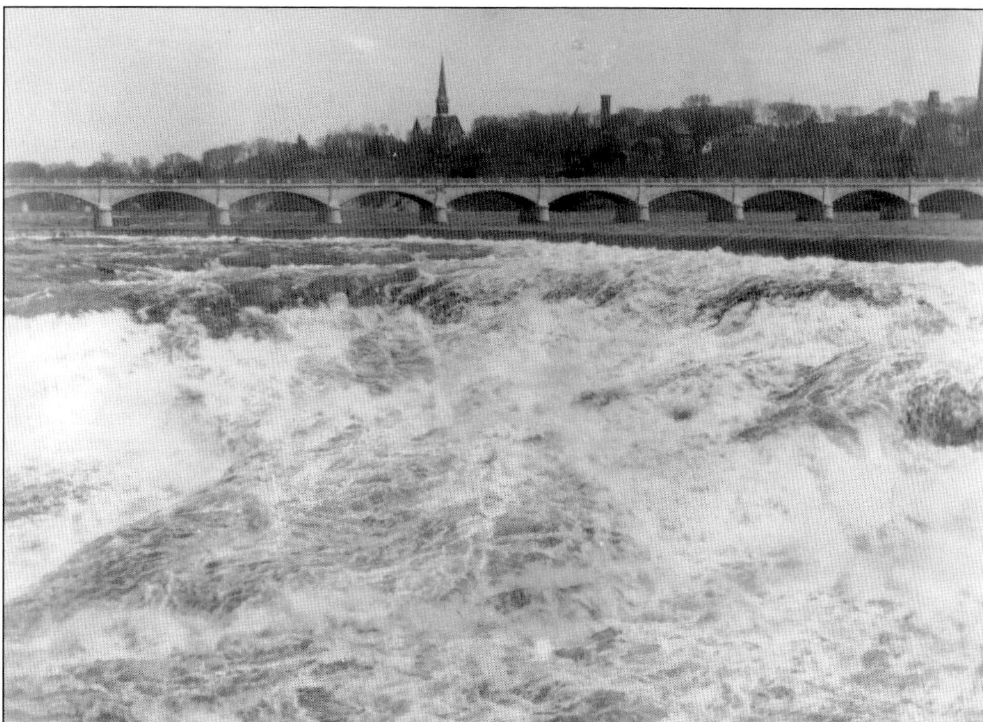

This springtime photograph shows the falls and the Fenimore Bridge.

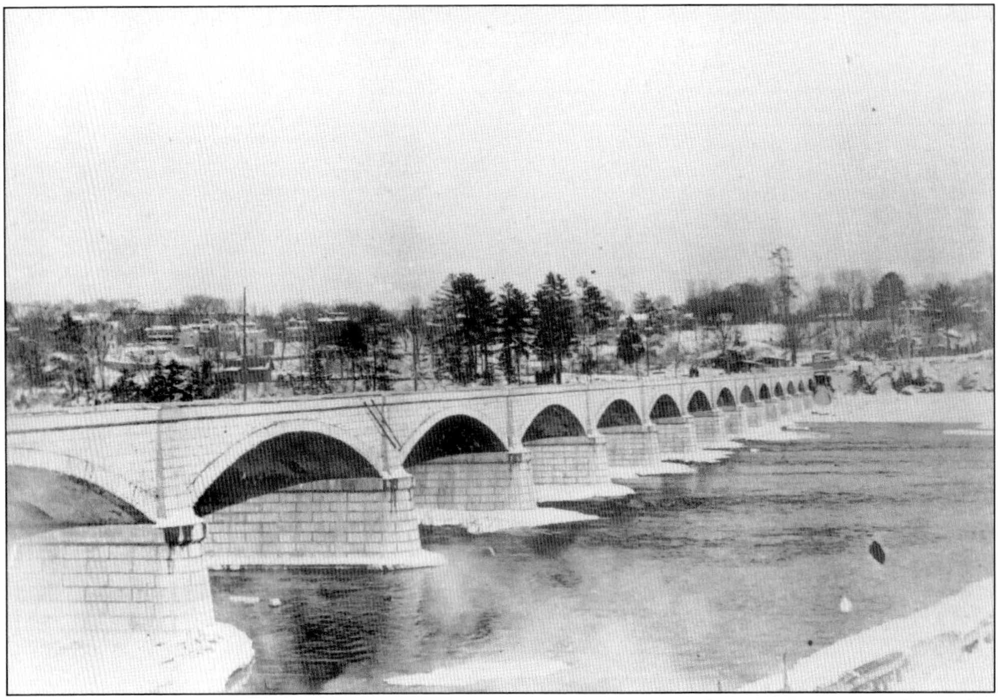

This view of the bridge offers a different perspective. It was taken looking east from the west shore. Behind the pole on the left of the bridge is the Hudson Falls railroad station, on Depot Street.

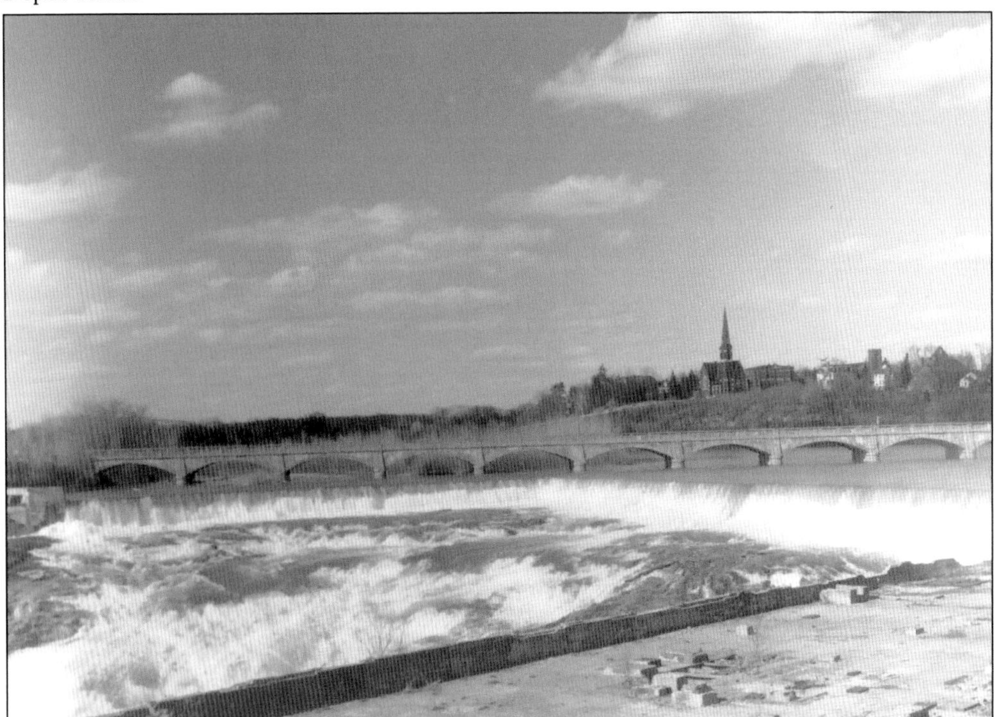

This 1960s view shows Bakers Falls and the Fenimore Bridge.

Two

Churches and Schools

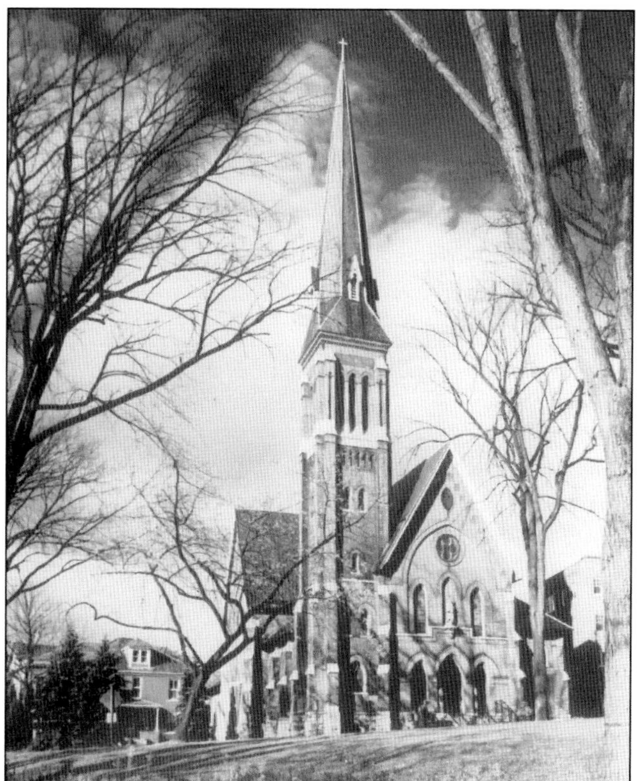

St. Paul's was founded in the 1870s to serve the French Canadian population of Sandy Hill. The group purchased the old Baptist Church, located at the top of River Street hill. Constructed in the 1890s, this beautiful structure was struck by lightning in the 1970s and burned in a spectacular fire.

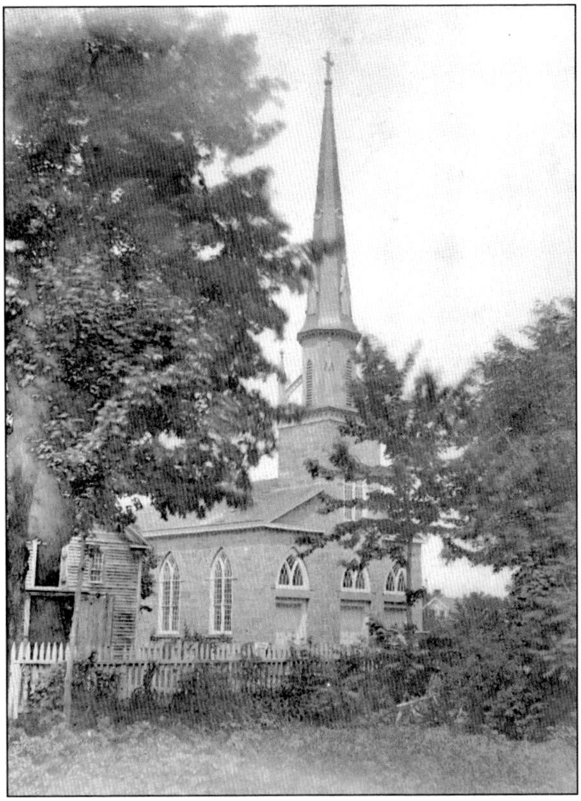

This was the first Roman Catholic church to be built anywhere between Albany and Canada. It was constructed on Wall Street (on the site of the present Catholic rectory) in the late 1830s. At that time it was named Christ Church. It was renamed St. Mary's some 10 ten years later. It was destroyed by fire in the late 1870s or early 1880s.

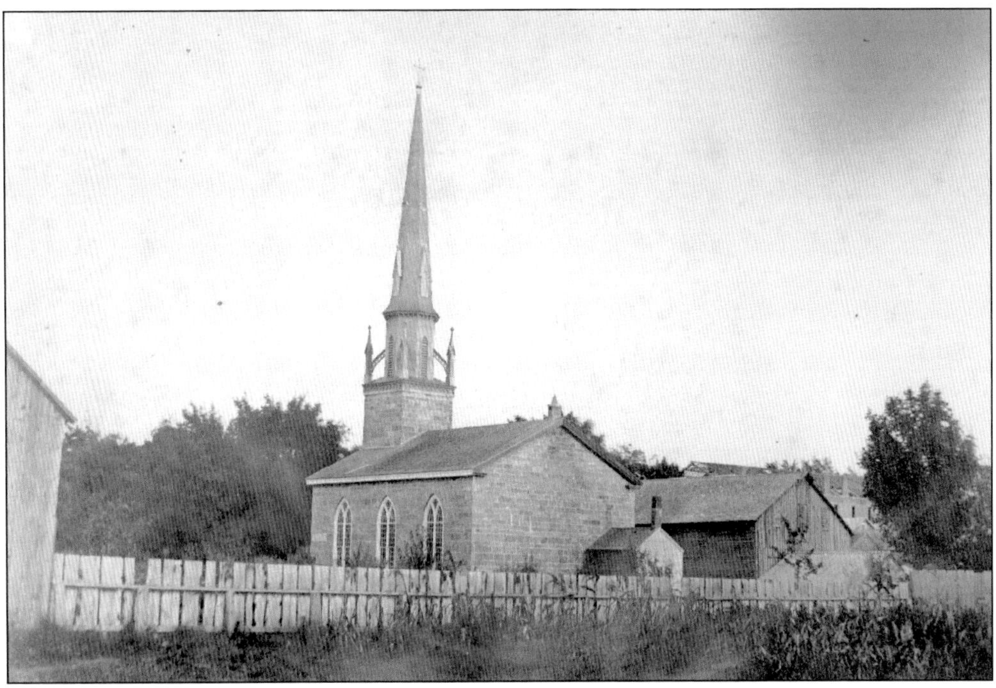

This photograph of St. Mary's Church was taken from the rear *c.* 1870. Notice the decoration at the base of the steeple.

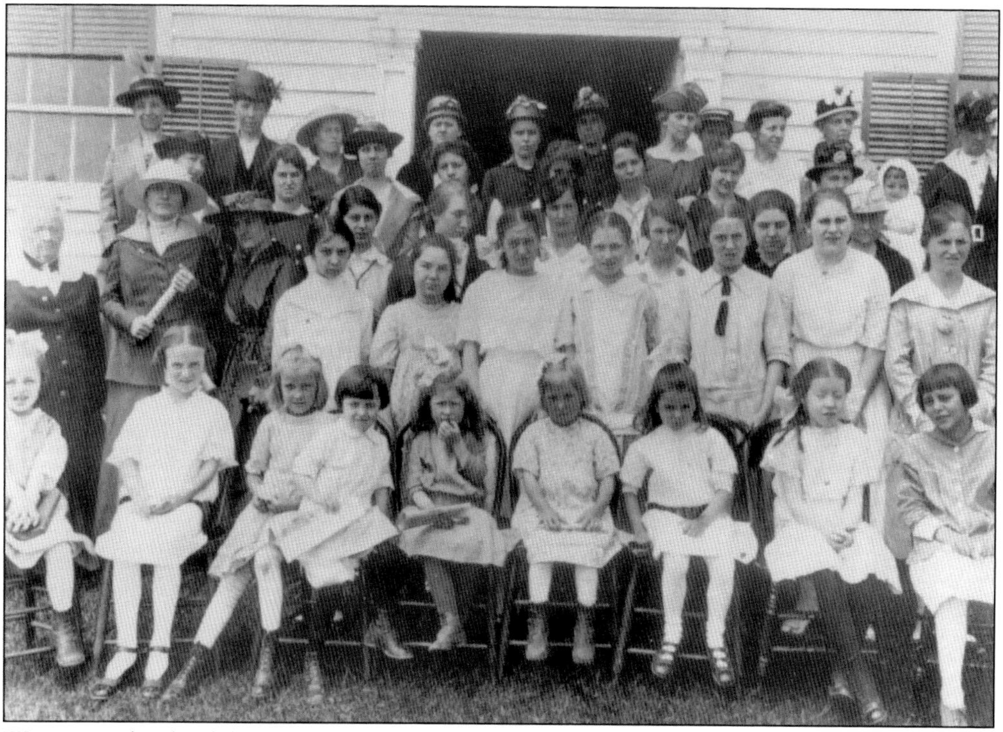

Women and girls of the Sandford's Ridge United Methodist Church attend a gathering *c.* the 1920s or 1930s. The church is on the western border of town next to Queensbury and a couple of miles north of Warren County Airport.

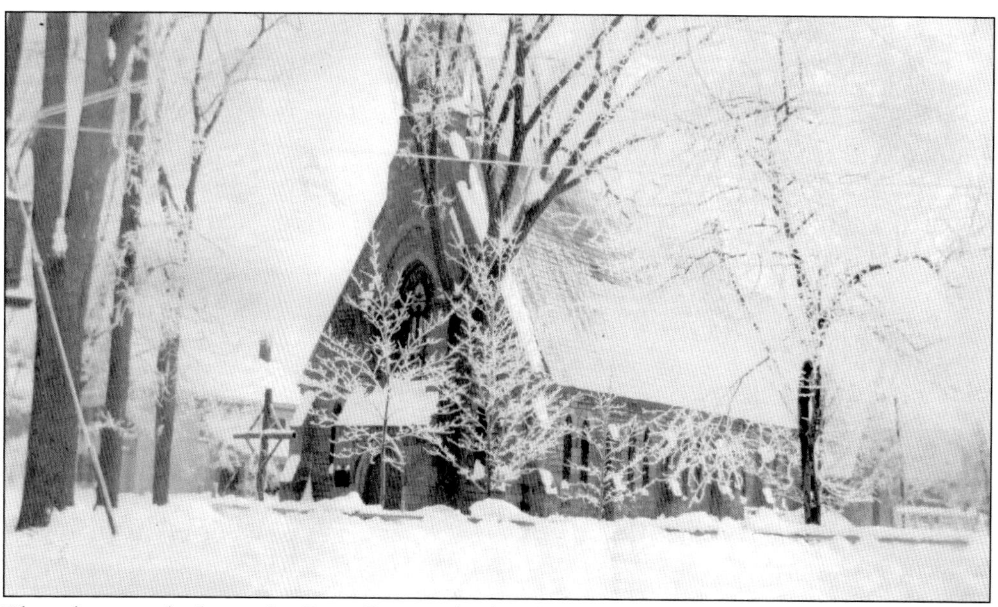

This photograph shows the Zion Episcopal Church, on Main Street, after the snowstorm of February 14, 1914.

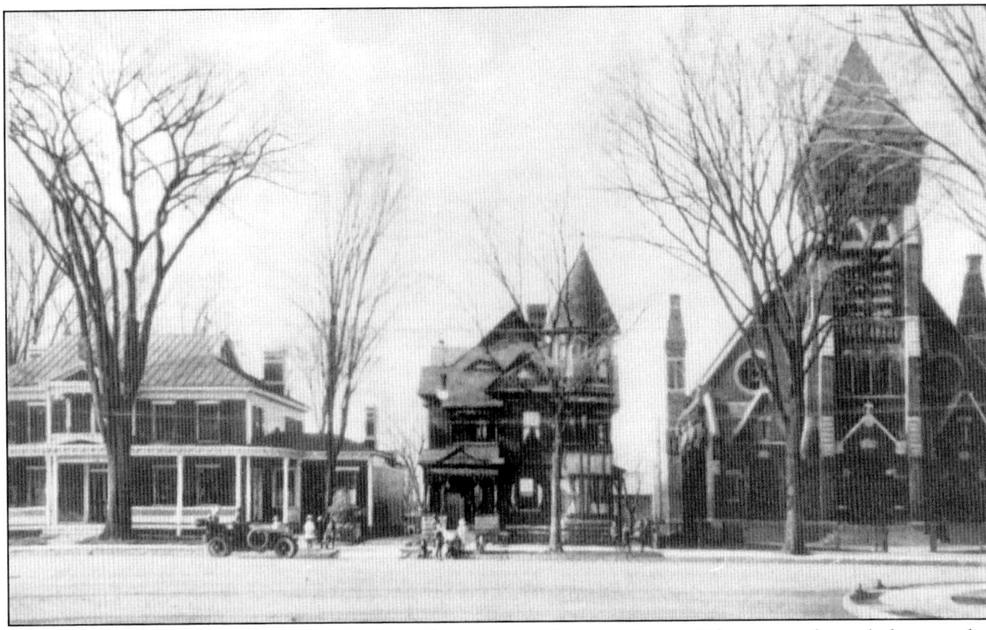

These buildings were all on Park Place but are no longer there. They are, from left to right, the home of the Gov. Nathaniel Pitcher, the rectory of St. Mary's Church, and the second St. Mary's Church, which was built following the fire that destroyed the one on Wall Street.

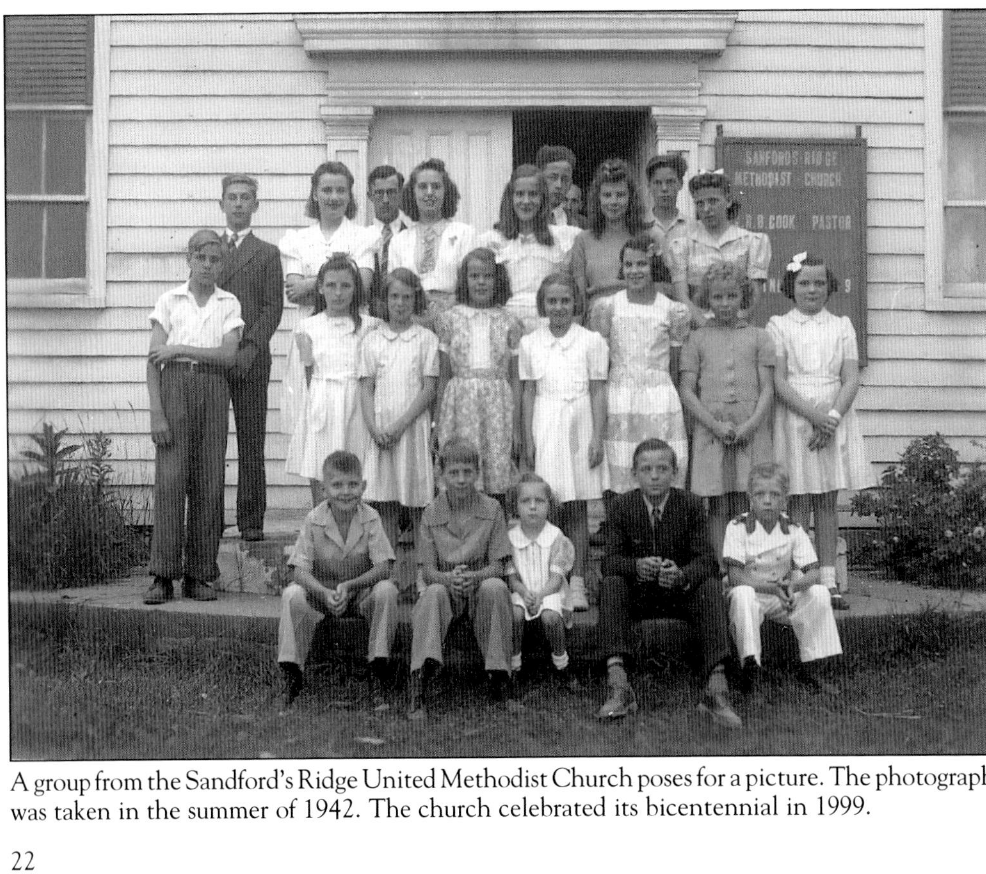

A group from the Sandford's Ridge United Methodist Church poses for a picture. The photograph was taken in the summer of 1942. The church celebrated its bicentennial in 1999.

To the right of the courthouse is the second building that the First Baptist Church used. This second church was built in the 1870s to replace a smaller one, which was sold to St. Paul's Church. The tall steeple was lost many years ago, and the trees are gone now, too.

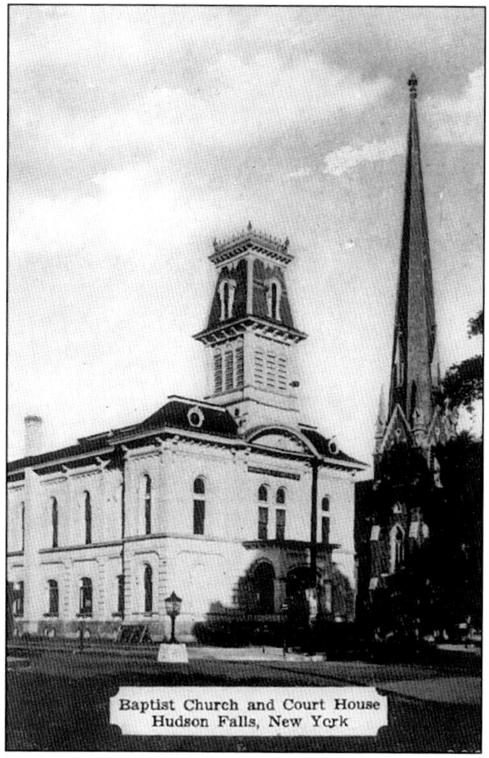

Baptist Church and Court House
Hudson Falls, New York

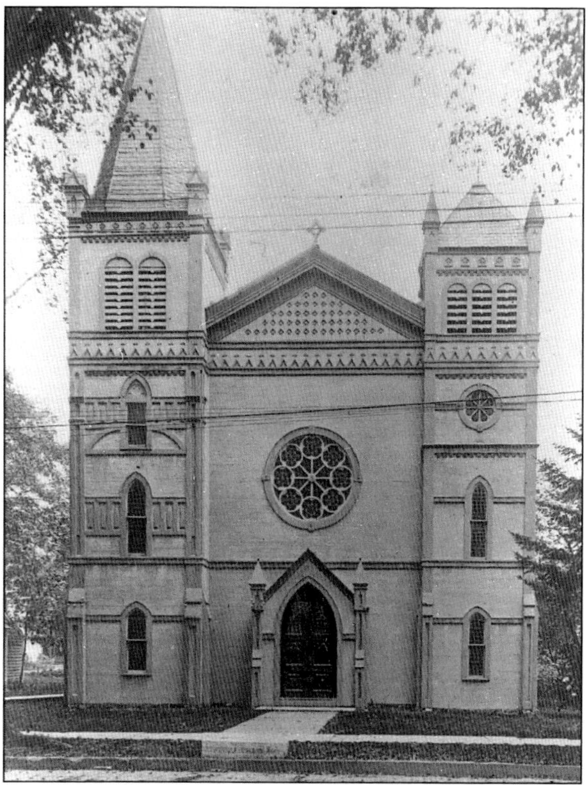

This Hudson Falls United Methodist Church dates from the mid-1800s. Located on Main Street across from the village hall, it was replaced in the 1920s by the present church.

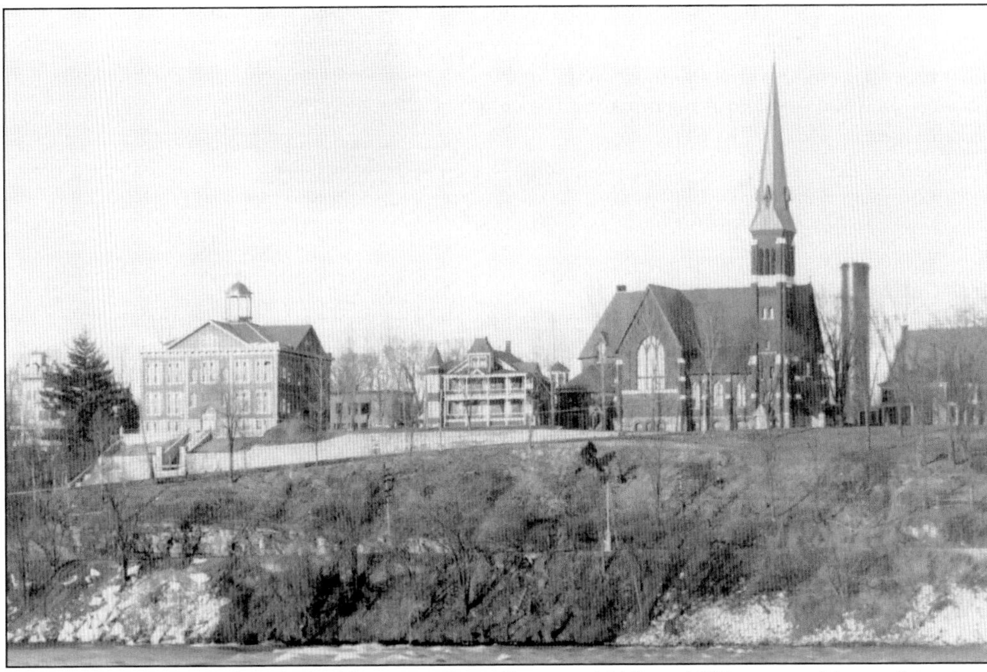

All of the Catholic church buildings in the village *c.* 1915 to 1920 are visible in this view, taken from the west side of the Hudson River. The structures, from left to right, are St. Paul's School and Convent and Rectory and Church, the Wall Street water tower, and St. Mary's Rectory and Church. All except the buildings that housed St. Paul's School and Rectory are gone, and those two are now owned by Washington County Head Start.

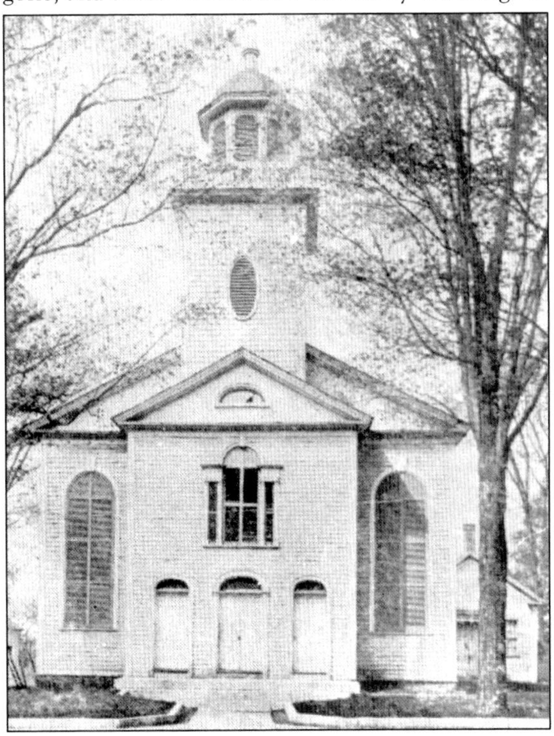

This church has undergone many changes since the time that this photograph was taken. It began as an Advent Christian church and went through several other hands over the years before becoming an Evangelical church, which it is today. It is located at the corner of Main and Willow Streets.

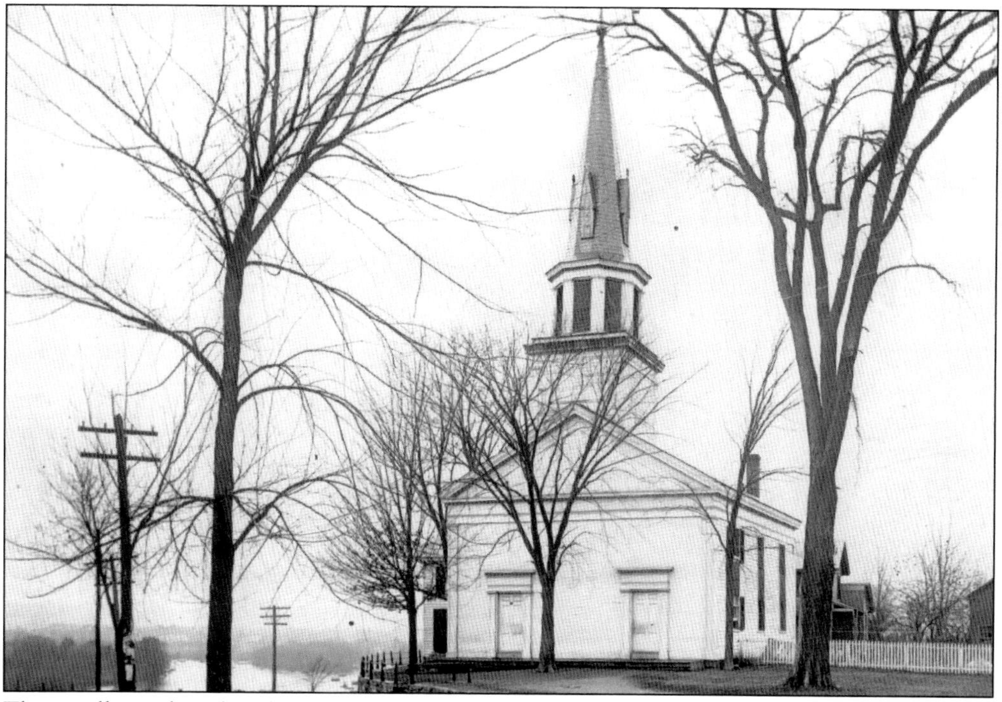

This small wooden church was built by the Baptists, sold to St. Paul's, and torn down to make way for the brick St. Paul's that burned in the 1970s.

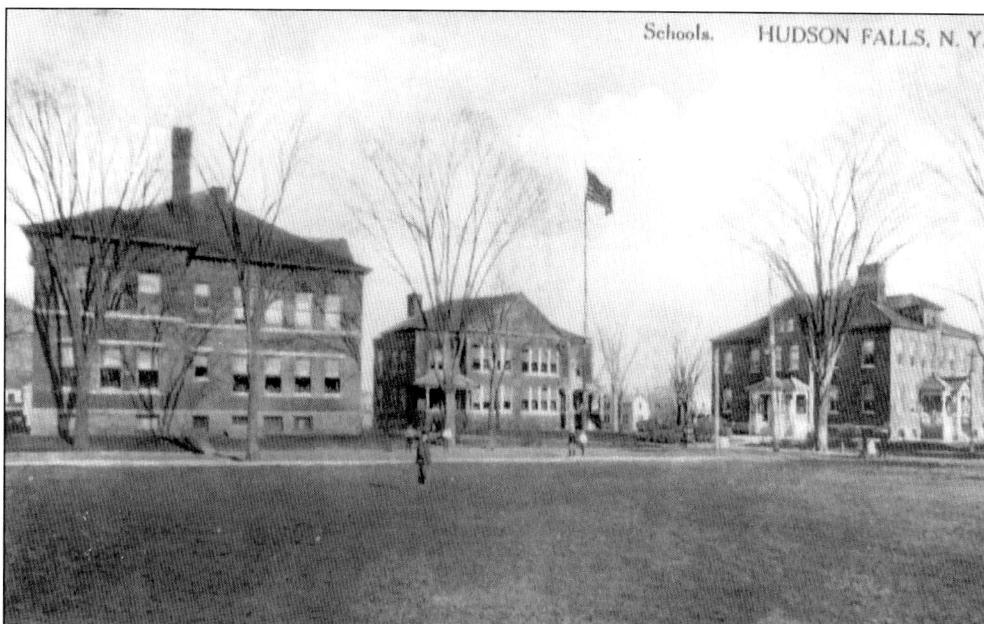

In the 1920s, the campus of the Hudson Falls schools was located where the kindergarten is located today, on the east side of Paris Park. These buildings housed the high school, grade school, and industrial arts classes. They were gradually replaced during several decades from the late 1920s into the 1960s.

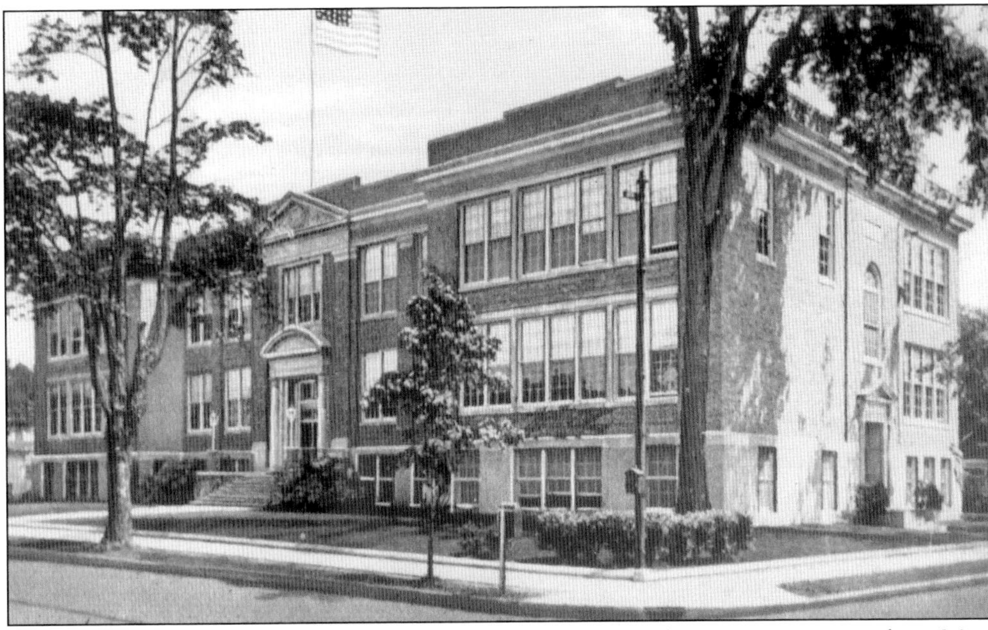

This high school building replaced the first one at Paris Park. It was constructed on Main Street, between Hudson Place and Mechanic Street, taking half of the whole block. The high school remained here until the present school on East LaBarge Street opened in the fall of 1955. This building then became the junior high school. Later, it was replaced by a chain drugstore.

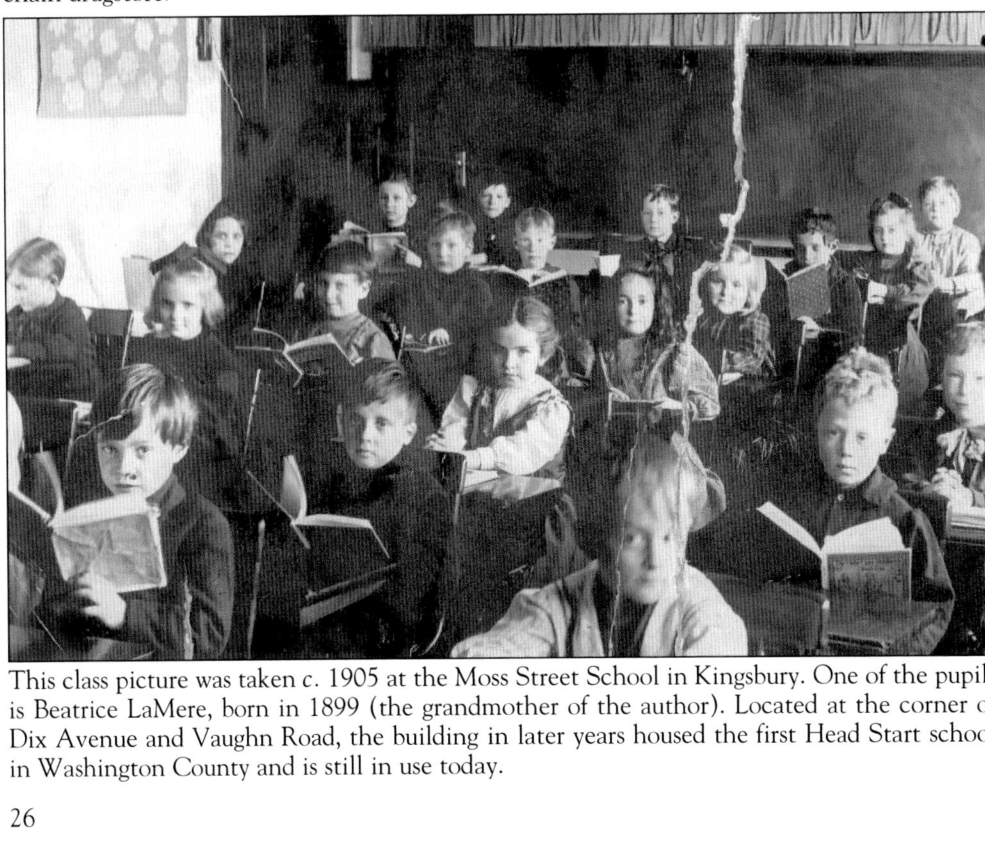

This class picture was taken *c.* 1905 at the Moss Street School in Kingsbury. One of the pupils is Beatrice LaMere, born in 1899 (the grandmother of the author). Located at the corner of Dix Avenue and Vaughn Road, the building in later years housed the first Head Start school in Washington County and is still in use today.

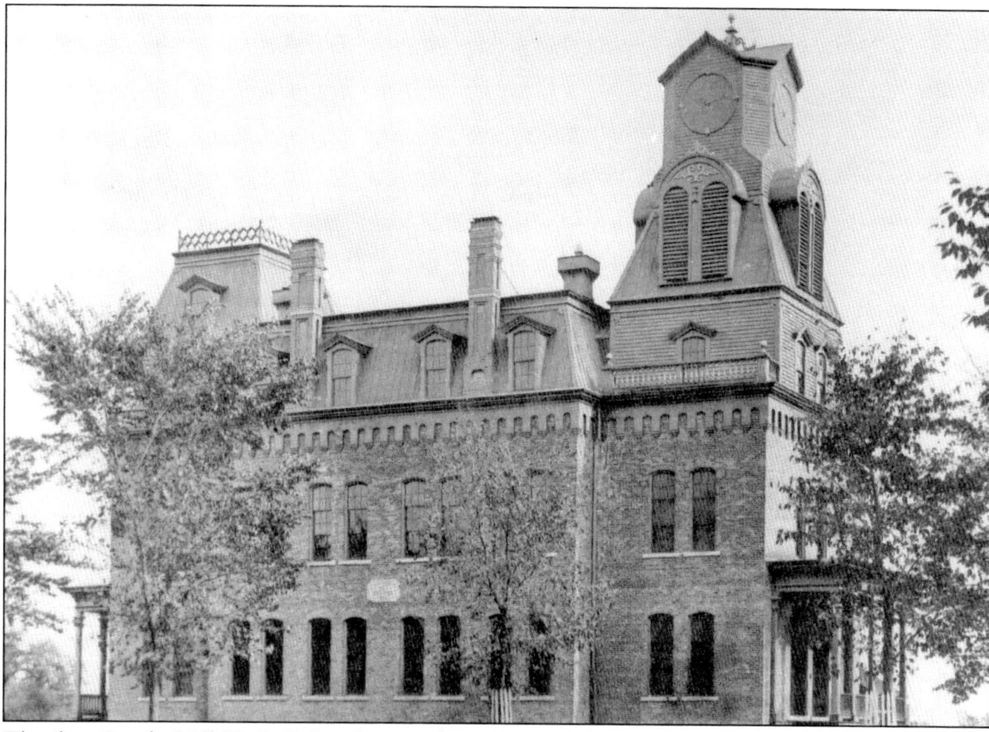

The first Sandy Hill High School opened *c.* 1890. It also appears on page 25, where it is the middle of the three school buildings. The earlier view shows a lot of Victorian decoration that was no longer there by the time the later photograph was taken.

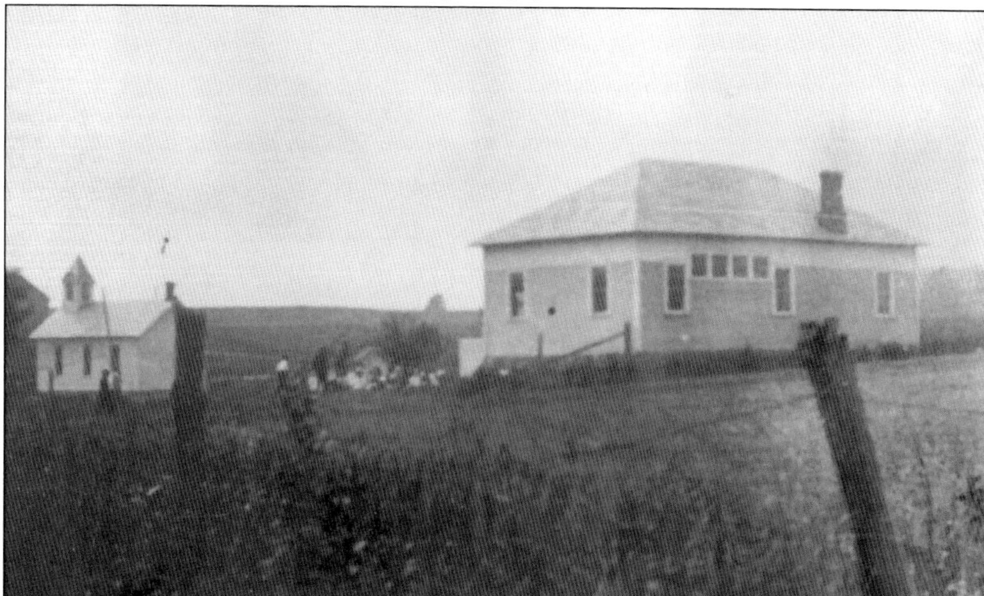

The Smiths Basin School was used as a two-grade school until the early 1960s. It was the last of the small rural schools to be incorporated into the Hudson Falls Central School. The smaller building, to the left, is a Methodist church, which only lasted a short while and was later torn down.

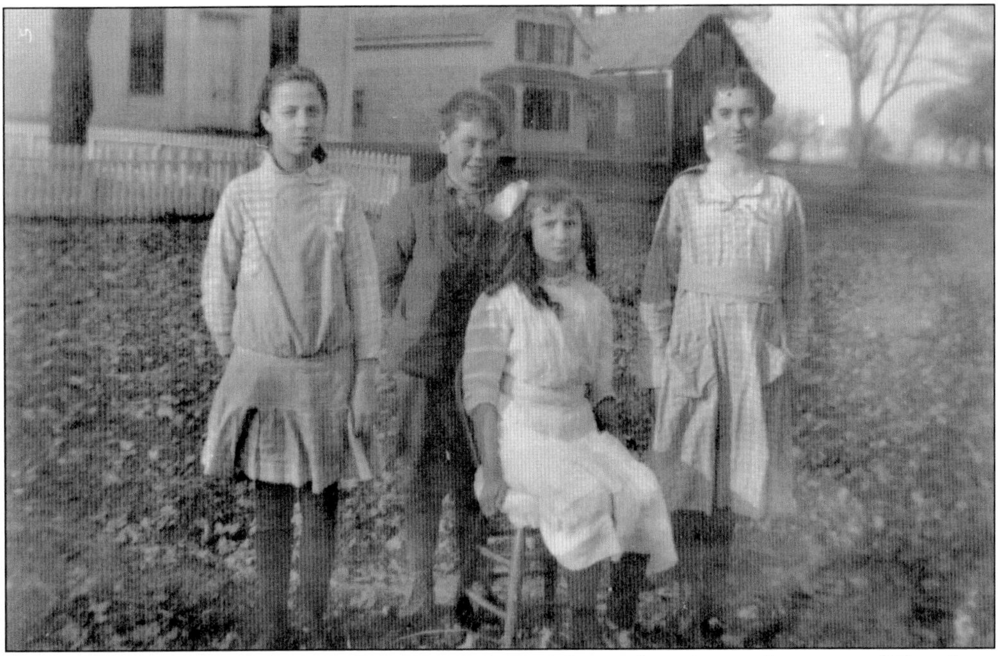

These students are from the Kingsbury Street School, located on the south corner of Kingsbury Road and state Route 4. They are sitting in front of the school, with the 200-year-old Kingsbury Baptist Church in the background. This photograph dates from the 1920s.

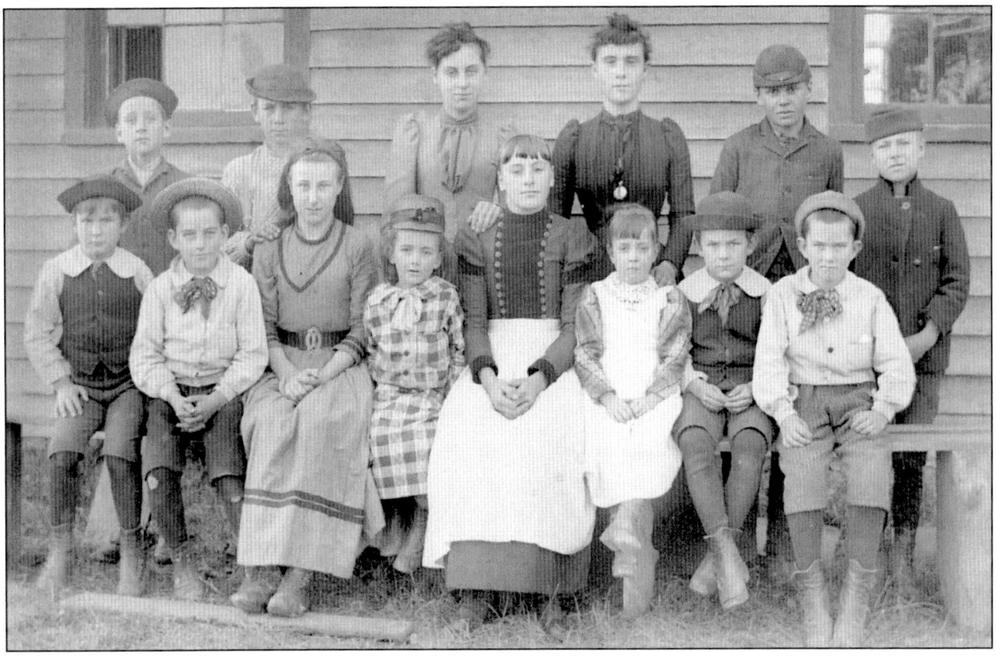

This class poses beside the one-room schoolhouse at the corner of Hartman Road and Notre Dame Street Extension. The picture dates from c. 1890. These children came from as far away as the area of the Kingswood Golf Course, about two miles away. Imagine walking that far to school in the winter. The boys appear to be full of energy and eager to have the picture-taking session end.

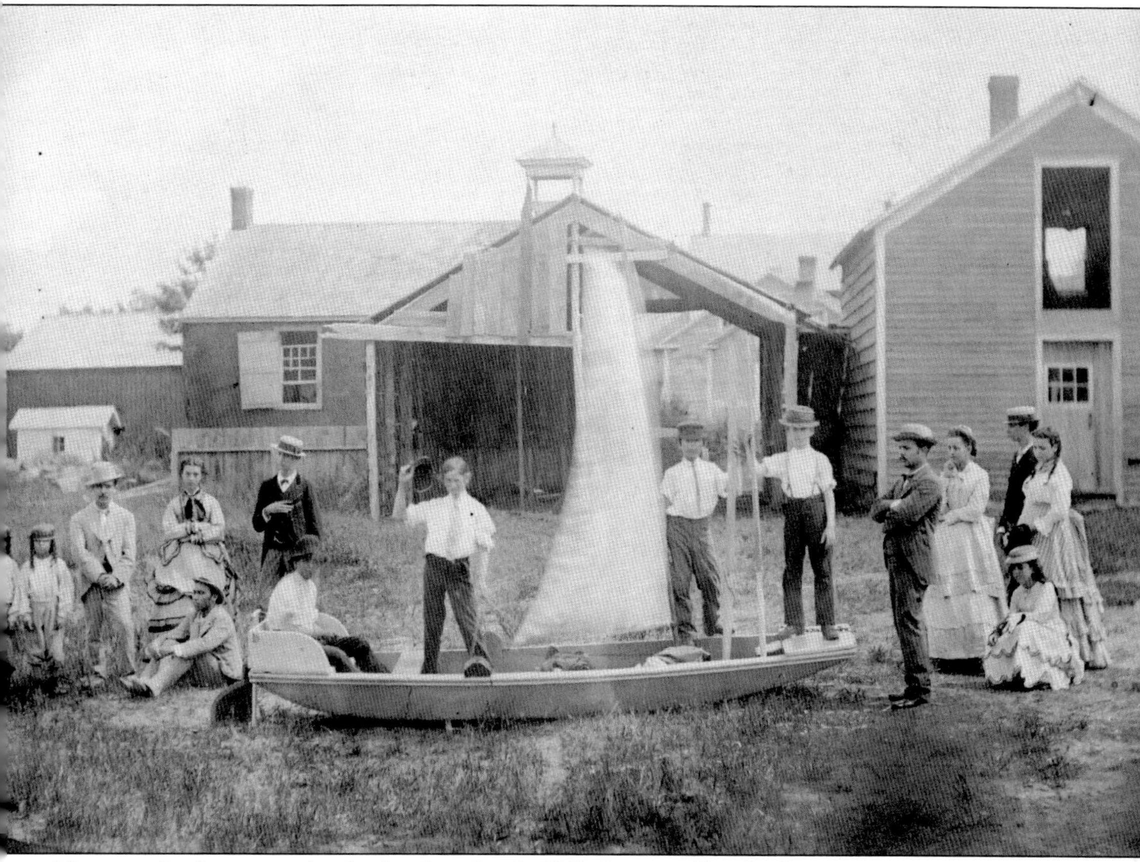

This was the first centralized school in Sandy Hill. It opened in the late 1860s. According to historian James Cronkhite, it was the Union Free School. There is some dispute as to where it was located. Some say it was on Wall Street, where Walnut Street is today. However, an early county history places it at the "head of Oak Street," where the later campus was built. Either way, this 1870 photograph shows the school, with the small bell tower, behind the barn.

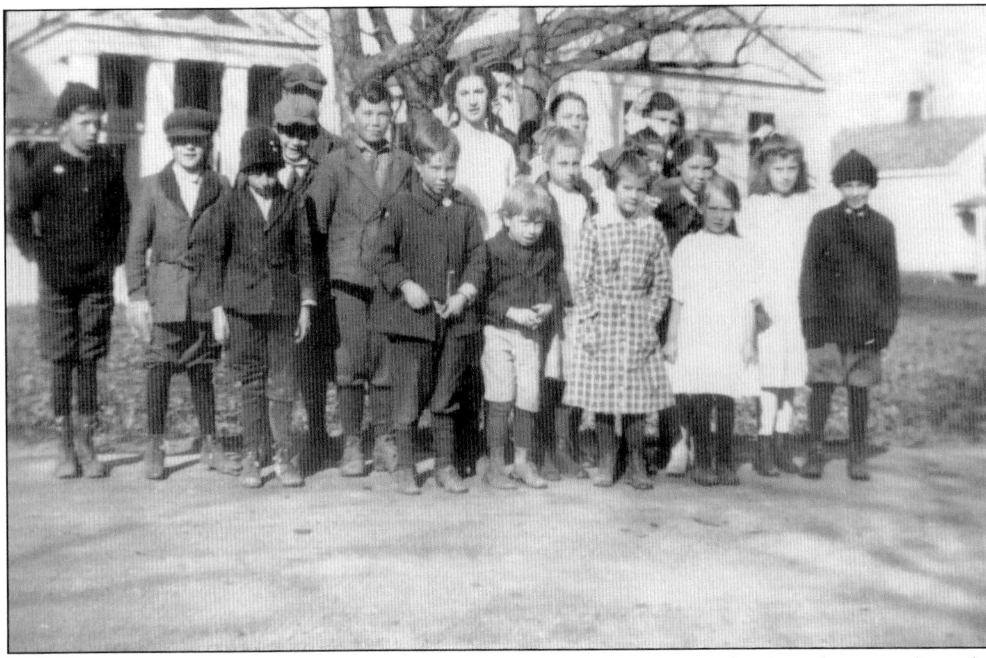

Standing in the road, a class from the Kingsbury Street School poses for this photograph in the 1930s. Imagine a class trying to do that today on busy Route 4.

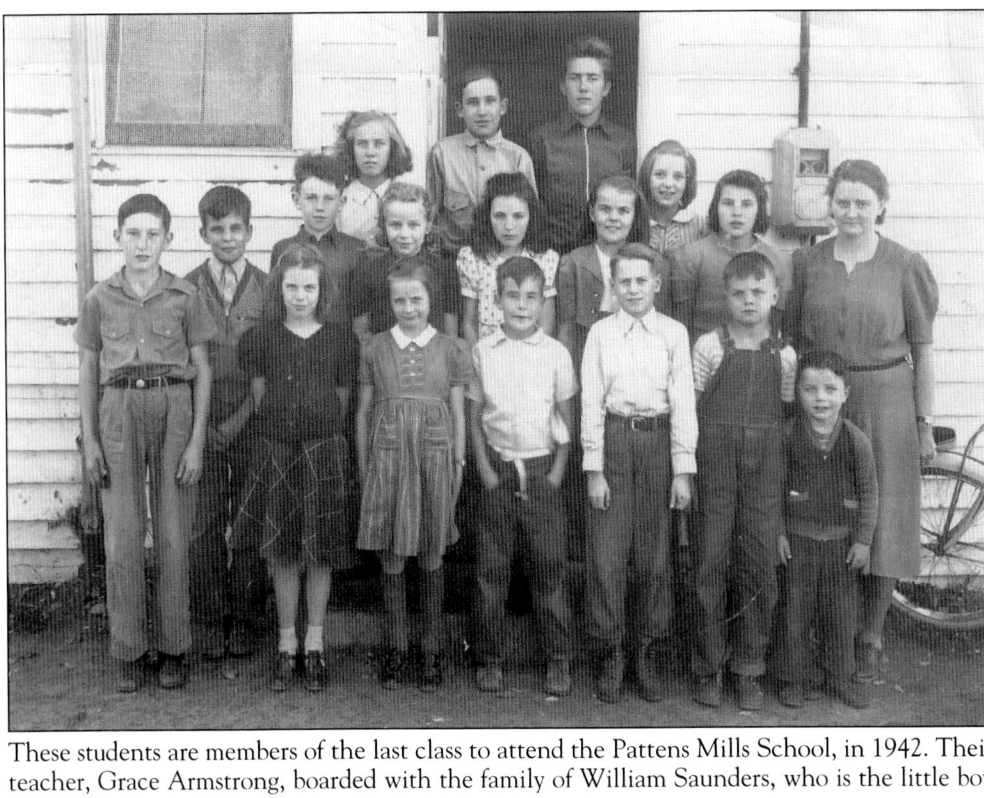

These students are members of the last class to attend the Pattens Mills School, in 1942. Their teacher, Grace Armstrong, boarded with the family of William Saunders, who is the little boy standing in front of her.

Three

SANDY HILL AND HUDSON FALLS

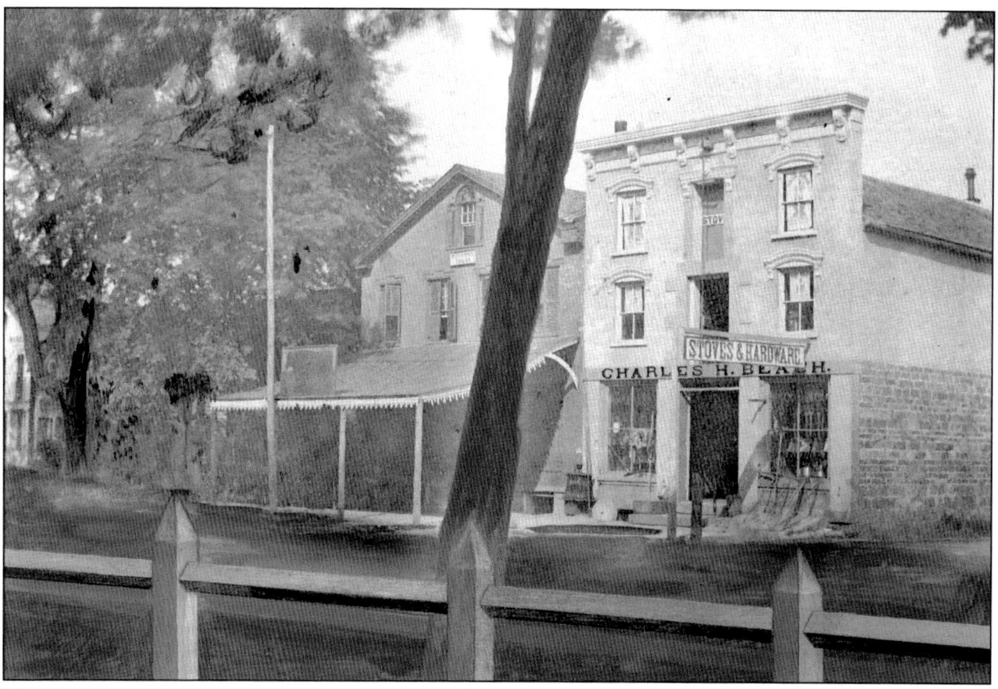

This is an 1870 view looking out of the village park to the east side of Main Street. At that time the fence went all the way around the park. The building with the large awning over the sidewalk is located where McCann's Pharmacy is today. It was in this store that Townsend Harris was born, in 1803. A few years after this picture was taken, all of the buildings on the east side of the street were destroyed by fire.

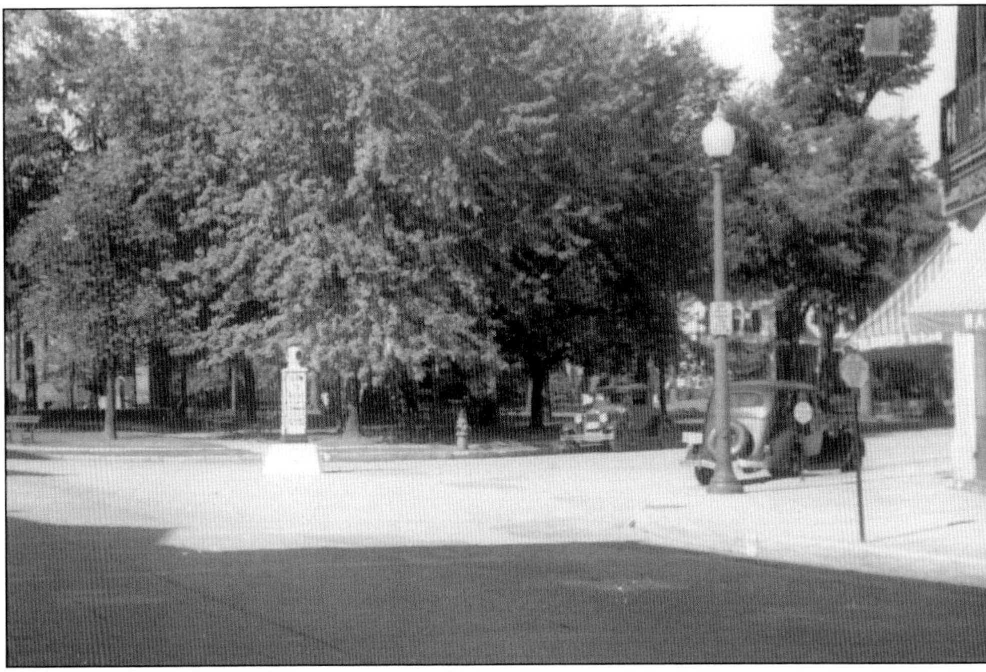

This photograph shows the intersection of Main Street and Park Place c. the late 1930s. The object in the middle of the intersection has directions to Glens Falls and Fort Edward on it. With the size of modern trucks, such a fixture would not last long today.

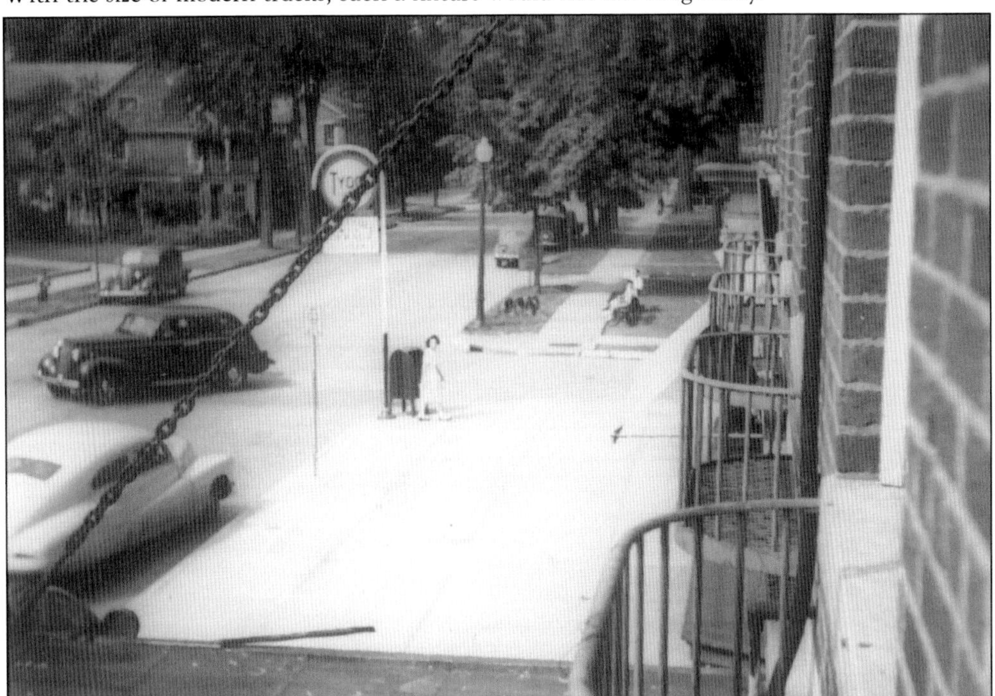

This early-1950s photograph was taken looking north on Main Street from an upstairs window of the old Strand Theatre. In 1969, the theater became the Kingsbury Town Hall.

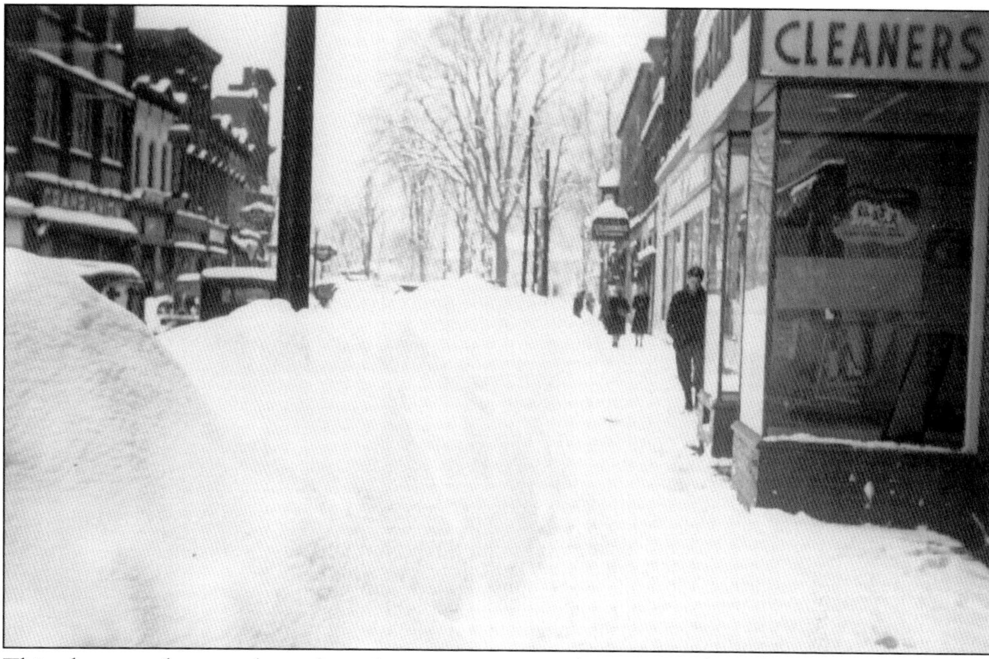

This photograph was taken after a big snowstorm in the 1940s. The sidewalk view is looking south on the west side of Main Street, north of Park Place.

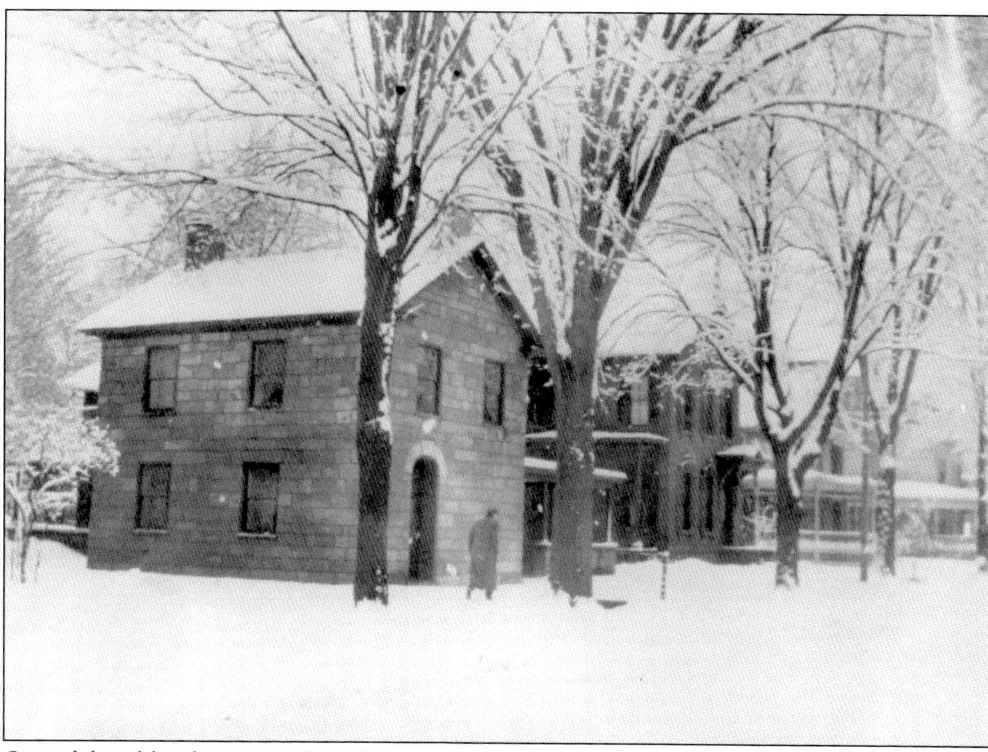

One of the oldest houses in the village stands at 1 Pearl Street, just behind the post office. The street looks much the same today as when this photograph was taken in the 1940s.

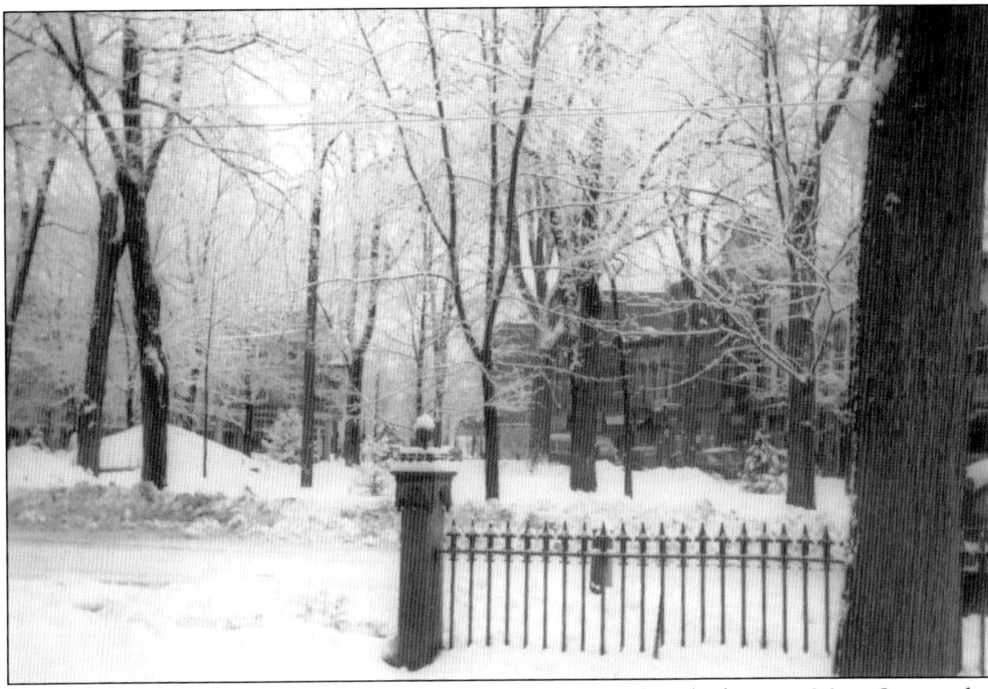

This photograph of the west side of the village park was taken looking up Main Street after another big snowstorm in the 1940s.

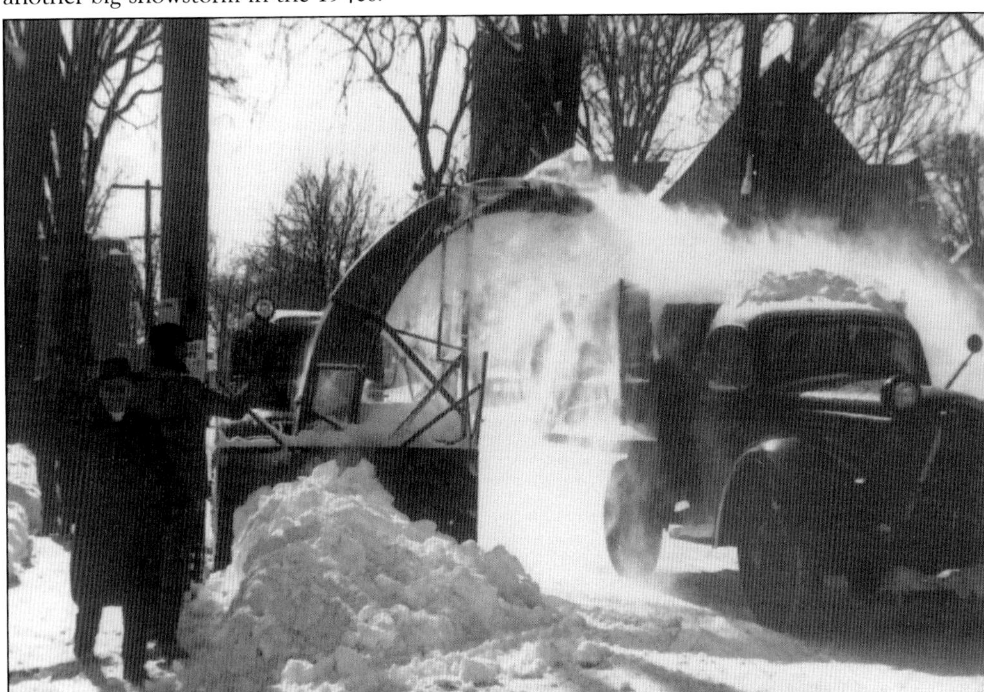

Hudson Falls has always been known for cleaning up quickly after a snowstorm. A dump truck, not much larger than a modern pickup truck, and a snowblower seem to be doing a good job on Wall Street in the 1940s. St. Mary's-St. Paul's Church rises in the background.

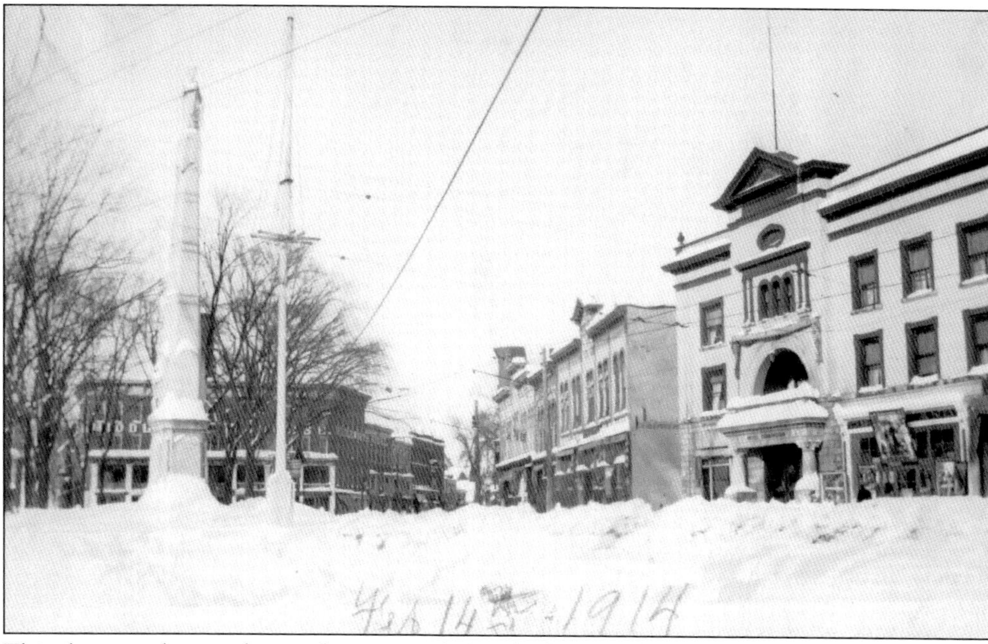

This photograph was taken in the winter of 1914, looking north from the front of the courthouse. Note the huge flagpole and the old Middleworth House in the center background.

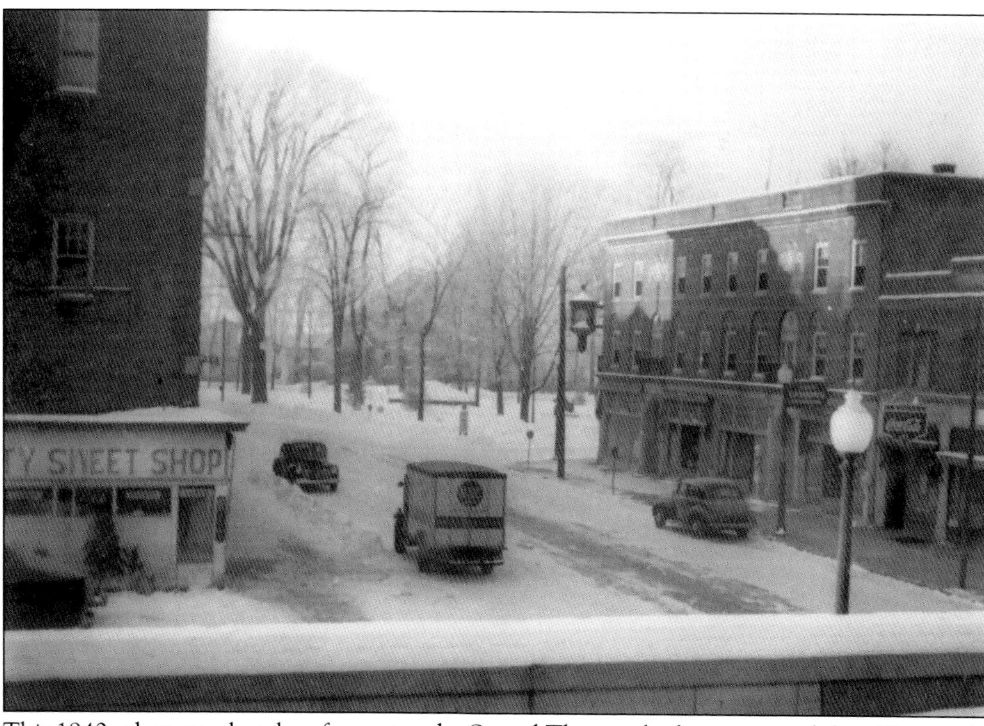

This 1940s photograph, taken from atop the Strand Theatre, looks out toward the village park. The village crew has done a good job in removing the snow.

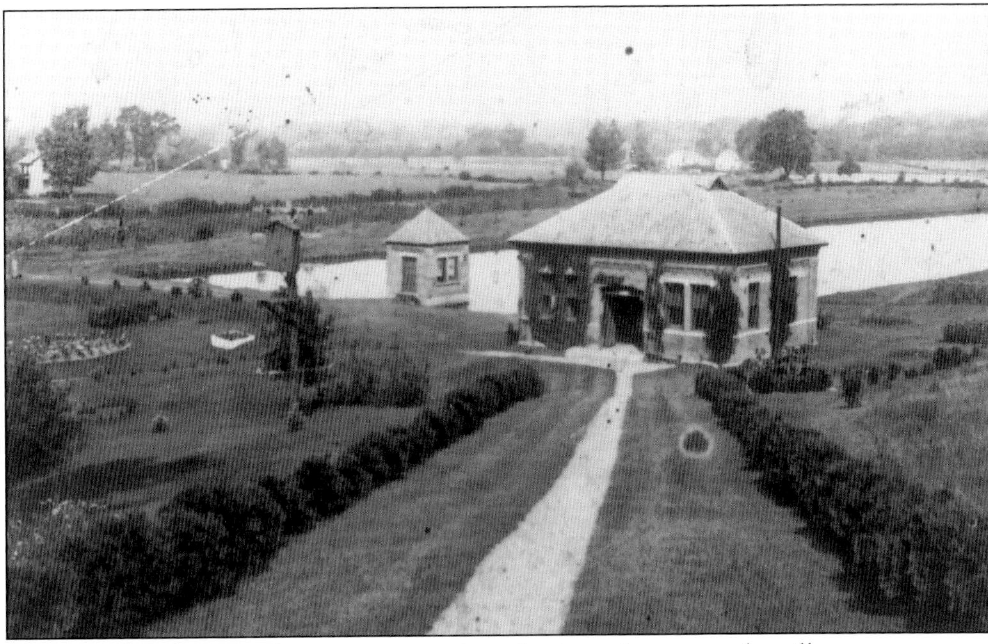

The Springbrook Water Company was a private business that set up the village water system. The village later took over the system. This photograph shows the pumping station for the waterworks. At the time this photograph was taken, the water tower was on Wall Street on the north side of the large parking lot.

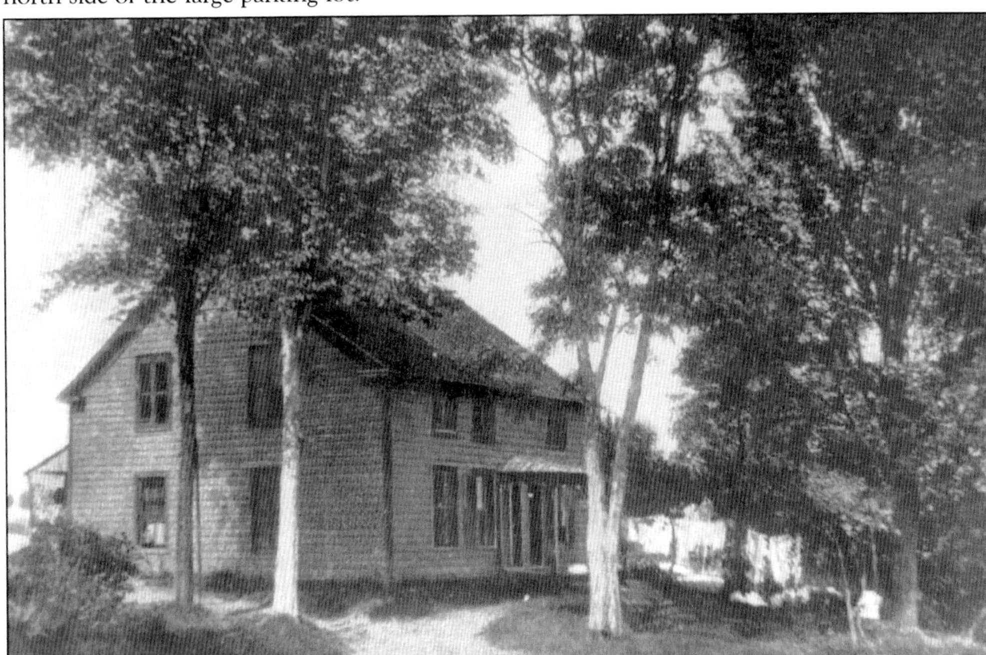

This is the first- or second-oldest house in the village. It was built in the early 1770s, before the Revolutionary War. During the summer of 1777, Lt. Gen. John Burgoyne used it as his military headquarters for a few days. In the 1830s, the house became a canal tavern, near the Five Combines. The house is still standing today at the corner of Pine Street and Burgoyne Avenue.

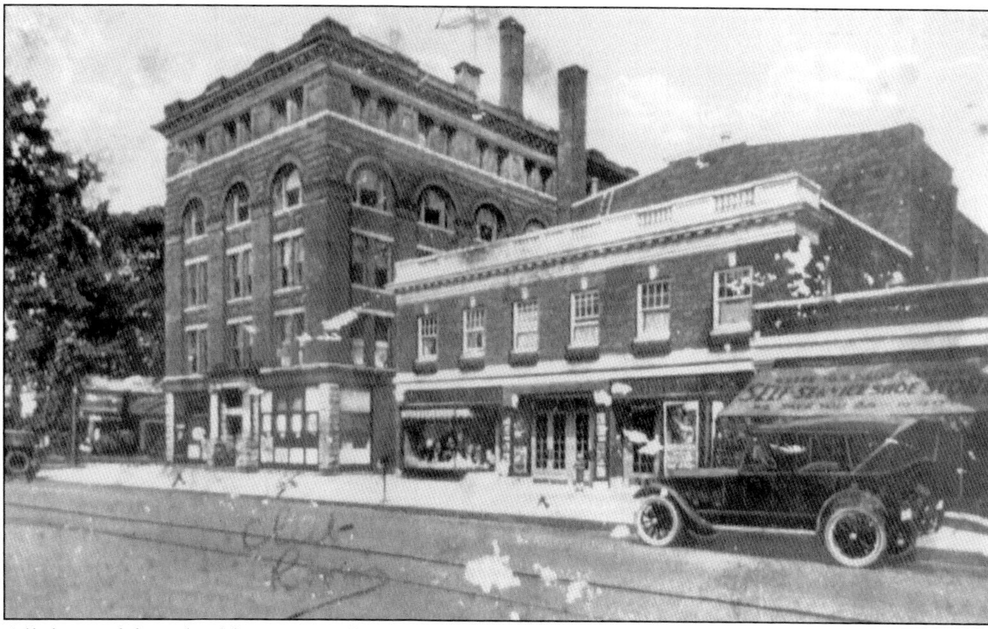

All three of these buildings are still standing. The first floor of the Masonic Temple, the five-story building, was the post office of Hudson Falls until the present one was built. The Strand Theatre is today the Kingsbury Town Hall. The self-service shoe store is today a tavern.

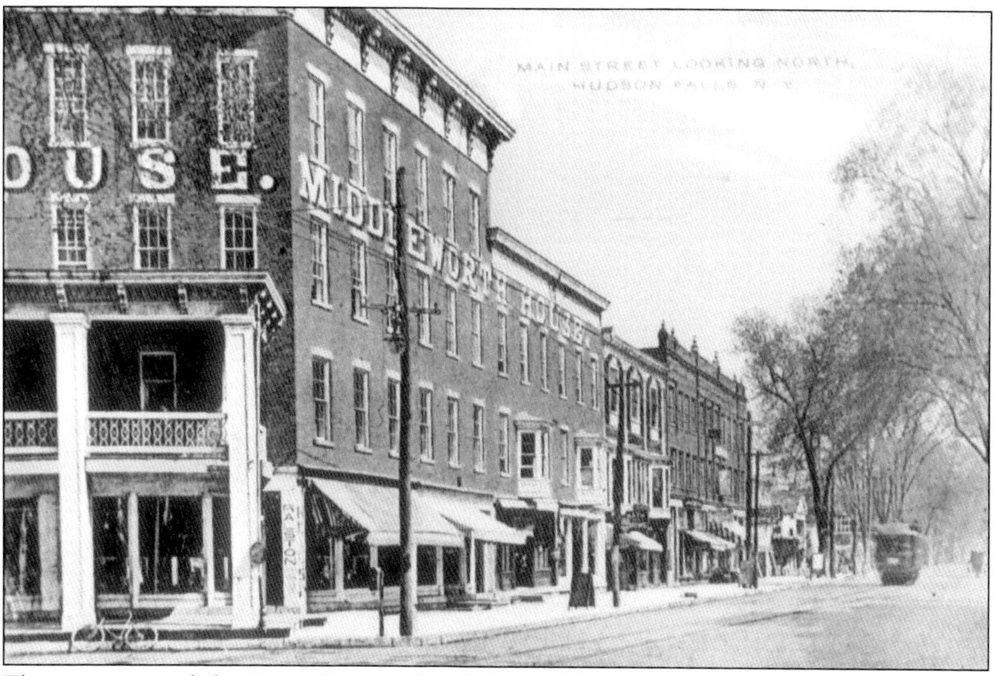

This is a view of the Main Street side of the Middleworth House. Built in 1863, it was considered one of the finest hotels between Albany and Plattsburgh. The main part stood four stories tall and covered a whole block. When the Middleworth burned in 1920, the fire began in the building to the north of the three-story section. This photograph was taken between 1910 and 1915.

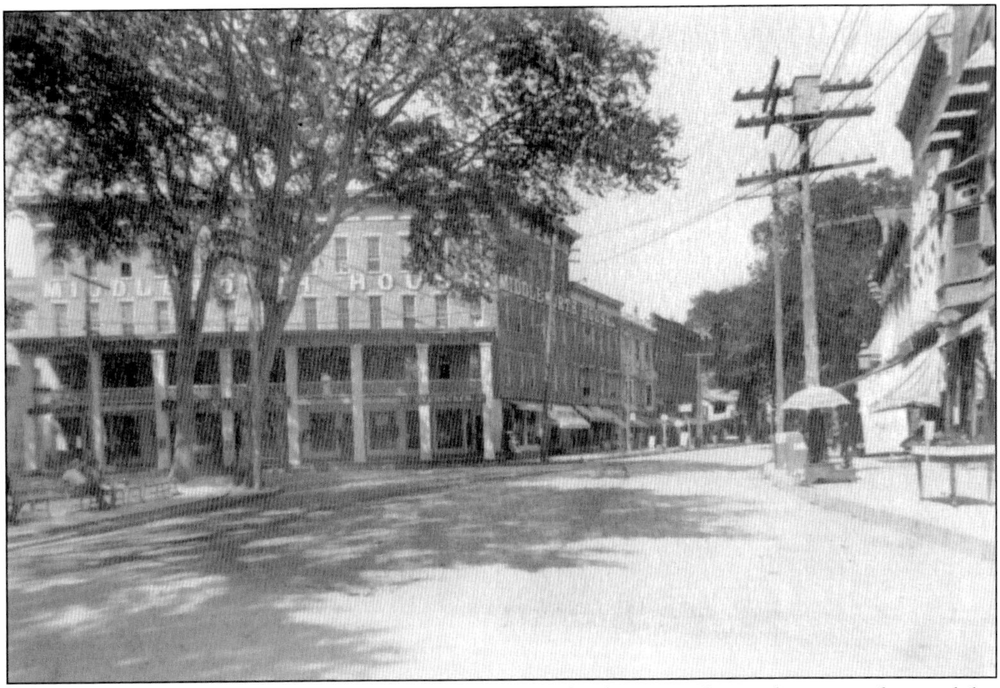

Taken about the same time as the previous photograph, this view shows the entire front of the Middleworth House. Across the front was a two-story veranda on which guests and townspeople could sit and watch the world pass by—at a much slower pace than that of today.

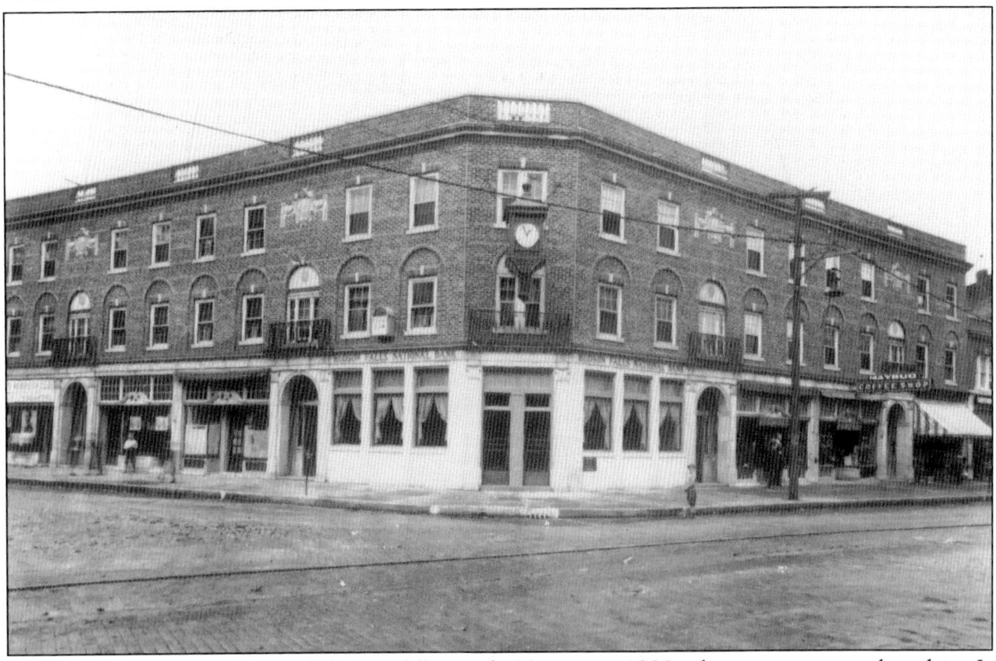

Following the destruction of the Middleworth House in 1920, this structure replaced it. It opened as the Hudson Falls National Bank, after the bank's original building burned. Upstairs were a large number of apartments, some of which had small fireplaces. Today, Custom Corners Frame Shop is located on the first floor.

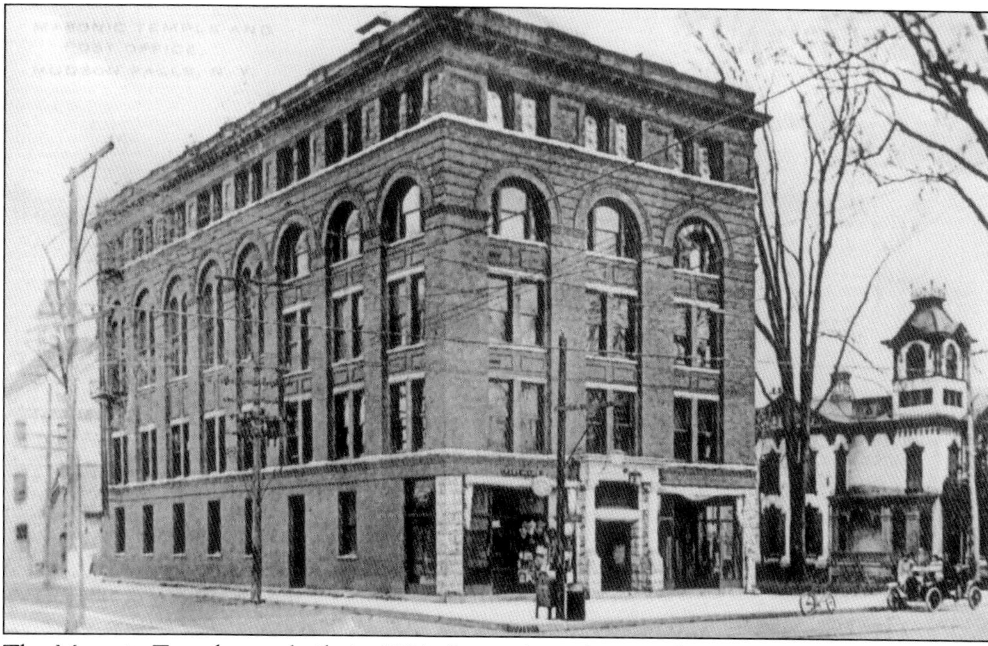

The Masonic Temple was built in 1901. It stood on the site that was later occupied by the Strand Theatre. This ornate building had a basketball court on the top. When the structure was being built, George LaMere, a youth at the time, climbed to the top of the building and carved his name in one of the rafters. Relating this tale to his nephew (the author) in later years, LaMere added that his mother would have grounded him for a year had she known what he had done.

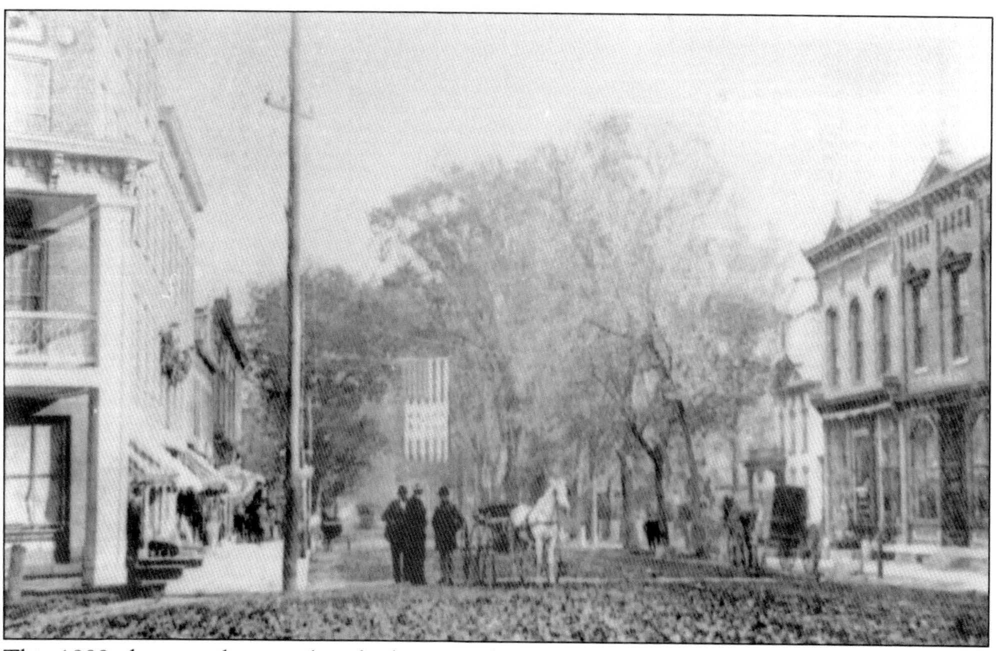

This 1888 photograph was taken looking north on Main Street from the intersection of Park Place, with the Middleworth House to the left. A national election was going on, and what appears to be a large flag hanging over the street is actually a political banner.

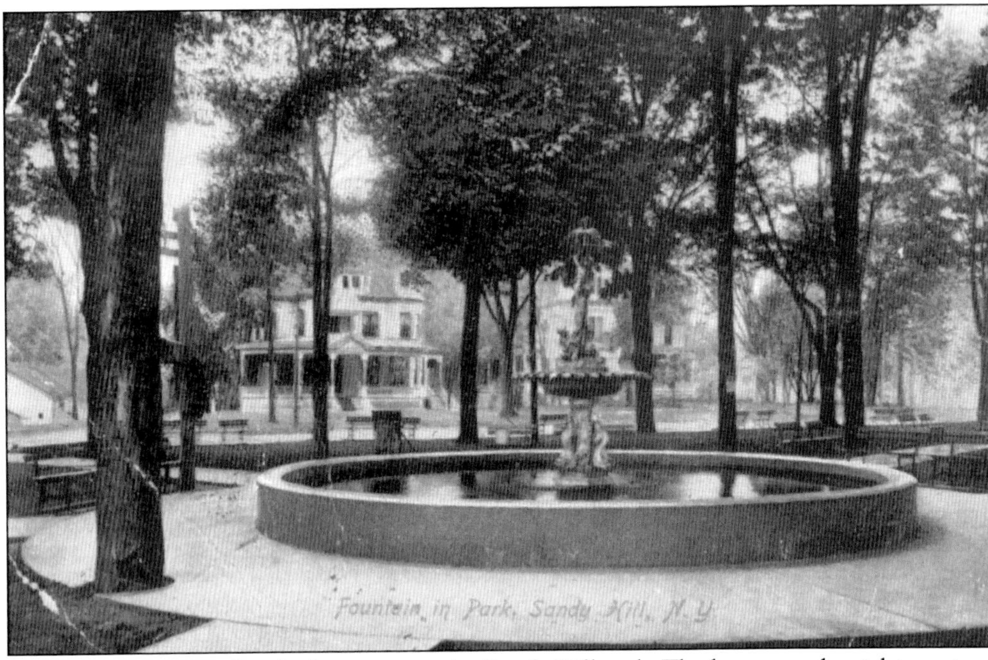

This 1907 view was taken looking west at the Sandy Hill park. The house on the right was torn down in the 1970s. The fountain is still in use each summer season and is covered with a large wooden pyramid during the winter.

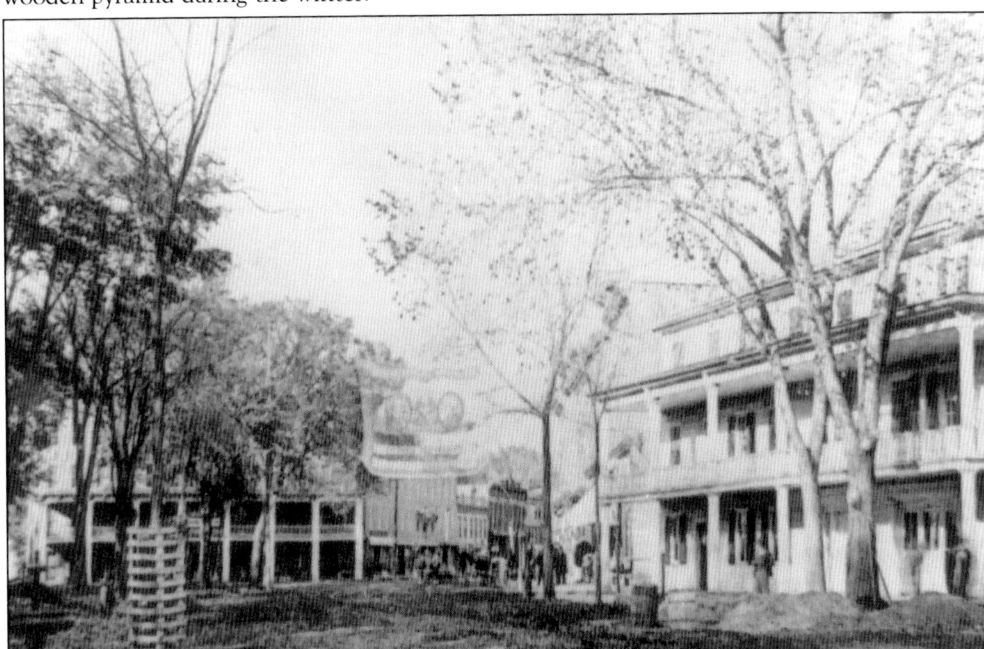

This view of view of Main Street was taken in 1888. The political banner has candidates pictured on it. To the left is the Middleworth House, and to the right is the Park House, another local hotel. Sandy Hill had four or five large hotels because it was the Washington County seat and, as such, had people coming into town for county meetings and court proceedings.

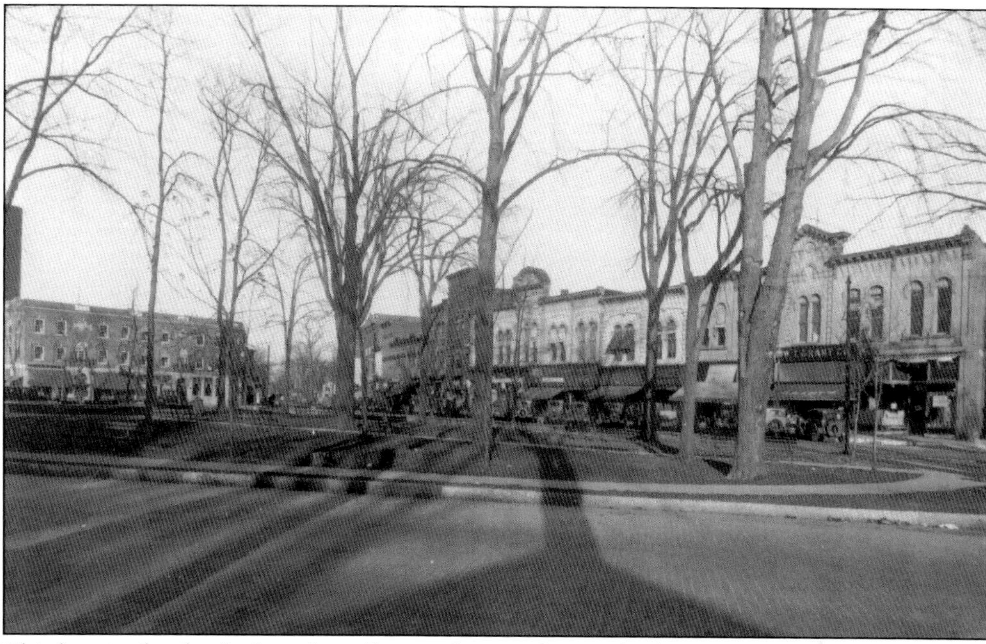

This late-in-the-day-look at the village park was taken *c.* the late 1920s or 1930s. It is hard to tell whether the season is autumn or spring. The only building that has changed is the last one on the right. In this picture it is a W.T. Grants, which was a five-and-dime department store. In the 1960s, it was completely remodeled and a new front facade was added. Grants went out of business in the mid-1970s.

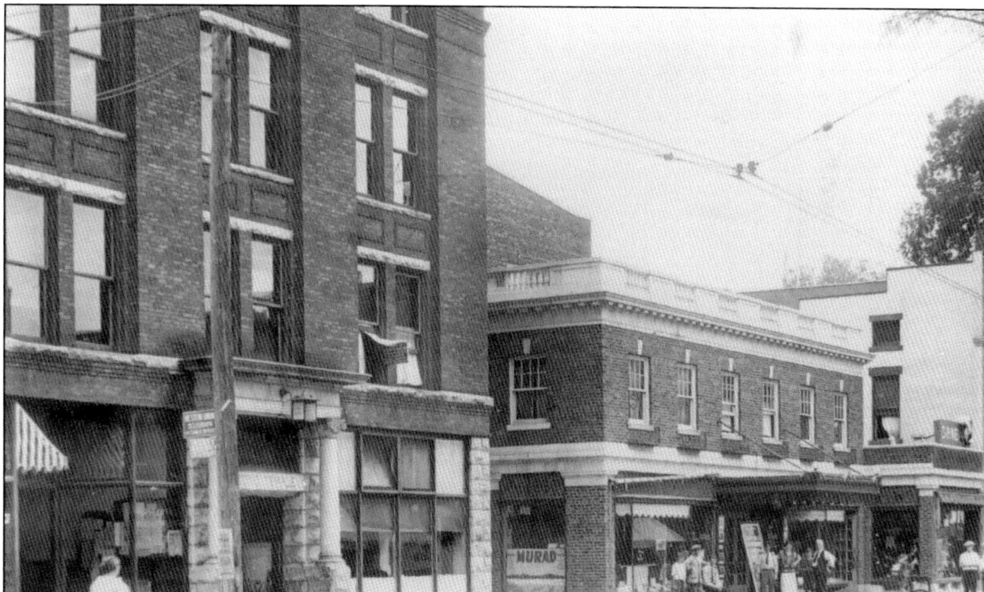

This close-up view shows the lower floors of the Masonic Temple and the Strand Theatre. The three-story building to the right burned down sometime in the 1940s. On either side of the theater entrance, there was a small business, such as a lunch counter or a newsstand.

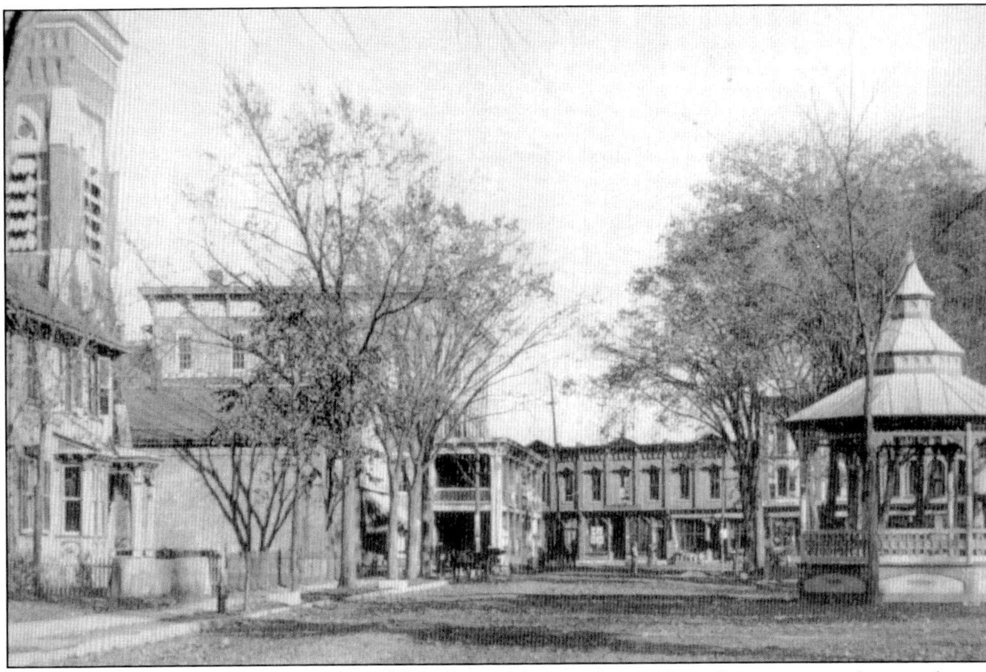

This is a rare look at the Sandy Hill bandstand. It was located in the street at the northwest corner of the village park. There is a bandstand in the Washington County village of Cambridge that looks very much like this one. Could it be the same one? The buildings, from left to right, are St. Mary's Church, the Sandy Hill National Bank, and the Middleworth House. The photograph dates from the 1880s.

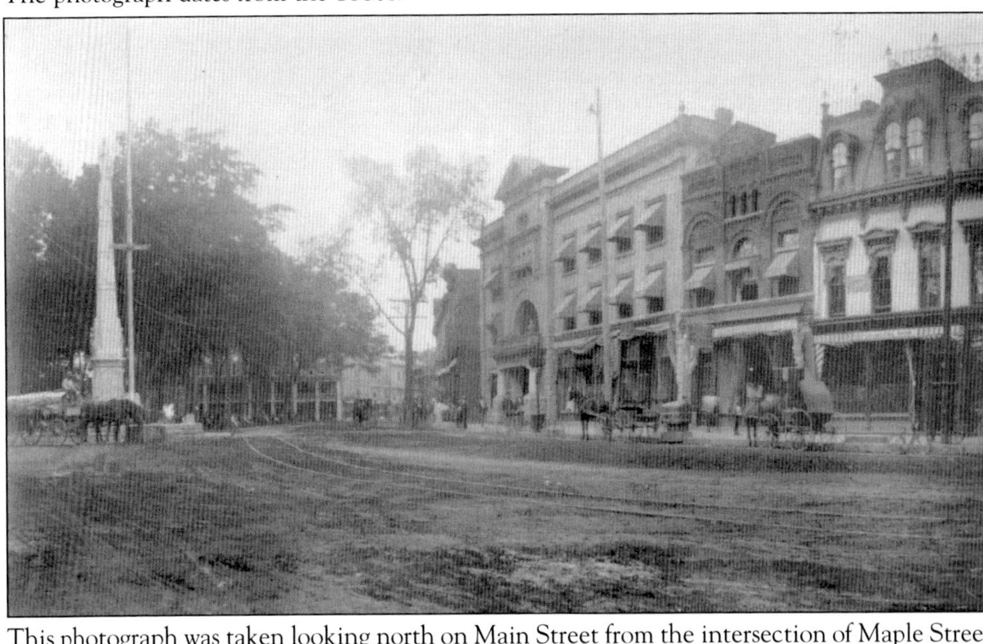

This photograph was taken looking north on Main Street from the intersection of Maple Street c. 1910 to 1915. The horse and wagon are stopped, and the horse is getting a drink from the village watering trough which, over the course of nearly 100 years, was located at various points around the village park. Notice that the street is still dirt.

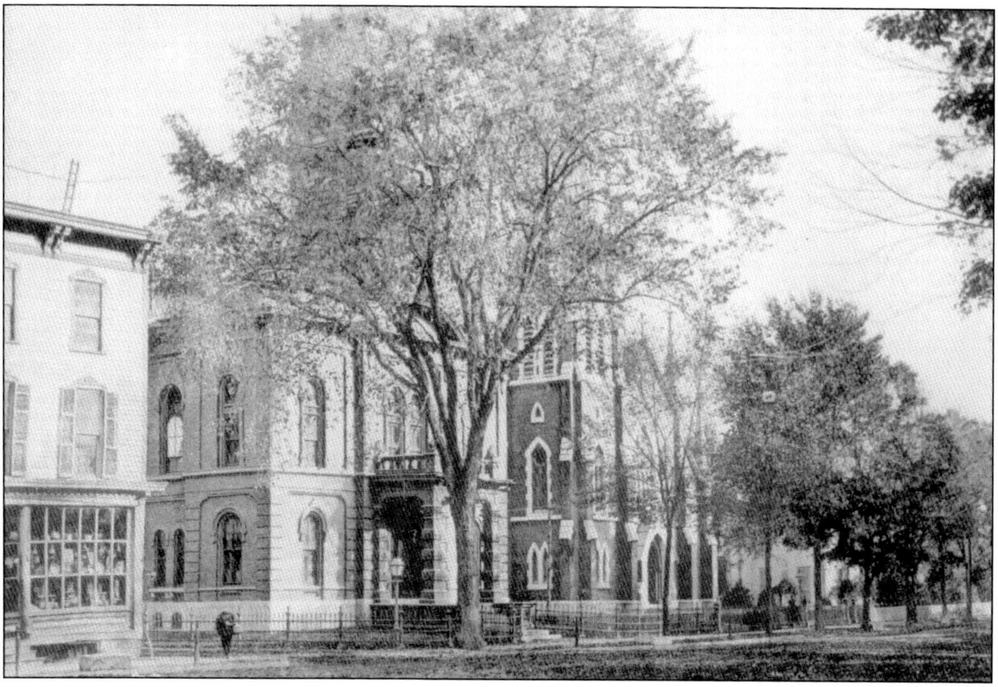

This photograph shows the Washington County Courthouse and the First Baptist Church. It was taken in the 1870s, when both buildings were quite new. Notice that the courthouse is unpainted (the only view of it unpainted that the author has seen) and is surrounded by a wrought iron fence.

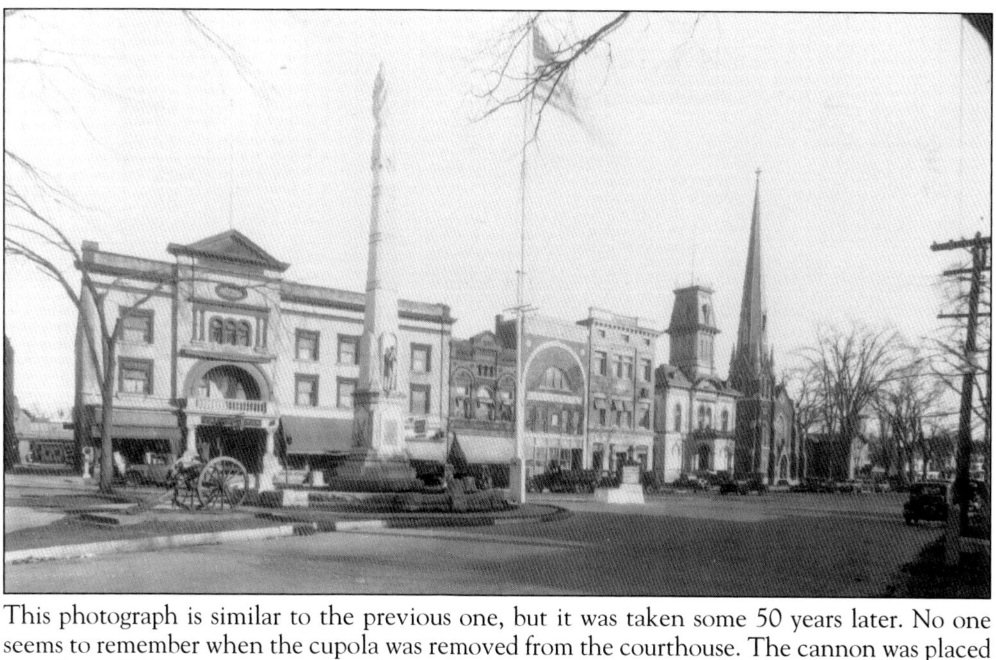

This photograph is similar to the previous one, but it was taken some 50 years later. No one seems to remember when the cupola was removed from the courthouse. The cannon was placed outside in 1908 as a memorial by the Collins Post, Grand Army of the Republic, a fraternal organization for Civil War veterans. It was cast in 1862 and saw action during the Civil War. In 2000, the carriage was rebuilt and rededicated.

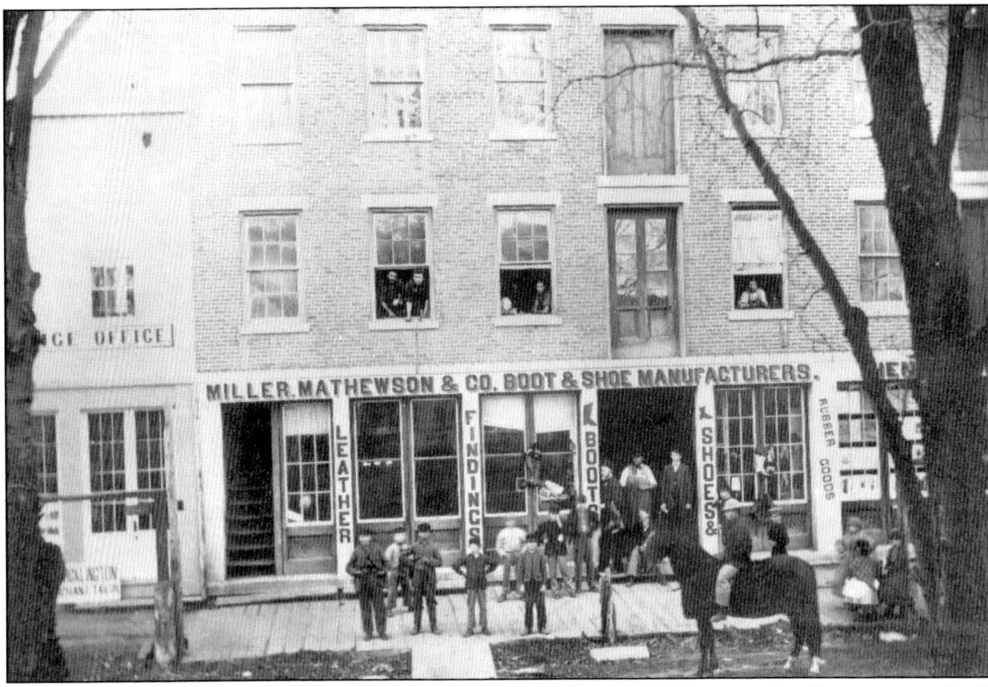

This late-19th-century photograph shows the Miller, Mathewson & Company, which manufactured various types of footwear. Most small villages of the time had a cobbler or two, but having a business of this type was rather unusual. The company was located on Main Street north of Park Place.

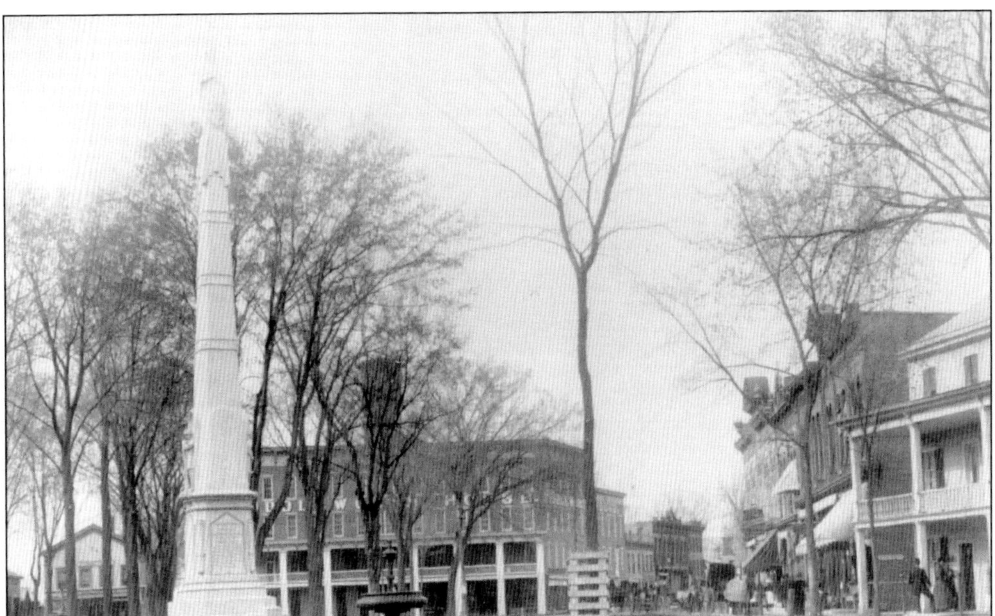

This 1880s view shows the Middleworth House and the new Soldiers Monument. The new monument was erected by Dr. Kellogg in honor all of the men from Washington County who served in the Civil War.

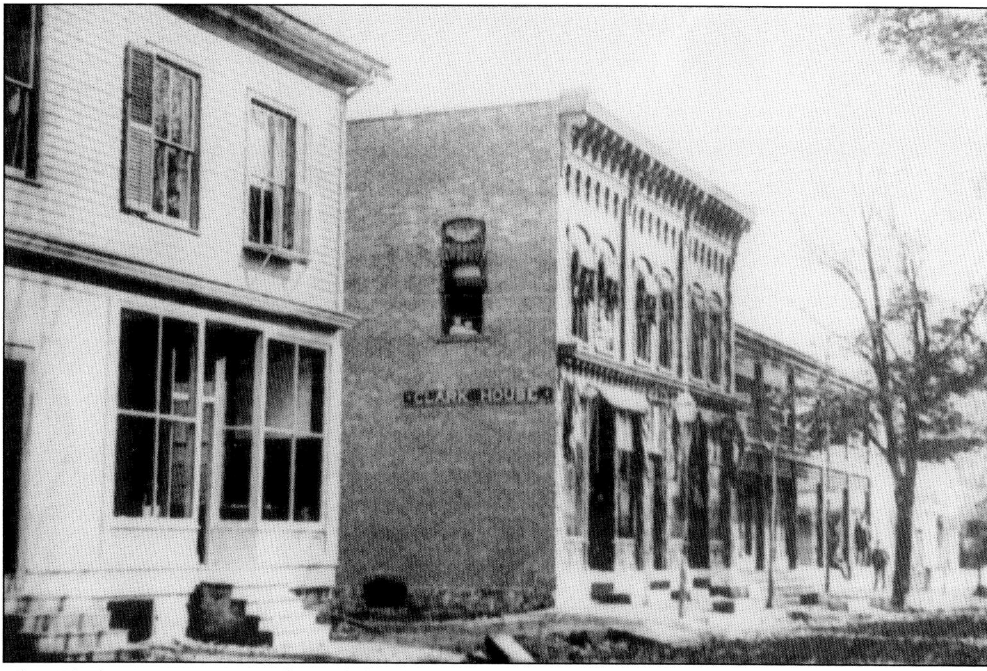

The Clark House was another of the hotels in the village. The building on the left is the first Washington County Courthouse. Located in Sandy Hill, it stood on the site where the large brick courthouse was built later. In the mid-1870s, the old courthouse was moved north across Maple Street and was turned into a commercial and residential building. It was torn down in the 1960s to make room for a parking lot.

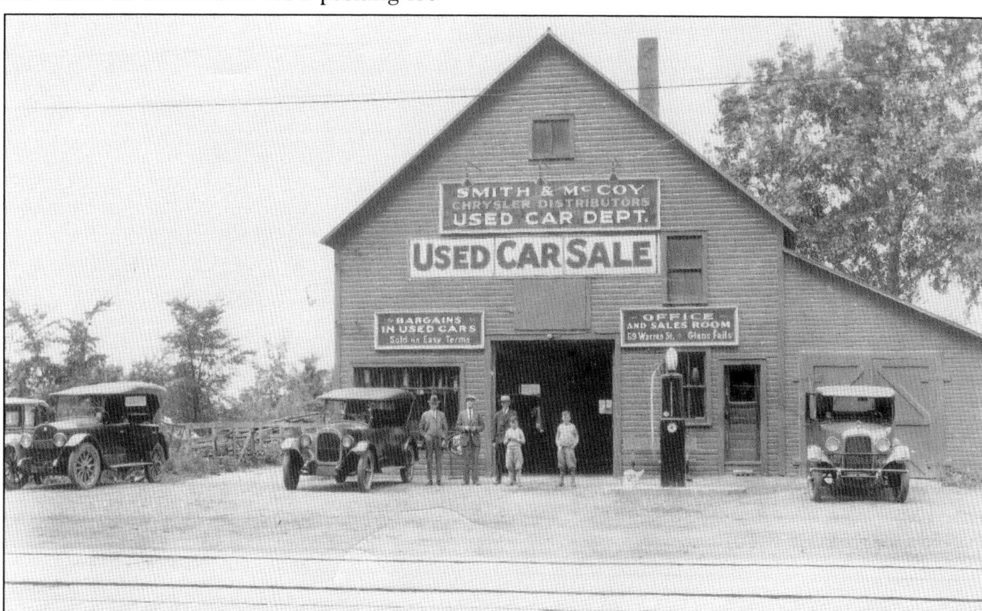

The used car department of Smith & McCoy was located on Feeder Street near the bend for the Boulevard. The Smith & McCoy Chrysler dealership was based in Glens Falls. The photograph dates from the 1930s.

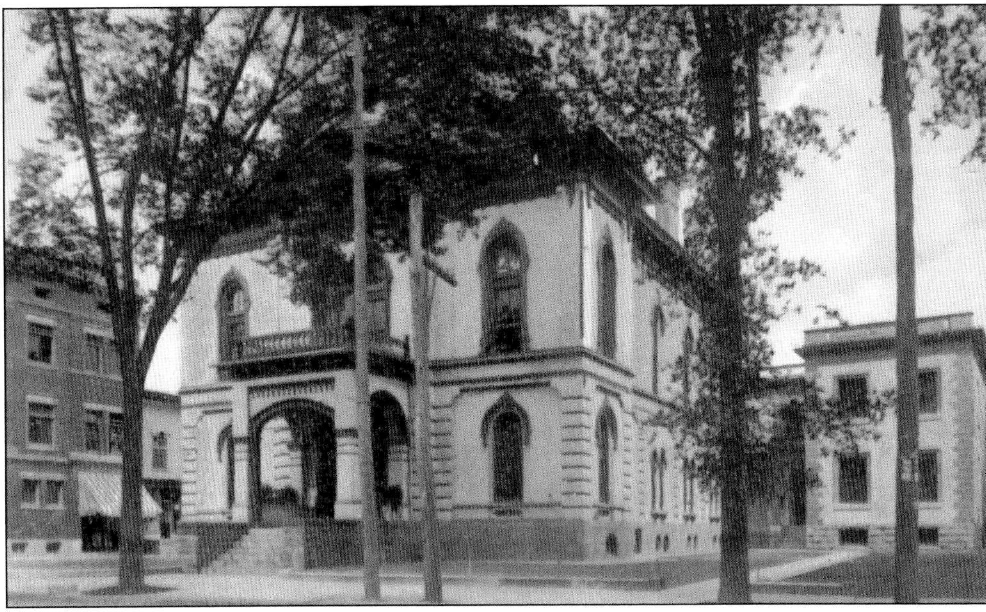

This 1909 view shows the painted Washington County Courthouse and the newly built office for the county clerks.

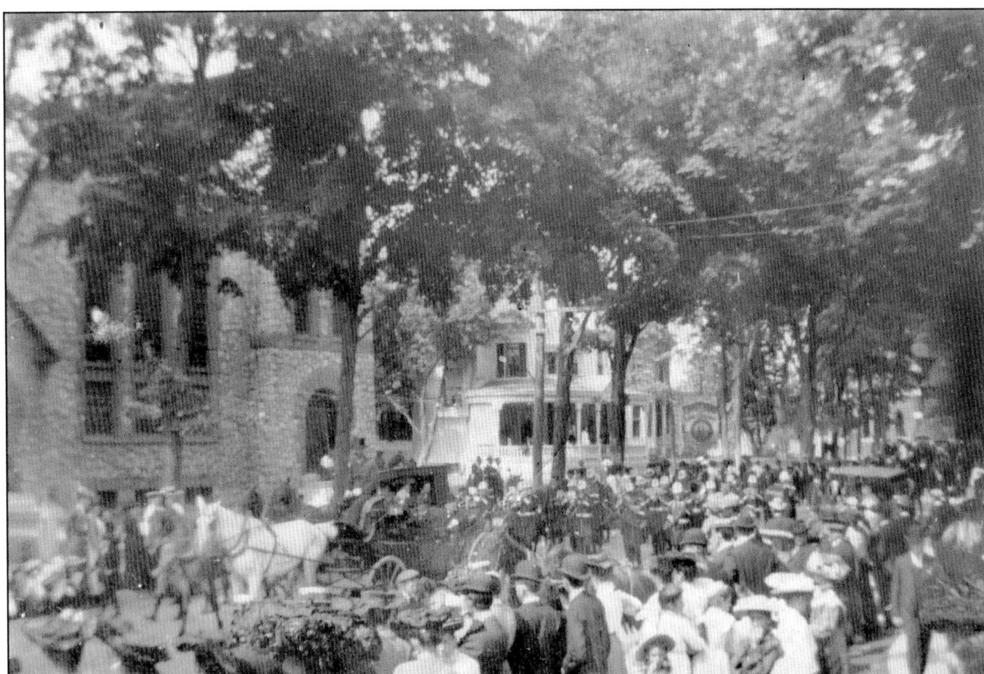

A 1920s-era parade heads south from the west side of the village park. The horses are pulling what may be the S & C steamer of the fire department. Next in the parade is a marching band.

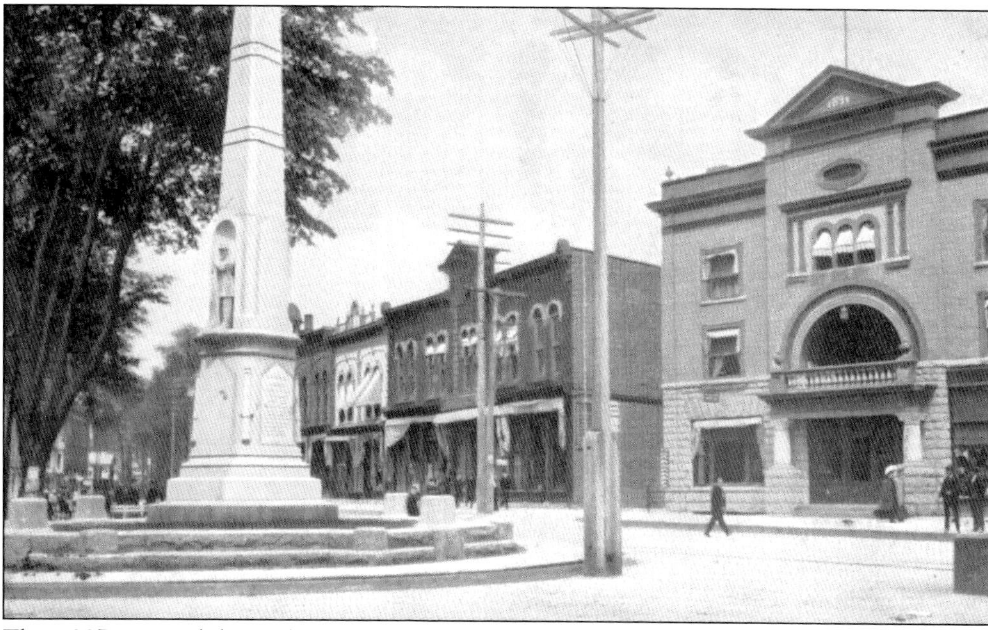

This 1907 postcard shows the center of Sandy Hill. The Cunningham Hotel, on the right, was built in 1895 and was destroyed by fire about 100 years later.

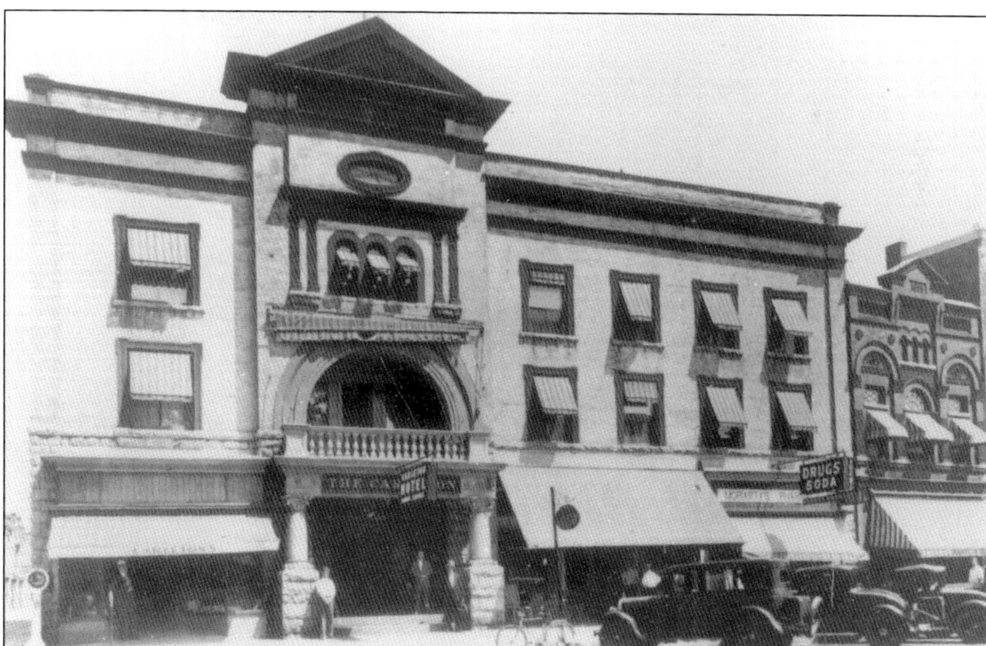

This picture of the Cunningham Hotel was taken some 20 years after the previous one was. In 1913, there was a movie theater located in the section to the right of the entrance. Moriarty's Drugstore and Soda Fountain was the last store on the right side of the hotel.

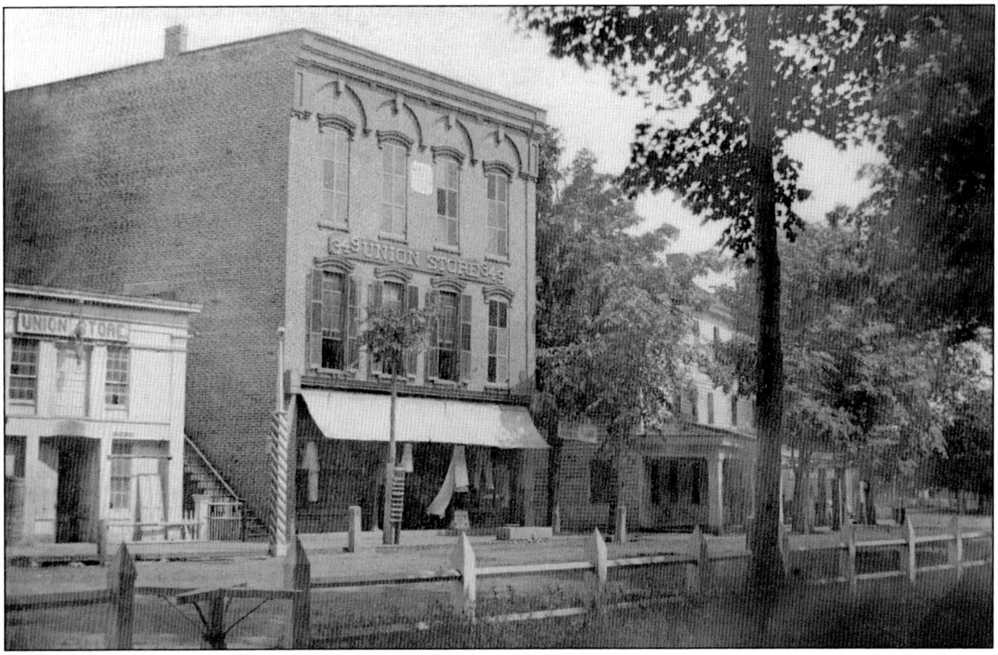

This view was taken looking out of the village park to the east side of Main Street. The building with the large porch, on the right, is the Coffee House, one of the three hotels around the park. It was the oldest of the three, dating from *c.* 1800. It burned down in the 1890s and was replaced by the Cunningham Hotel.

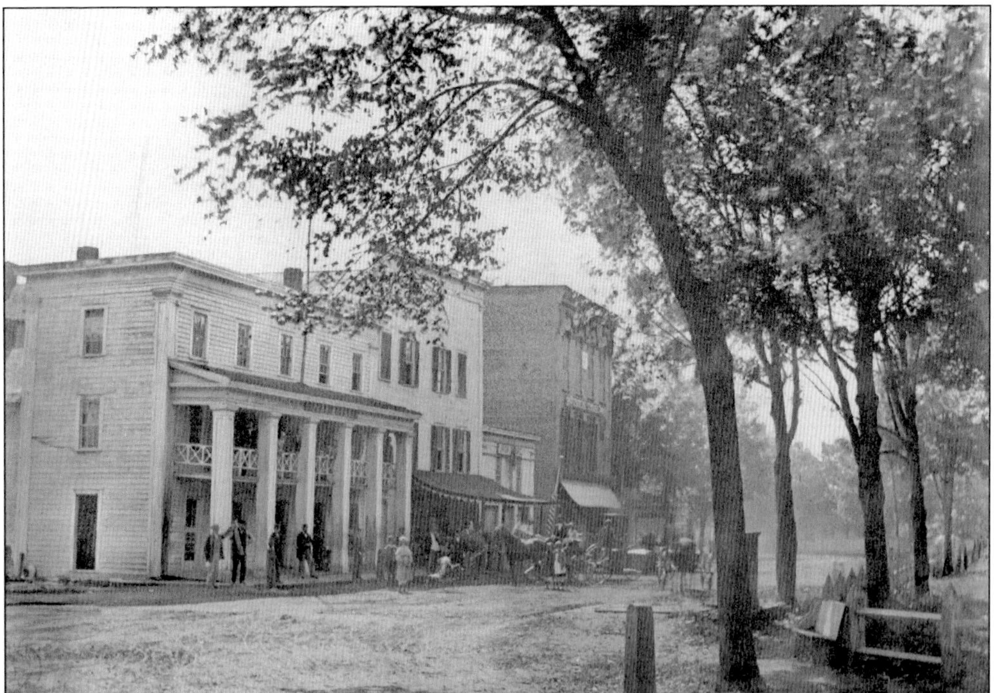

The second of the three hotels is the Park House. It was located about a half block north of the Coffee House. The fence that surrounded the village park is visible on the right.

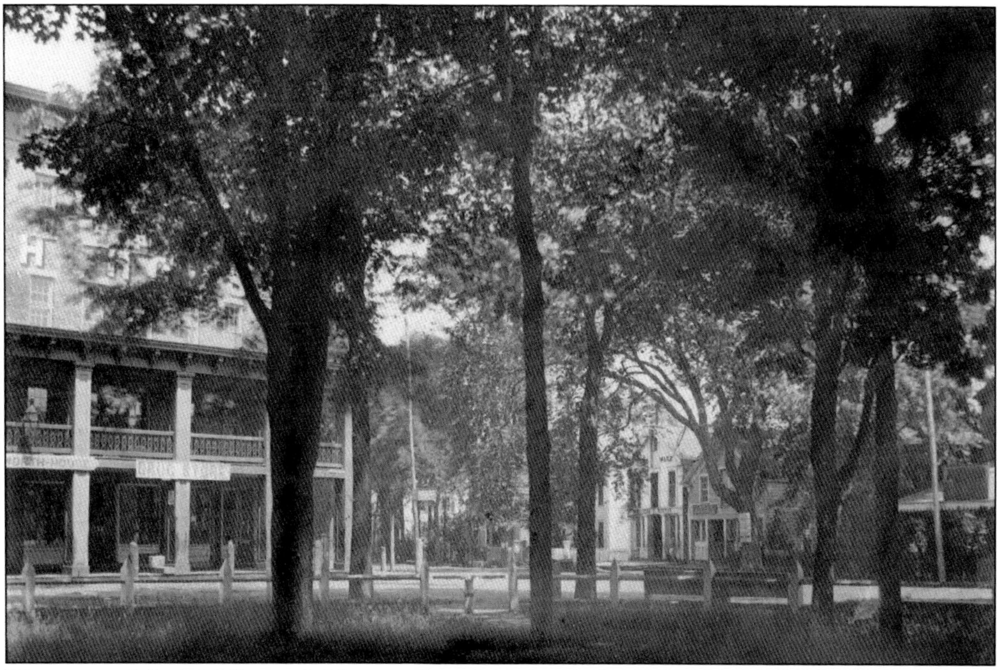

This view of the Middleworth House, taken from inside the village park, clearly shows the park fence. A turnstile, which kept large animals such as horses and cows from entering the park, is visible in the middle of the photograph.

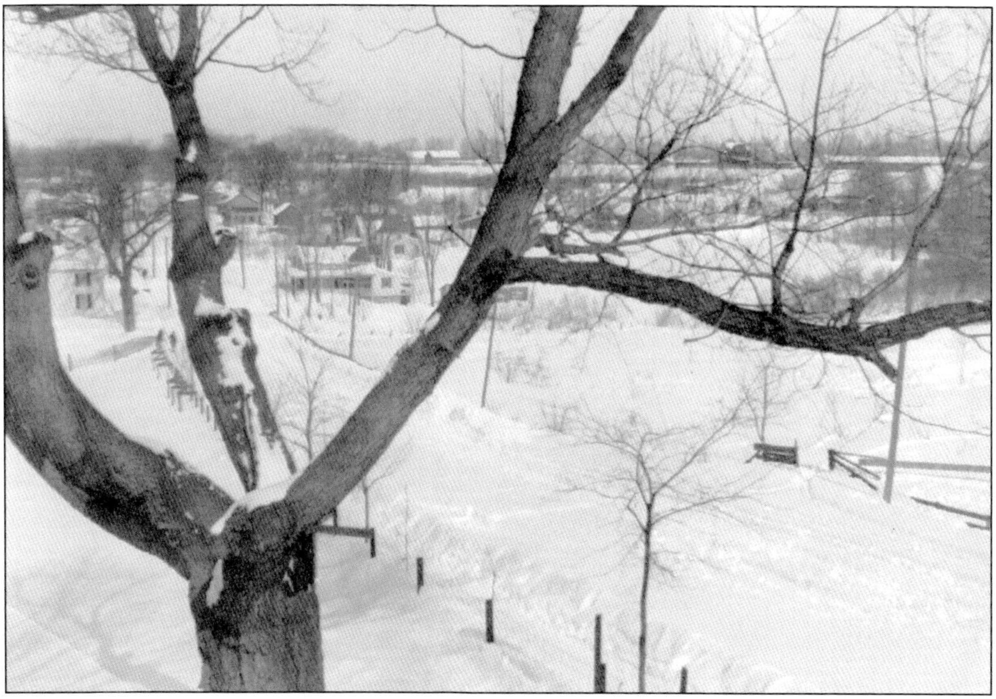

This winter scene was taken looking down Wall Street hill. In the background is the top of the hill on Melbourne Avenue, where the Glens Falls Feeder Canal is located. What is interesting is that there are so few trees in sight.

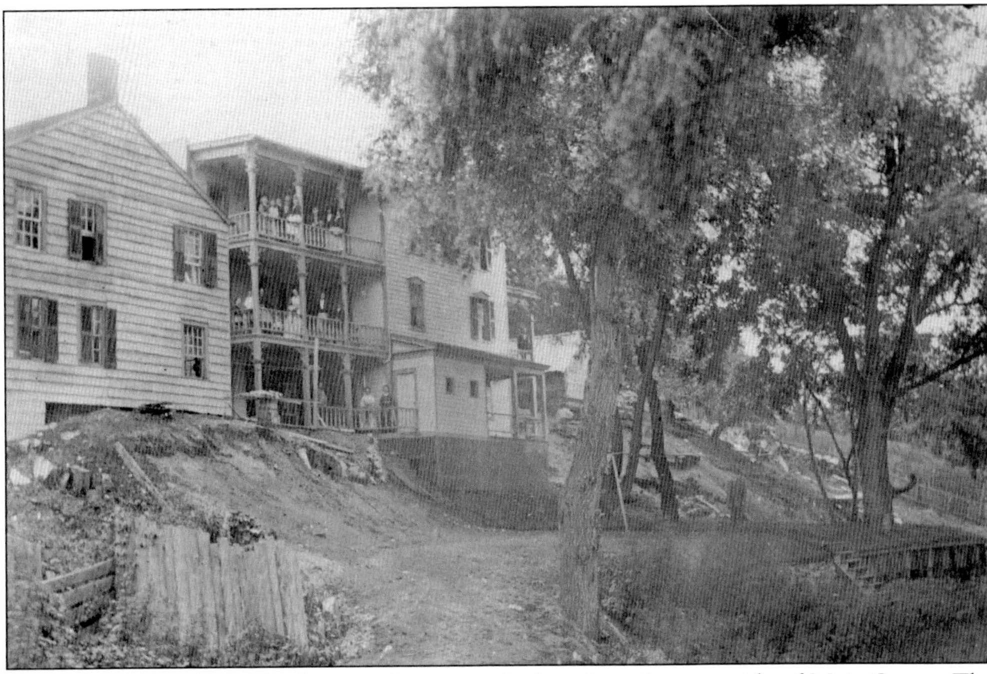

This view shows the back of a some houses and a hotel on the west side of Main Street. The photograph was taken from Depot Street near the bottom of the hill in the 1870s.

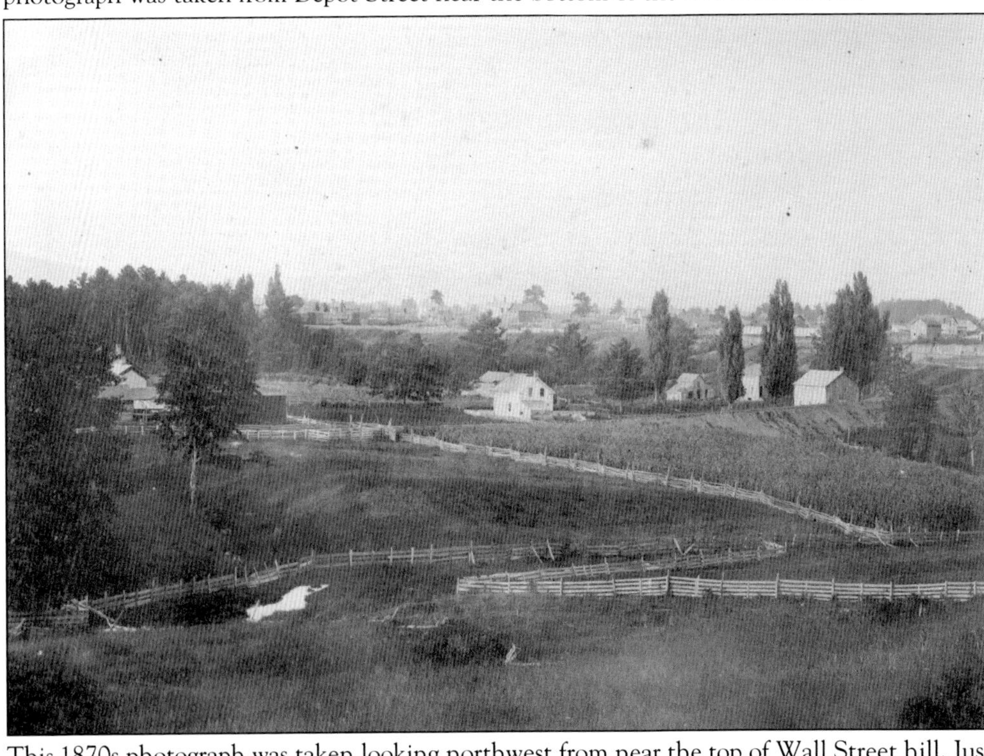

This 1870s photograph was taken looking northwest from near the top of Wall Street hill. Just behind the house, in the middle of the picture, is the narrow-gauge railroad that connected the Richards sawmill to the Glens Falls Feeder Canal.

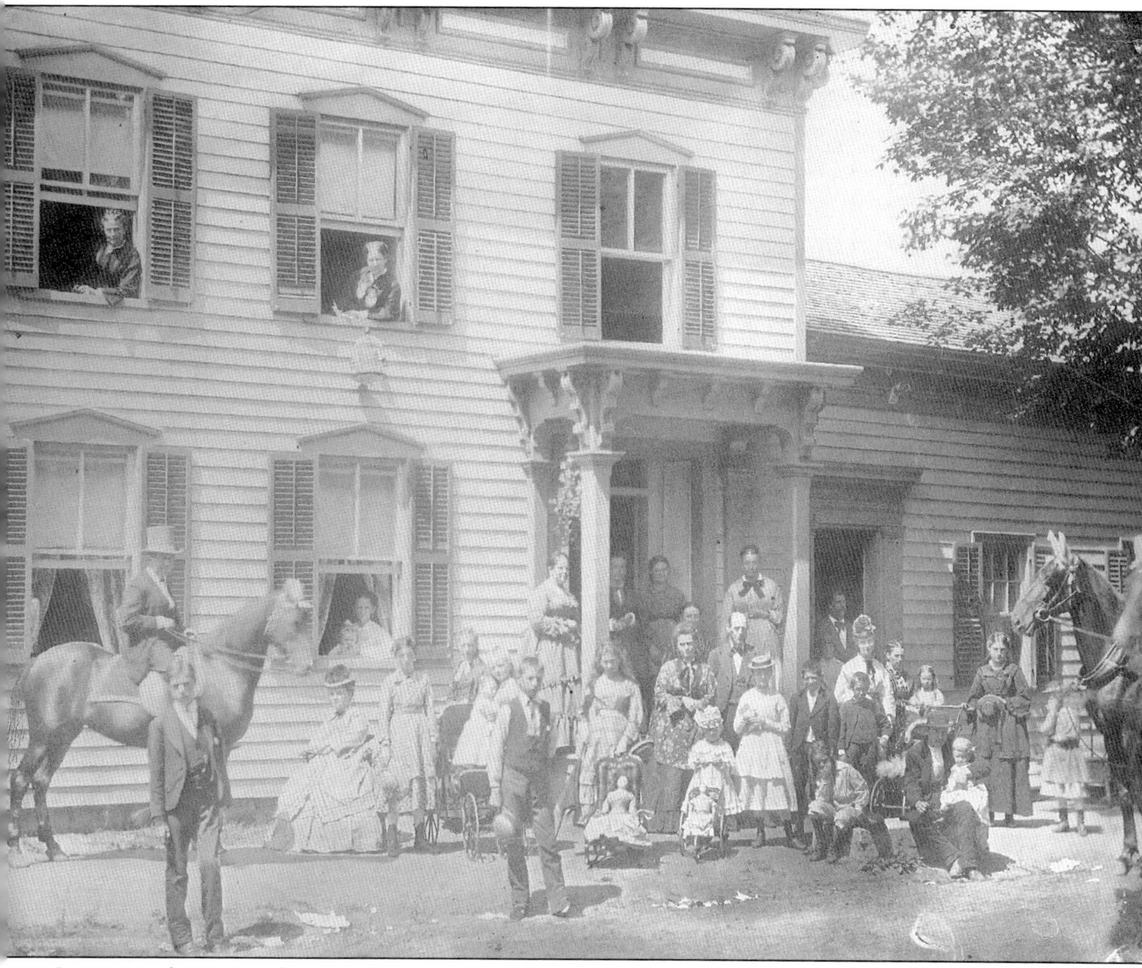

Some people pose in front of Pierson's Riverside Hotel, one of the other village hotels, located on Main Street near Hudson Place. Although this is an early-1870s photograph, some of the clothing appears to be from an even earlier period. Could it be that Sandy Hill fashions were a little behind the times?

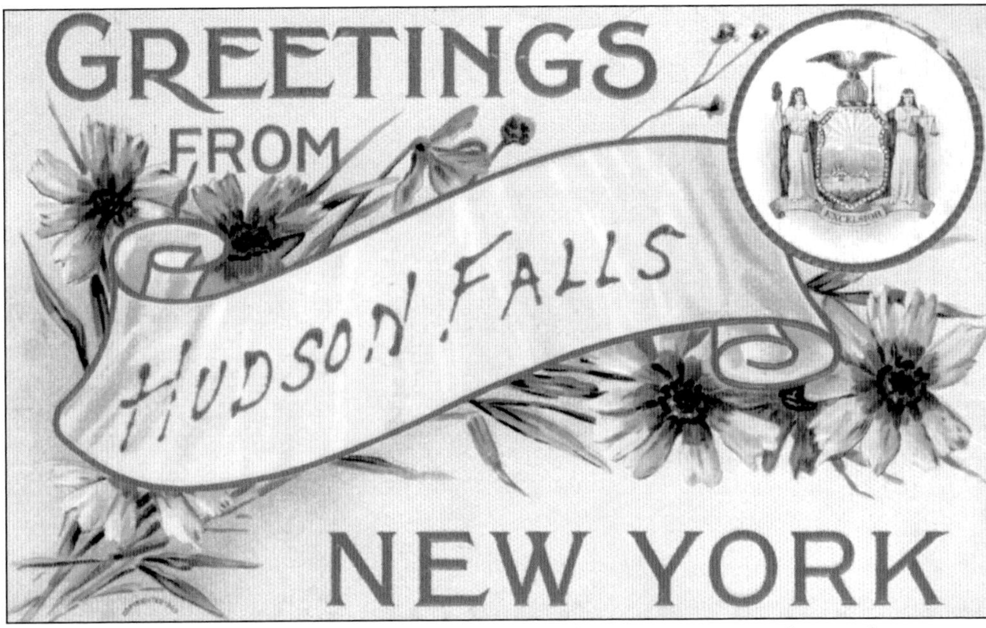

In the village election of March 1910, voters passed a proposition to change the name of the village from Sandy Hill to Hudson Falls. Although today that change may be viewed as a nonissue, at the time it was bitterly opposed by many voters, but not enough to defeat the proposition. Why was the name changed, you might ask. Some people thought it would entice tourists to stop here. This picture includes both sides of a 1910 postcard. What is interesting is that while the card says greetings from "Hudson Falls," it is postmarked March 29, 1910, two days before the name was officially changed.

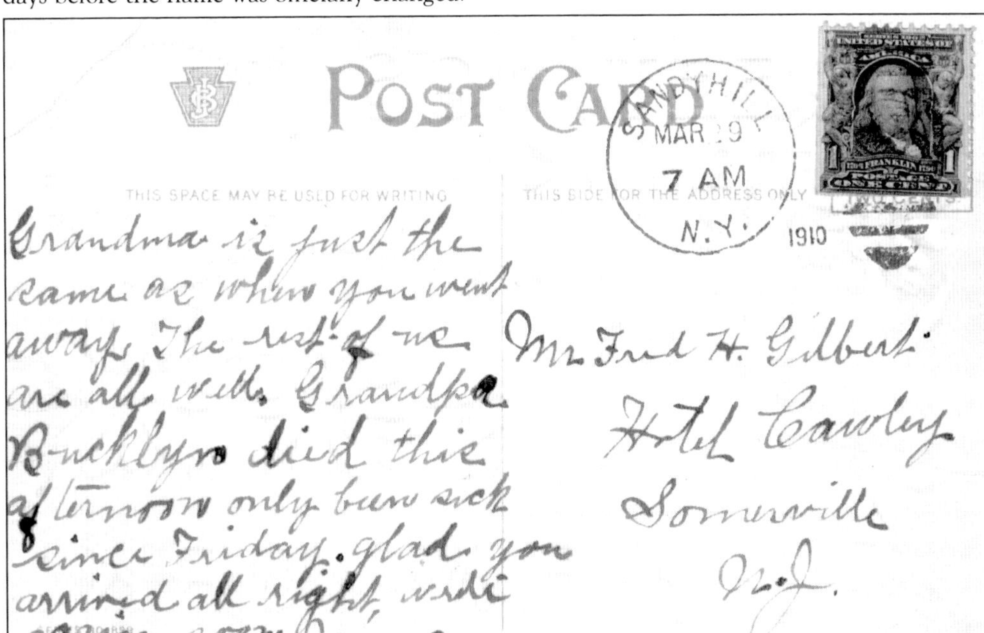

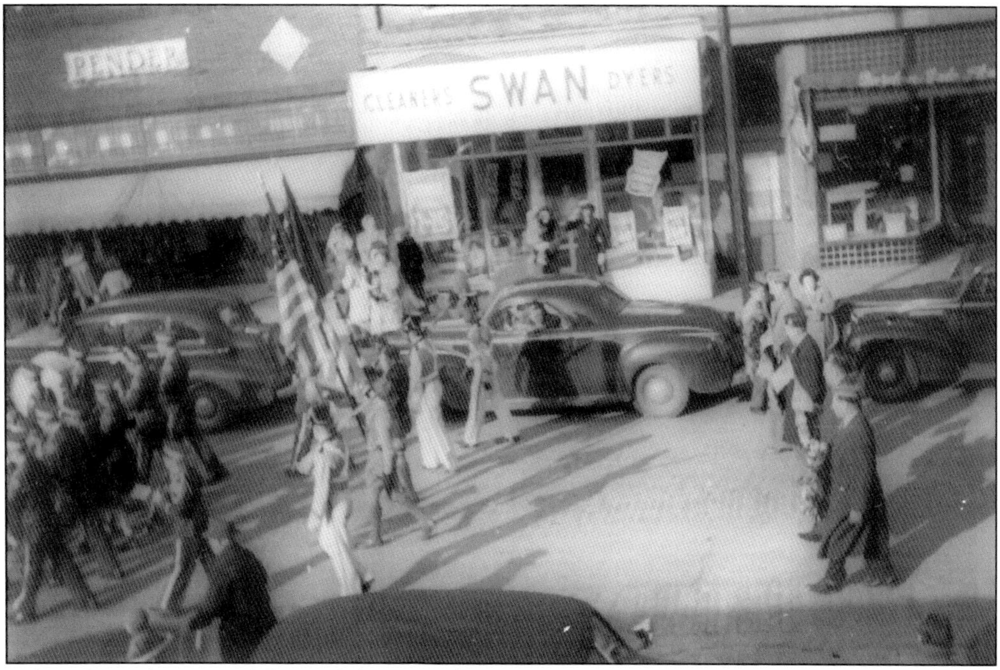

Taken from the second floor of the Strand Theatre, this photograph shows an early morning parade, with Boy Scouts marching south down Main Street. The date is *c.* 1950.

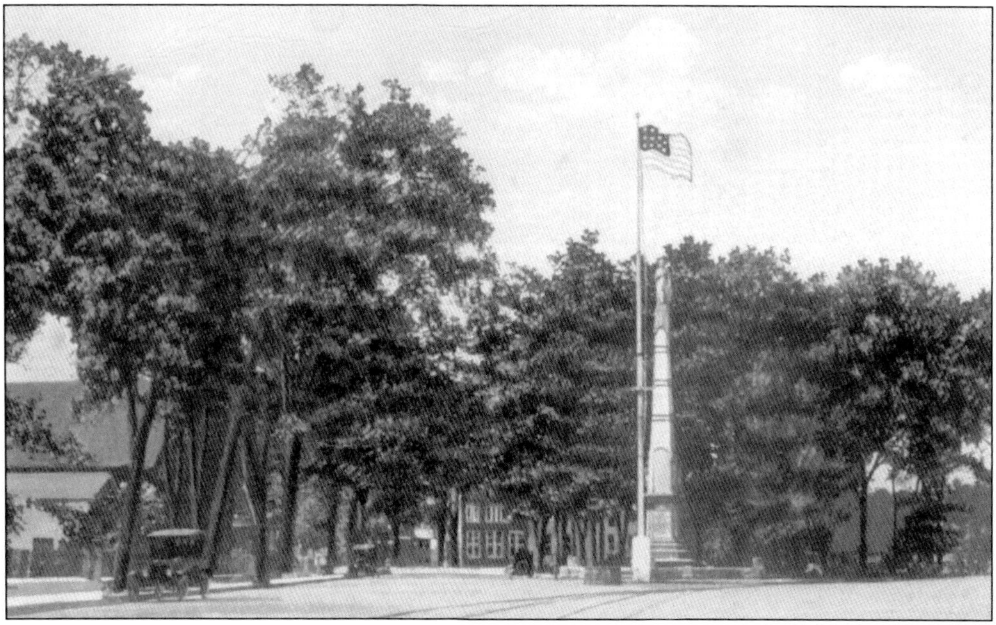

This view shows the flagpole and the Soldiers Monument. This view can be dated to *c.* 1920 or 1921 by noting the following: St. Mary's School is up beyond the left side of the village park, but the Middleworth House is not in the right background and the block that replaced it has not yet been constructed.

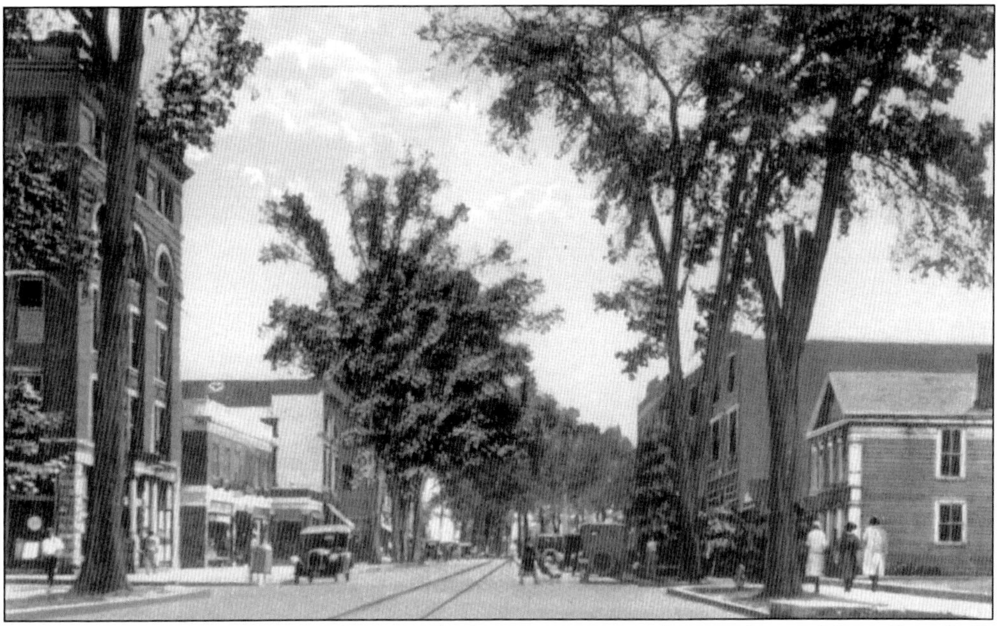

This *c.* 1920 view was taken looking south along Main Street from in front of the village hall. Note the trolley tracks down the middle of the street and the early-model automobiles.

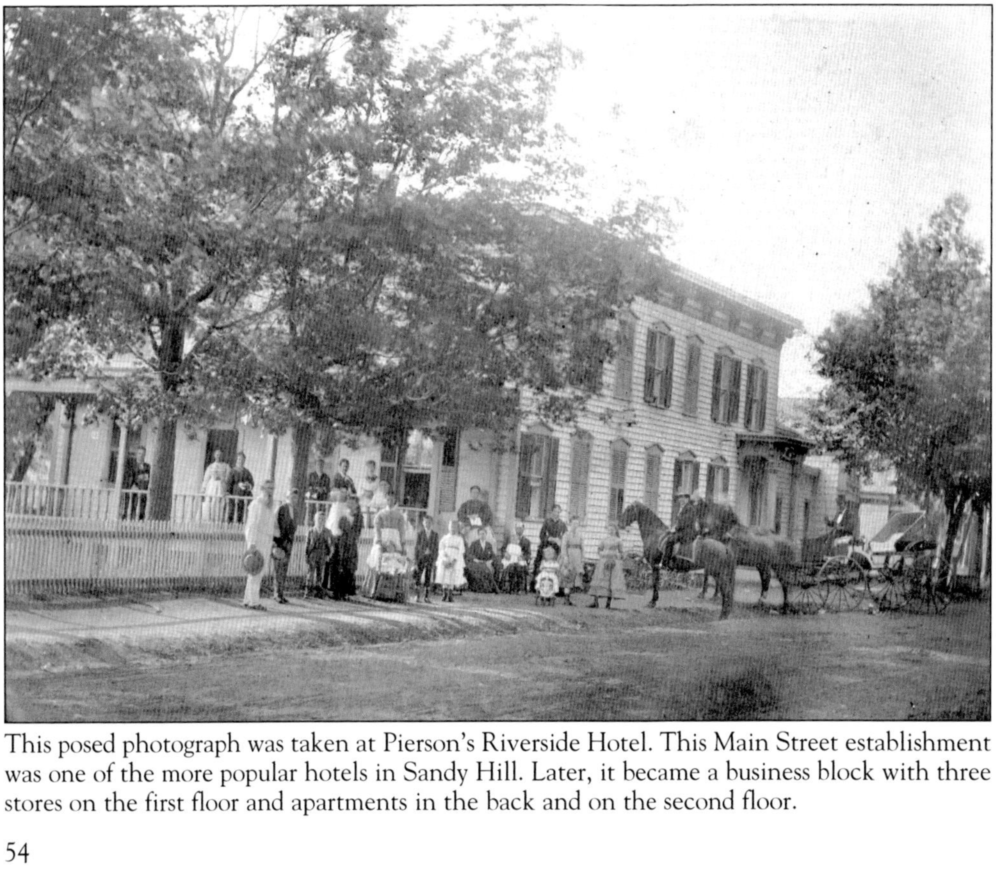

This posed photograph was taken at Pierson's Riverside Hotel. This Main Street establishment was one of the more popular hotels in Sandy Hill. Later, it became a business block with three stores on the first floor and apartments in the back and on the second floor.

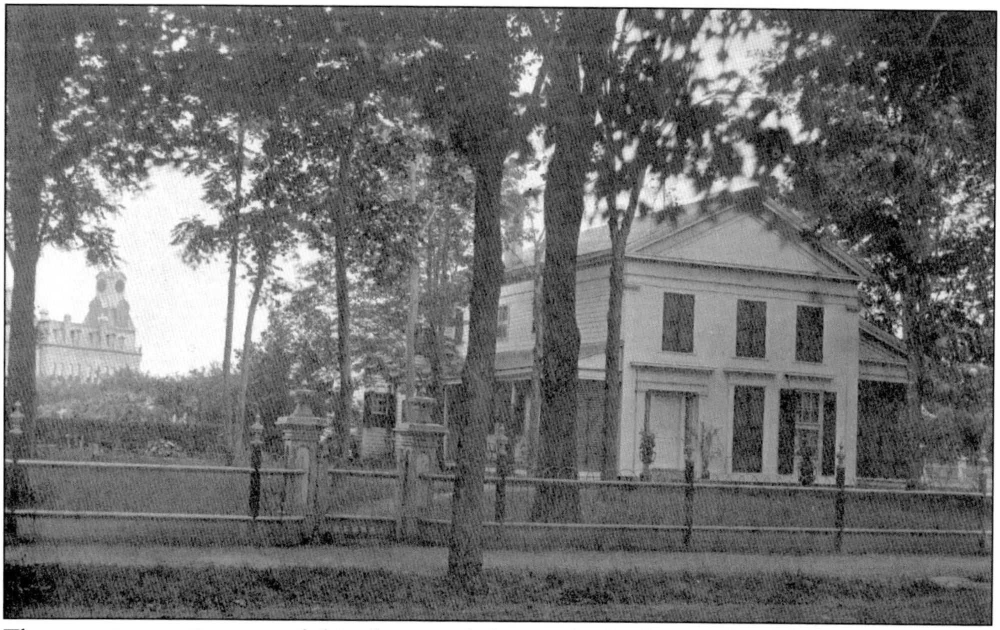

The most interesting part of this photograph lies in the background and helps in identifying the location. The building visible through the trees is the Sandy Hill High School. The house stands at the north corner of Clark and Main Streets and is in use today, with its yard still fenced.

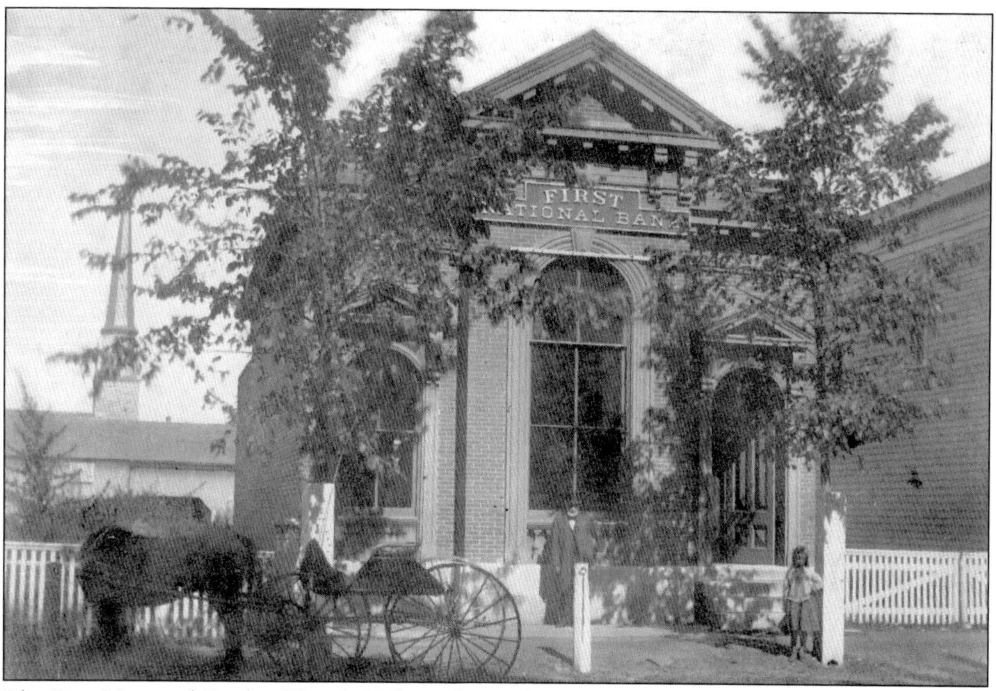

The First National Bank of Sandy Hill was located on Park Place, about where the sign for the Church of St. Mary's-St. Paul's is today. The bank remained here until it burned in 1920. In the background of this 1870 photograph is the steeple of the first St. Mary's Church, located on Wall Street.

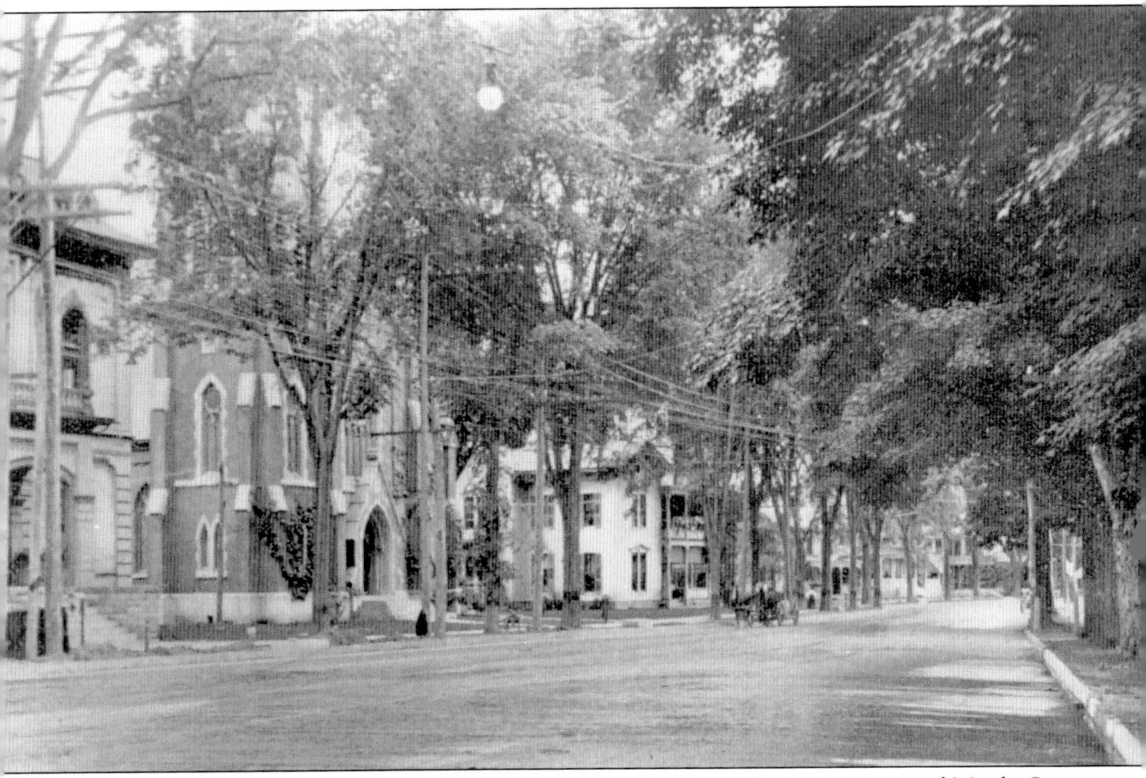

This picture was taken looking south on Main Street from the intersection of Maple Street. The courthouse and the Baptist church are just to the left. The next large house is the Griffin family homestead. The Griffin family owned Griffin Lumber Company, which was located on Pearl Street by the Glens Falls Feeder Canal.

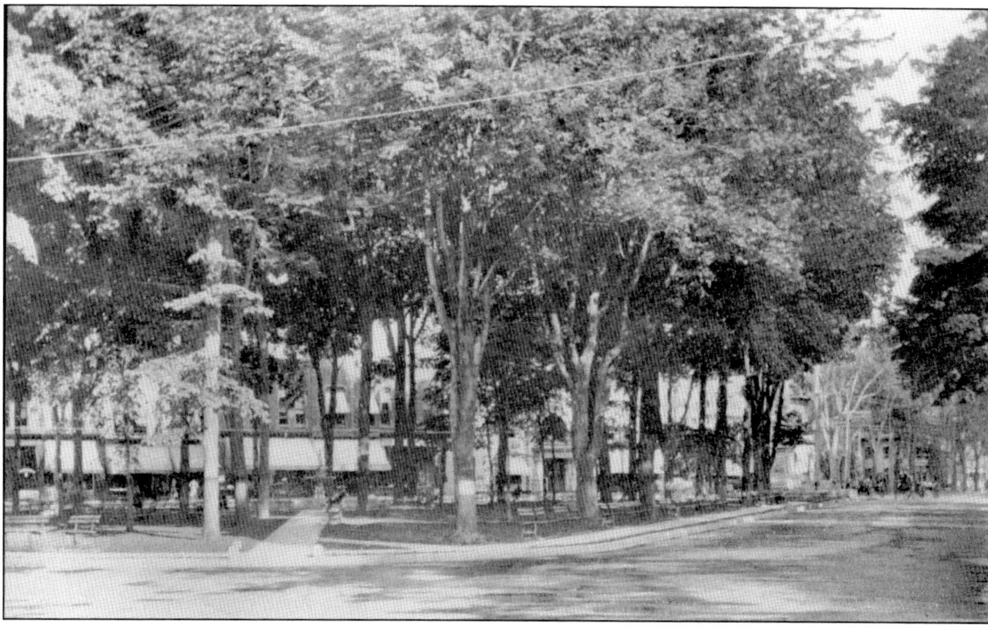

This view was taken looking east through the village park toward the Cunningham Hotel. The year is *c.* 1900, as the Civil War Cannon has not yet been placed at the south end of the park. Note that the sidewalks are set out in the same places as they are today.

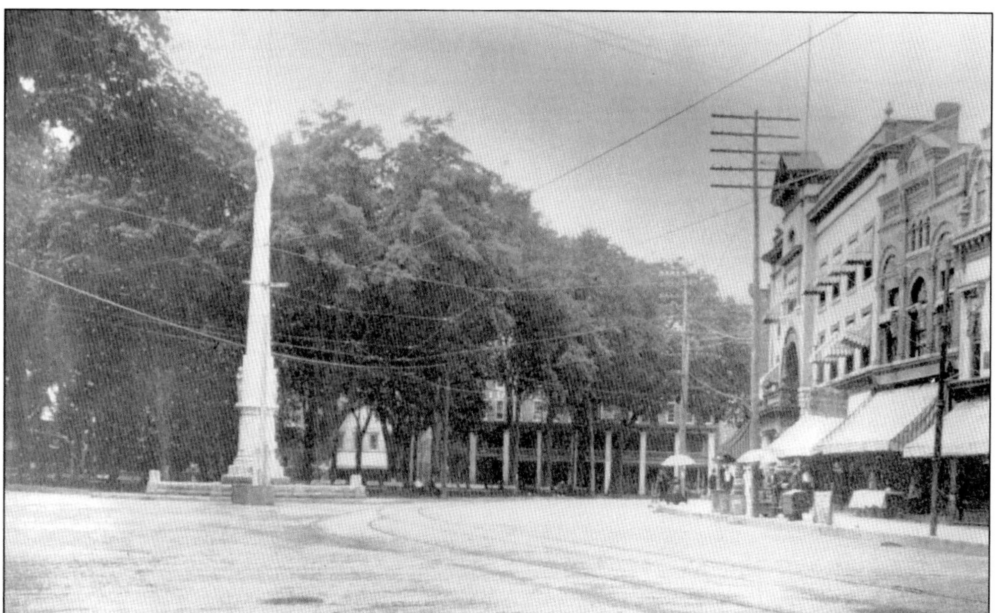

This picture shows the Middleworth House and some other buildings on Main Street. Also in clear view is the horse trough in front of the Soldiers Monument.

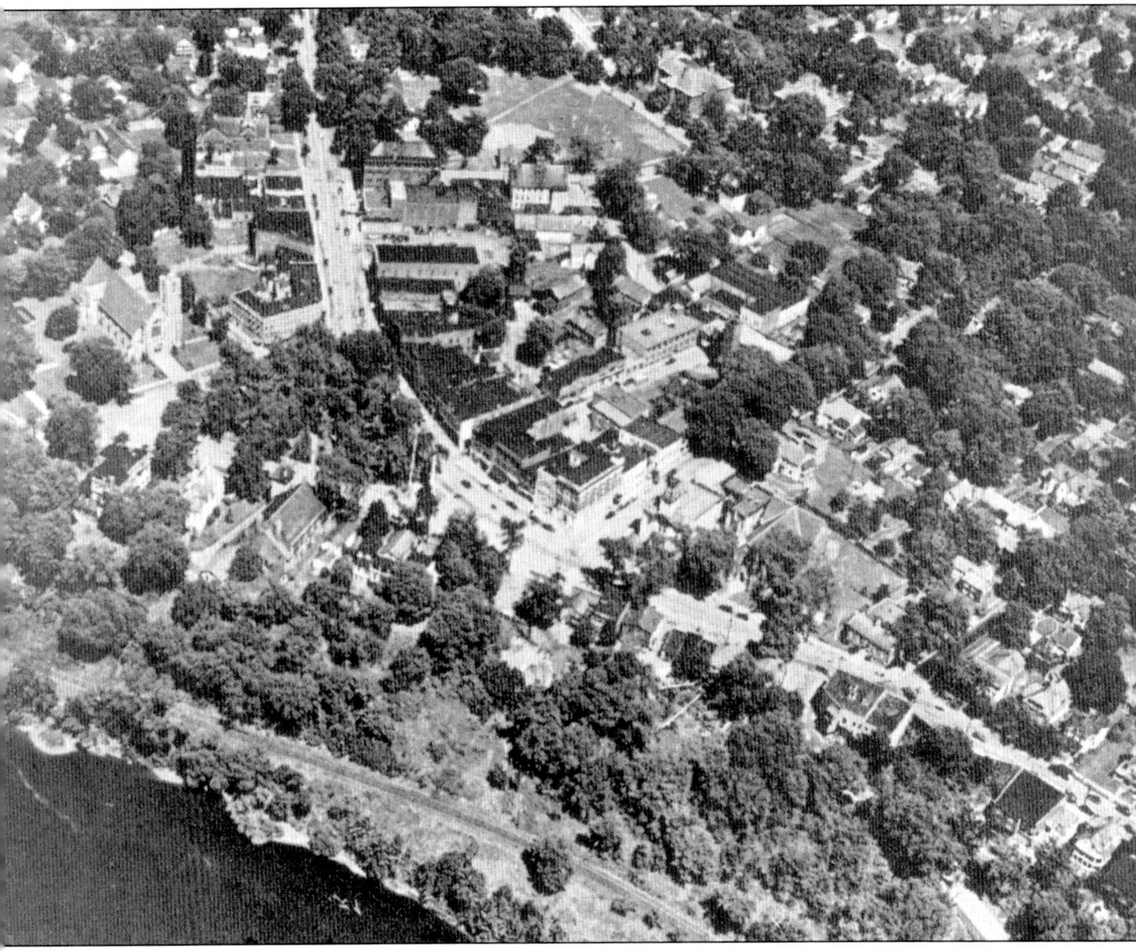

This bird's-eye view shows the village of Hudson Falls. Right in the middle is the large open square of Main and Maple Streets. The cupola is still on the courthouse and the new St. Mary's Church has been built, so that dates this picture from *c.* 1935.

Four

THE TOWN OF KINGSBURY

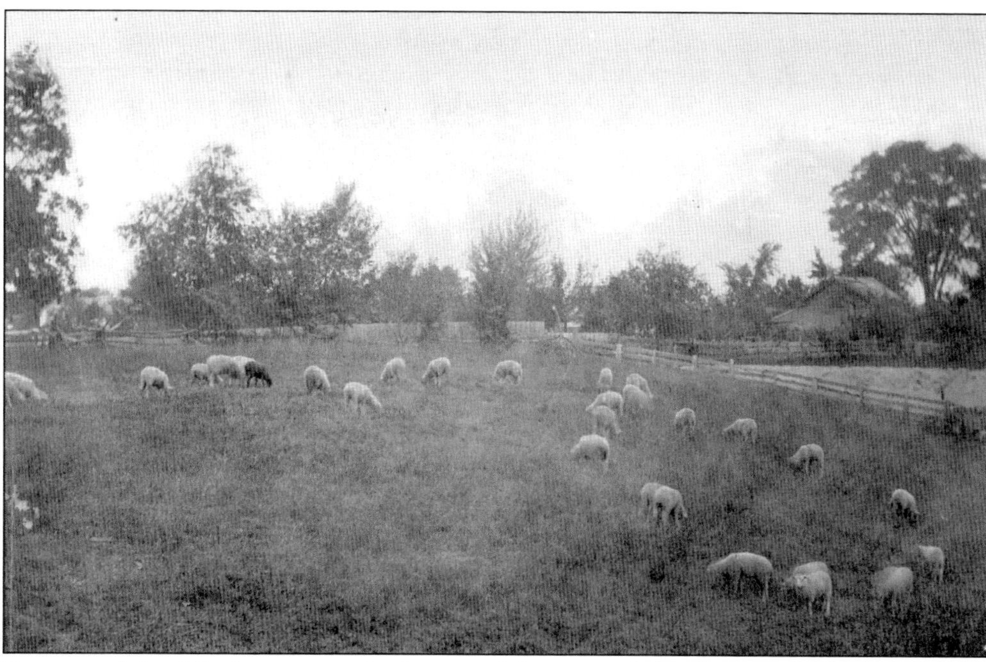

For most of the 230-plus years in the history of the town of Kingsbury, agriculture has played an important and prominent roll. The same is true for all of Washington County. During the mid-to-late 1800s, one of the strongest segments of the local agricultural industry was the raising of sheep. In fact, the county was one of the largest sheep-raising areas in the nation. This 1870s picture shows sheep grazing on a Kingsbury hillside.

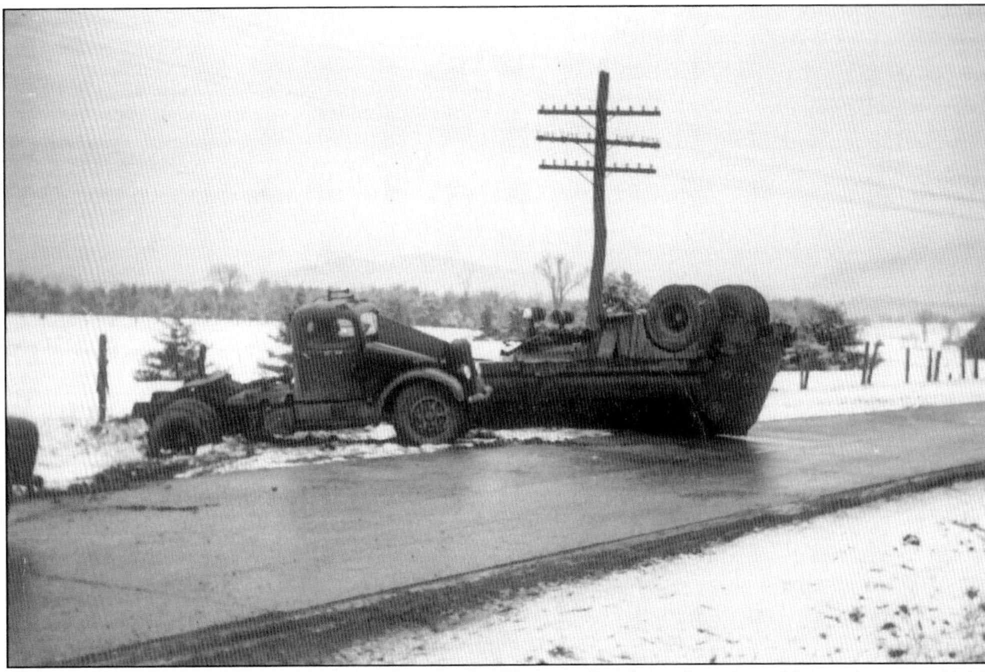

This accident took place on Route 4, several miles north of the hamlet of Kingsbury, *c.* 1940. The road appears to be icy, and the truck has jackknifed. In recent years this section of Route 4 has been the scene of similar but larger crashes.

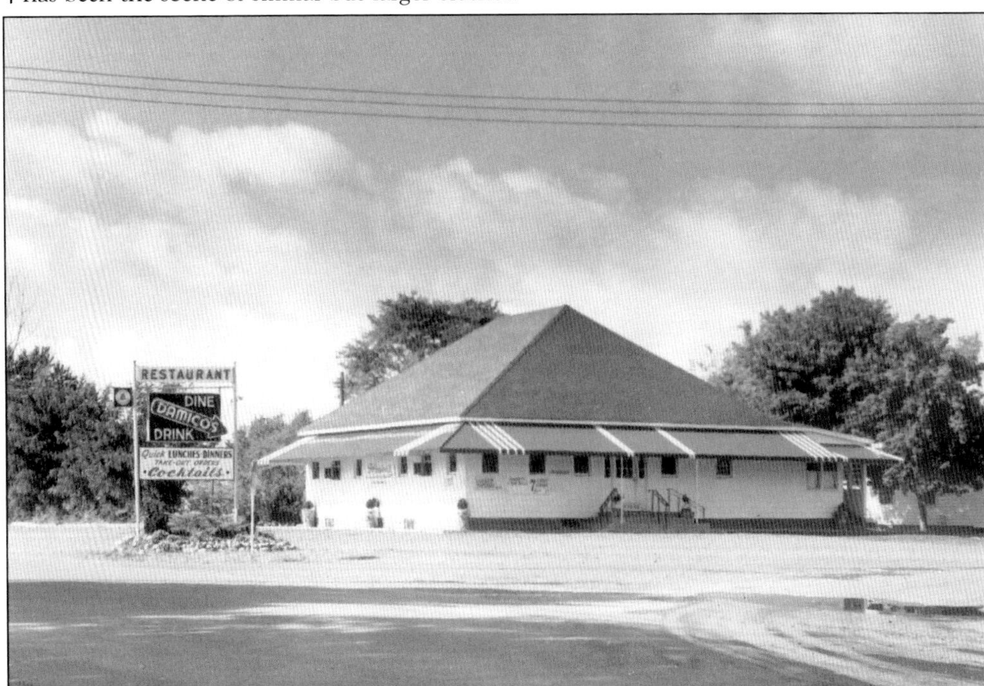

In 1948, D'Amico's was an Italian-American restaurant, located at the corner of Moss Street and Dix Avenue. In the 1980s, it became the Hong Kong Inn, a Chinese restaurant. Later, the building was destroyed by fire.

Although sheep raising was once a large business in town, it no longer is. However, the raising of dairy cattle has continued for a much longer period of time. Even today, dairy farming is the number one industry in Kingsbury. This agricultural scene dates from the 1870s.

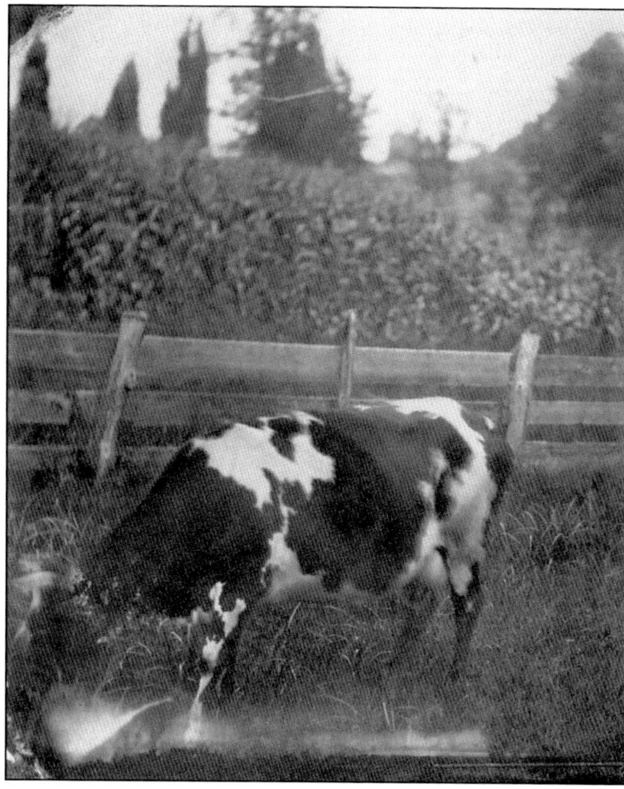

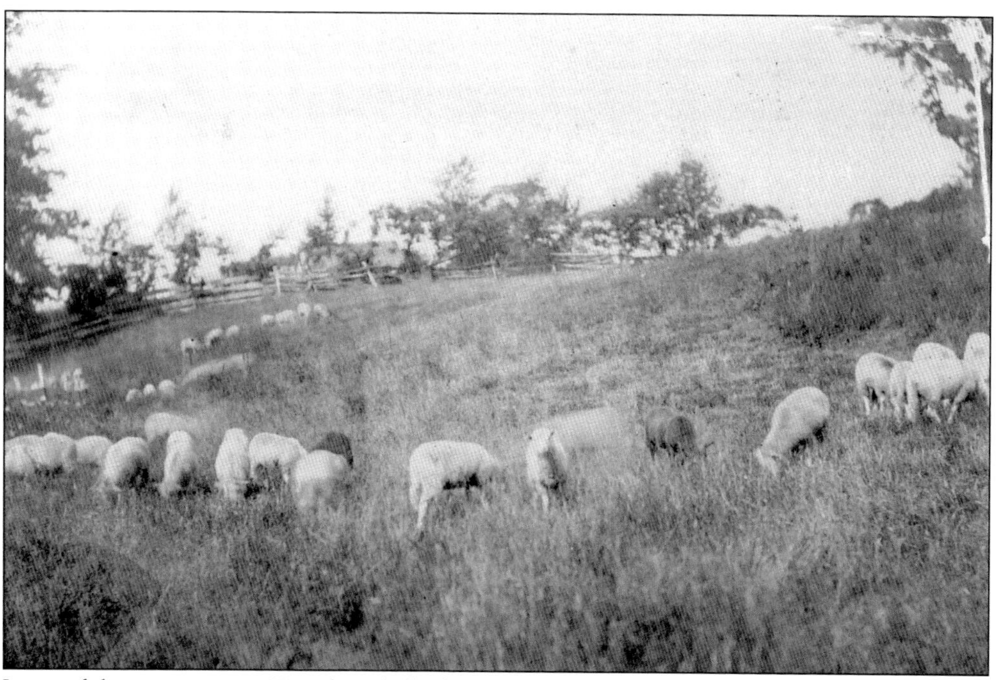

Lines of sheep graze on a Kingsbury hillside in the 1870s.

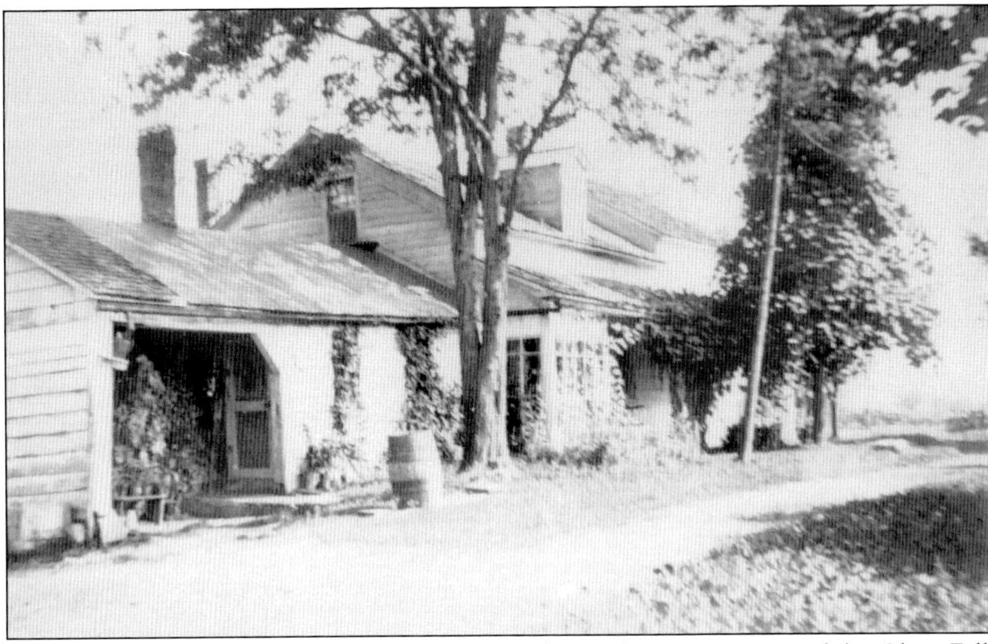

Before it burned in the 1970s, a picturesque farm lay at the east terminus of the Glens Falls Feeder Canal. It was the Sherman farm, which had a fine house and a good barn. This picture shows the woodshed loaded up, ready for the coming winter.

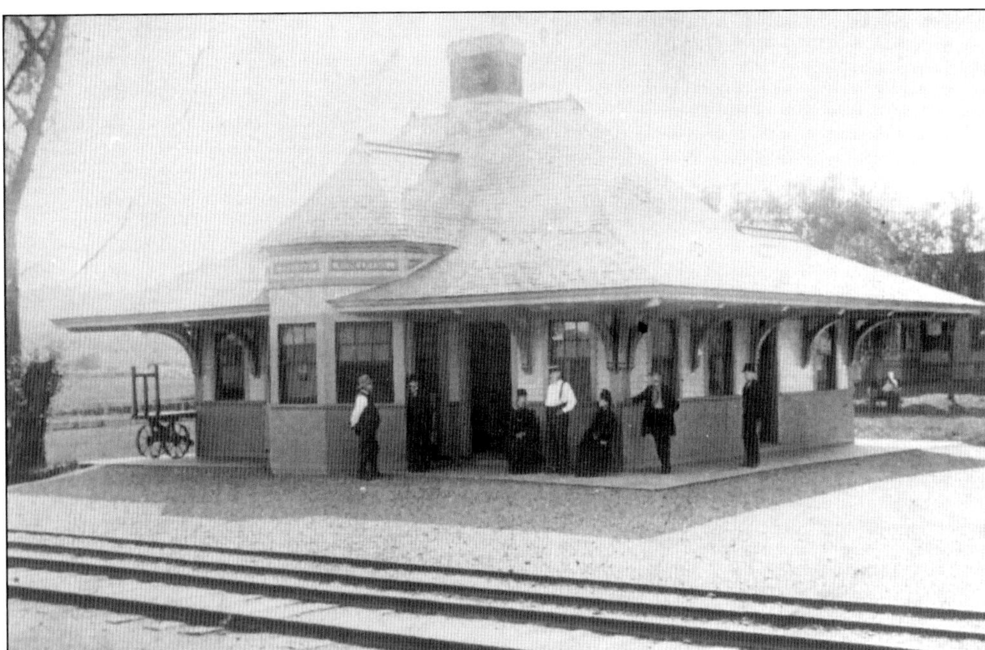

Smiths Basin was a very busy and prosperous hamlet in the late 1800s and early 1900s. In 1891, the Delaware and Hudson Railroad built this station in Smiths Basin to serve that part of Kingsbury and neighboring Hartford. Unfortunately, this architectural gem was torn down in the early 1960s.

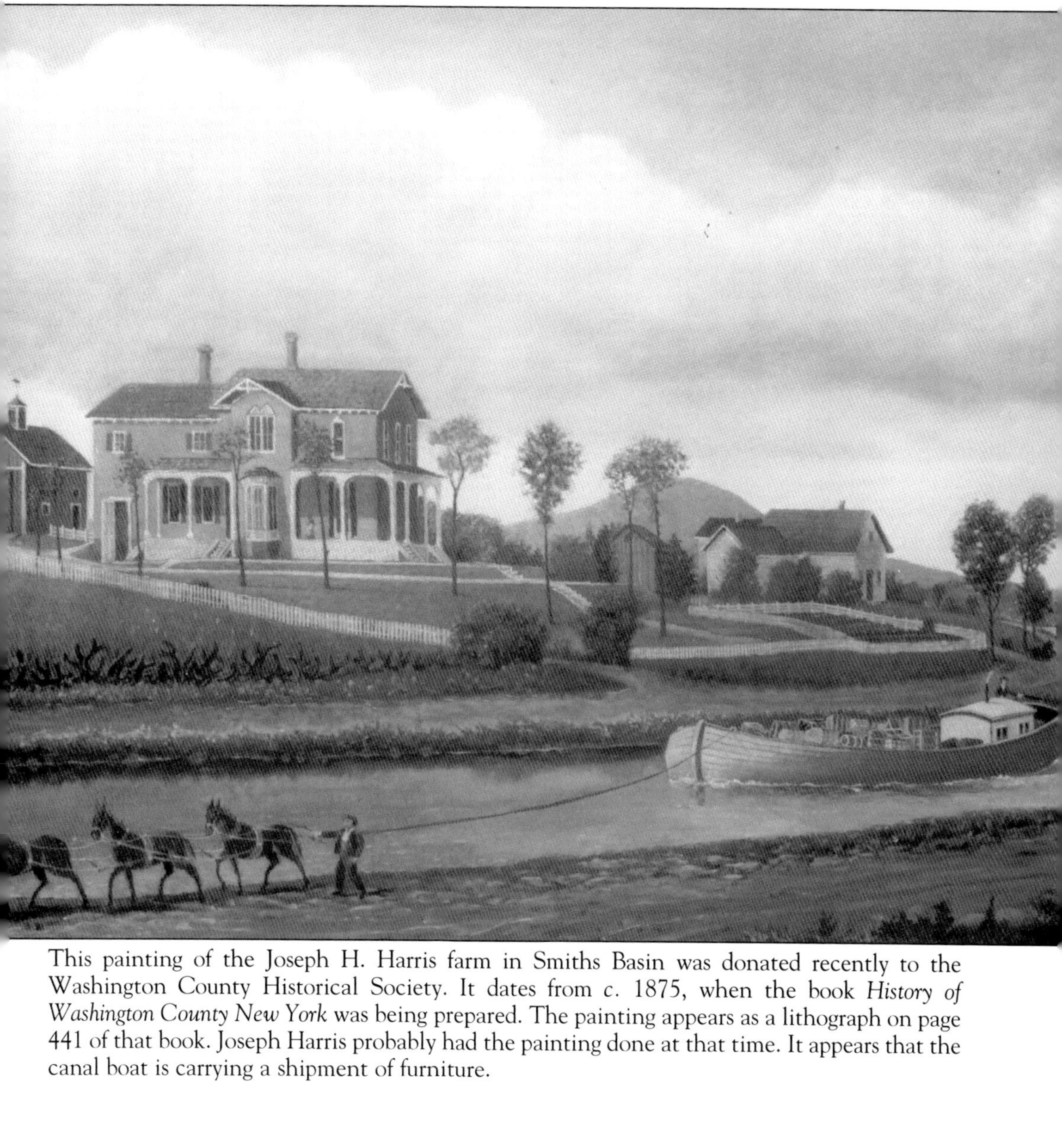

This painting of the Joseph H. Harris farm in Smiths Basin was donated recently to the Washington County Historical Society. It dates from *c.* 1875, when the book *History of Washington County New York* was being prepared. The painting appears as a lithograph on page 441 of that book. Joseph Harris probably had the painting done at that time. It appears that the canal boat is carrying a shipment of furniture.

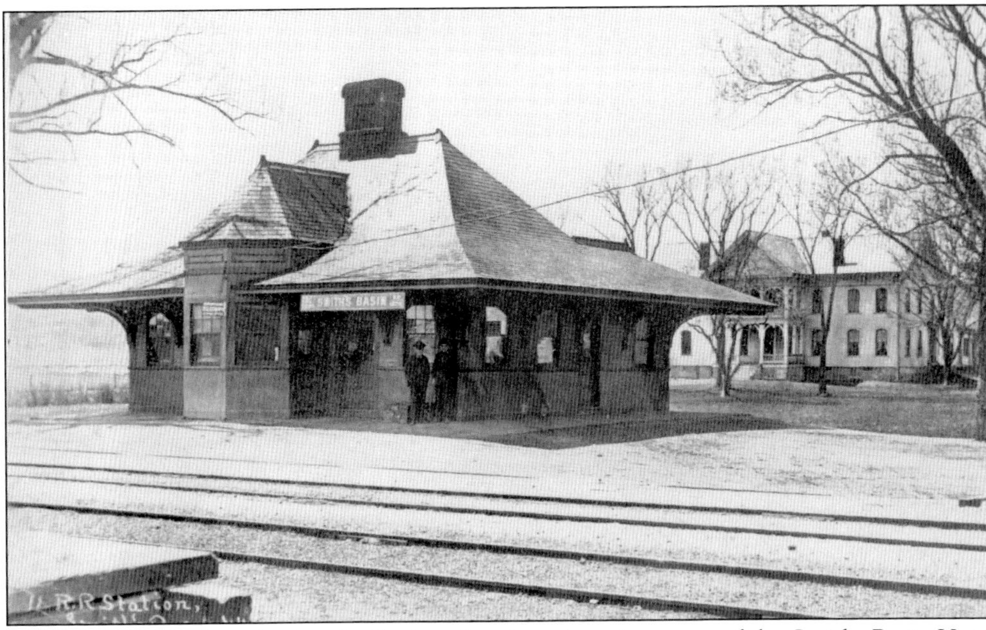

This is another look at the Smiths Basin railroad station. A portion of the Smiths Basin Hotel is visible in the background.

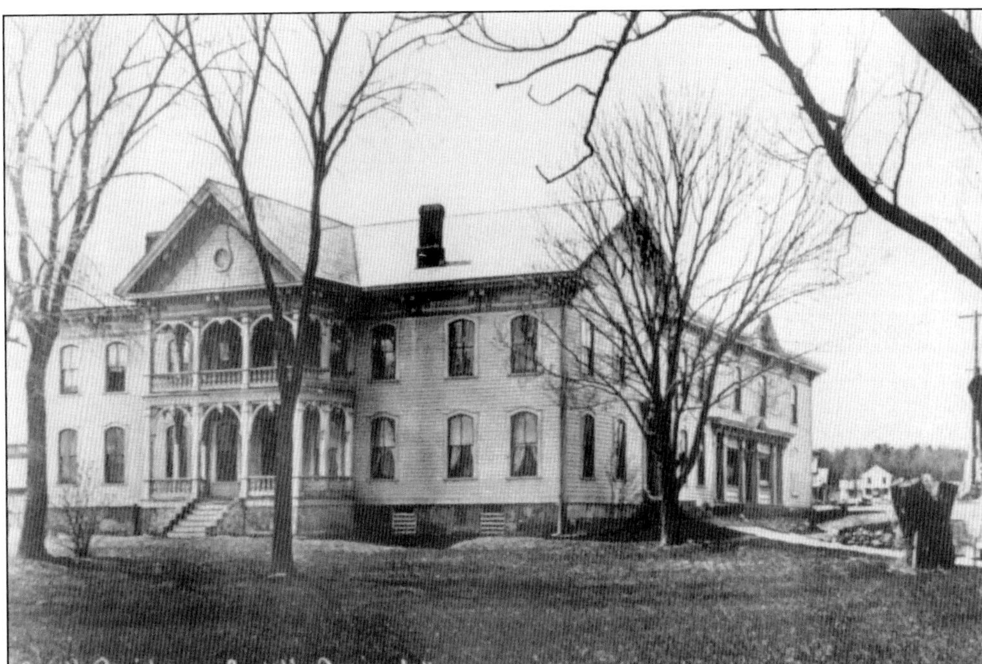

This is a close-up view of the Smiths Basin Hotel. To the left of the building is an addition, which served as a store and the post office. In the late 1980s, that wing was removed because it was collapsing. Since that time, several owners have done restoration work to save the main hotel, which is now used for public functions.

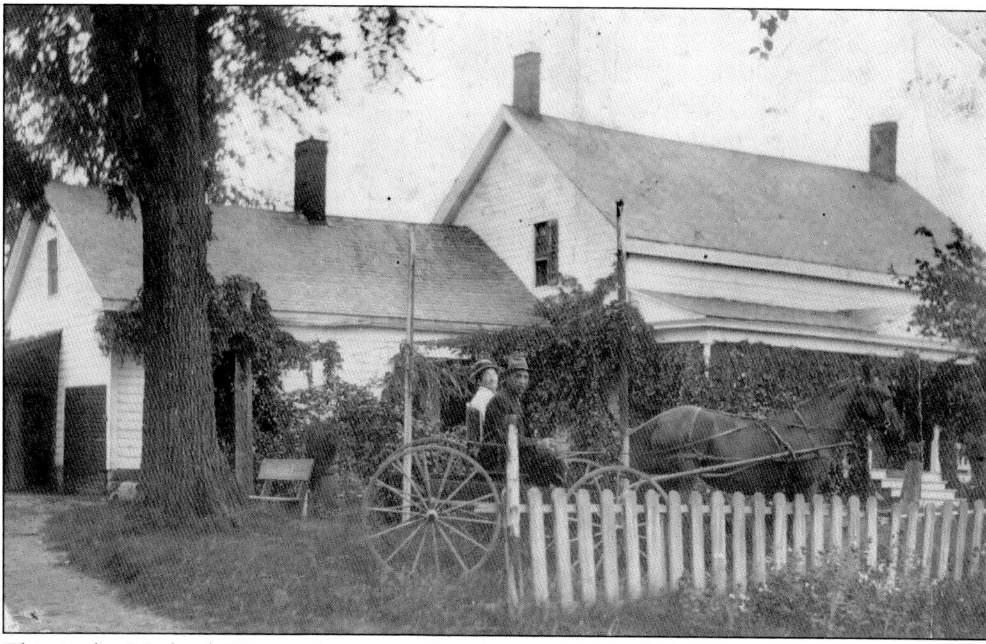

This is the Michael O'Leary home on Dix Avenue, located almost in front of the Board of Cooperative Educational Services (BOCES) complex. The picture was taken in the early part of the 20th century. The house burned down in the late 1940s.

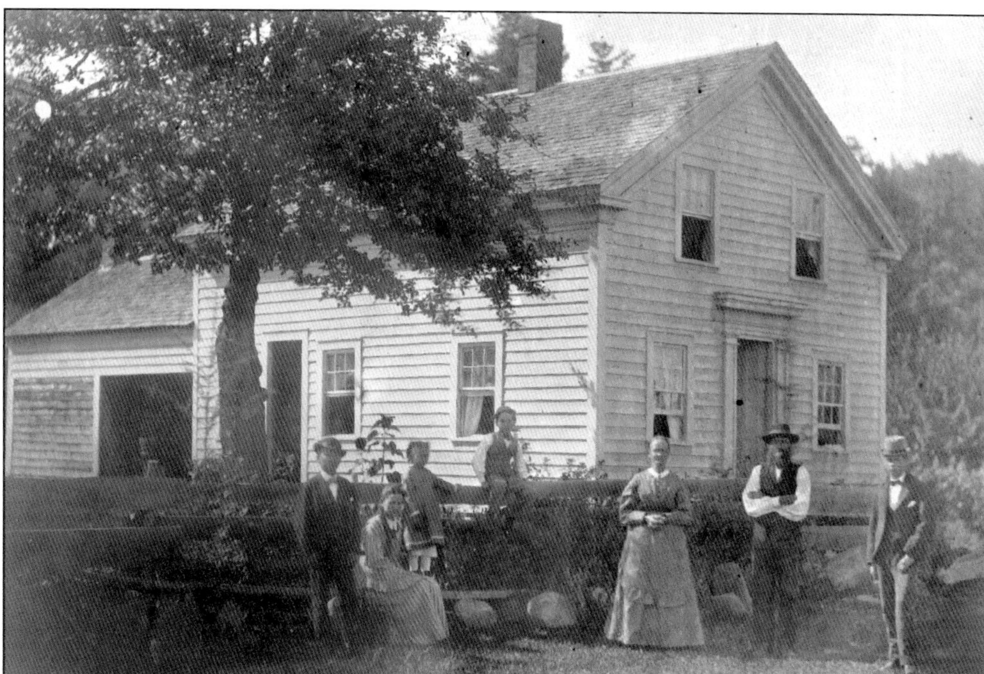

Family members pose for a portrait in front of their house *c.* 1870. The home may have been located near Bonds Creek, at Dunham's Basin.

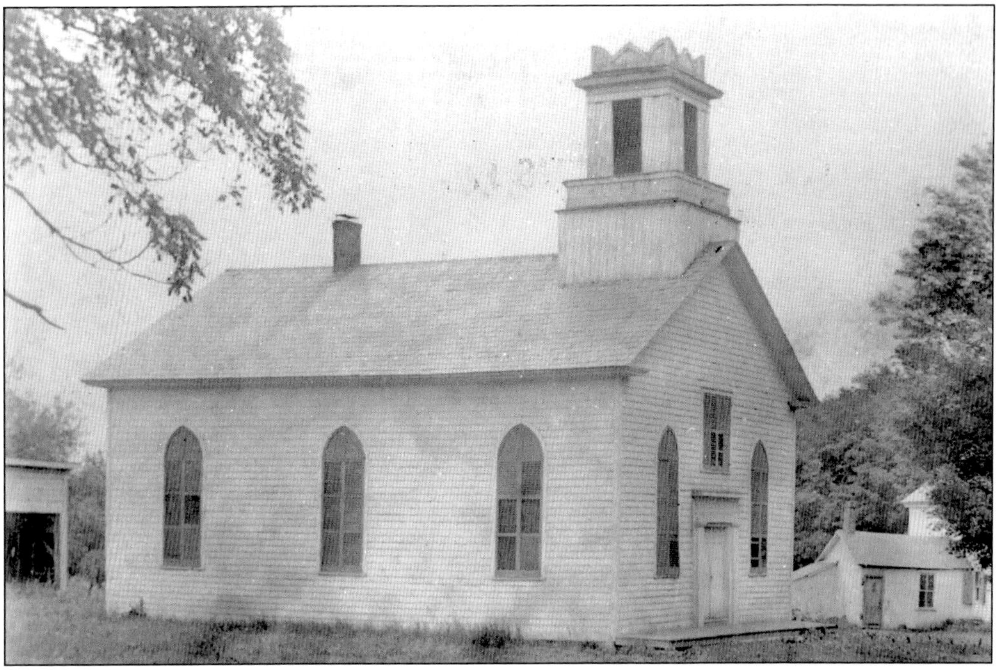

The Sandford's Ridge United Methodist Church is located near Pattens Mills, on the western border of Kingsbury and Warren County. The congregation was founded in 1799 and the church community is still active, having recently celebrated its bicentennial. This view dates from the late 1800s.

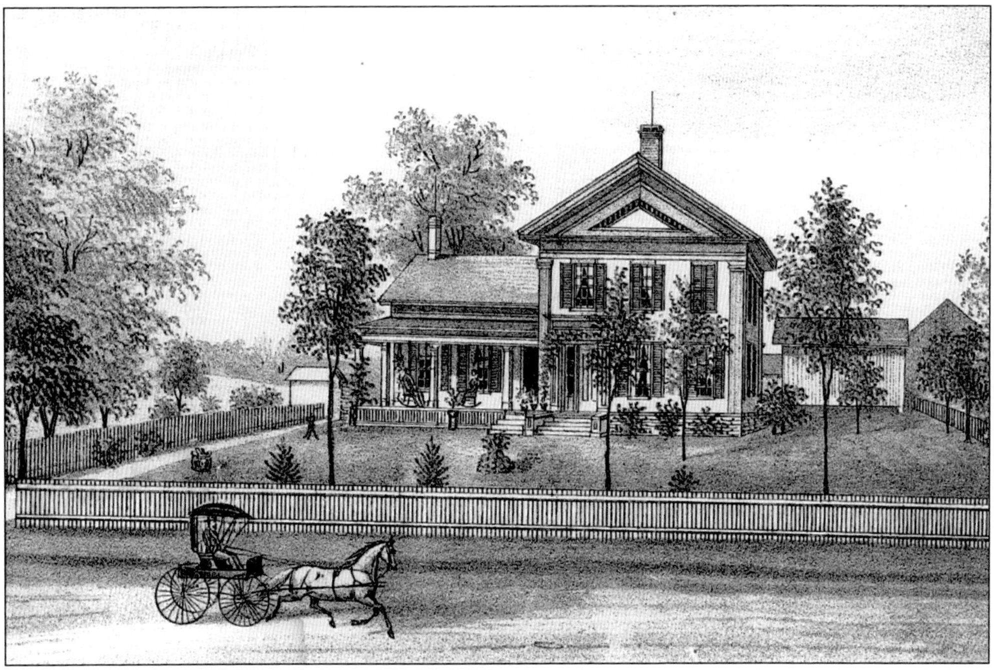

This picture from the 1878 *History of Washington County* shows the residence of T.M. Groesbeck *c.* the 1870s. It is the last house in the town of Kingsbury on the left side of Route 4, going north. Today, it is the home of Mrs. Leon Collins.

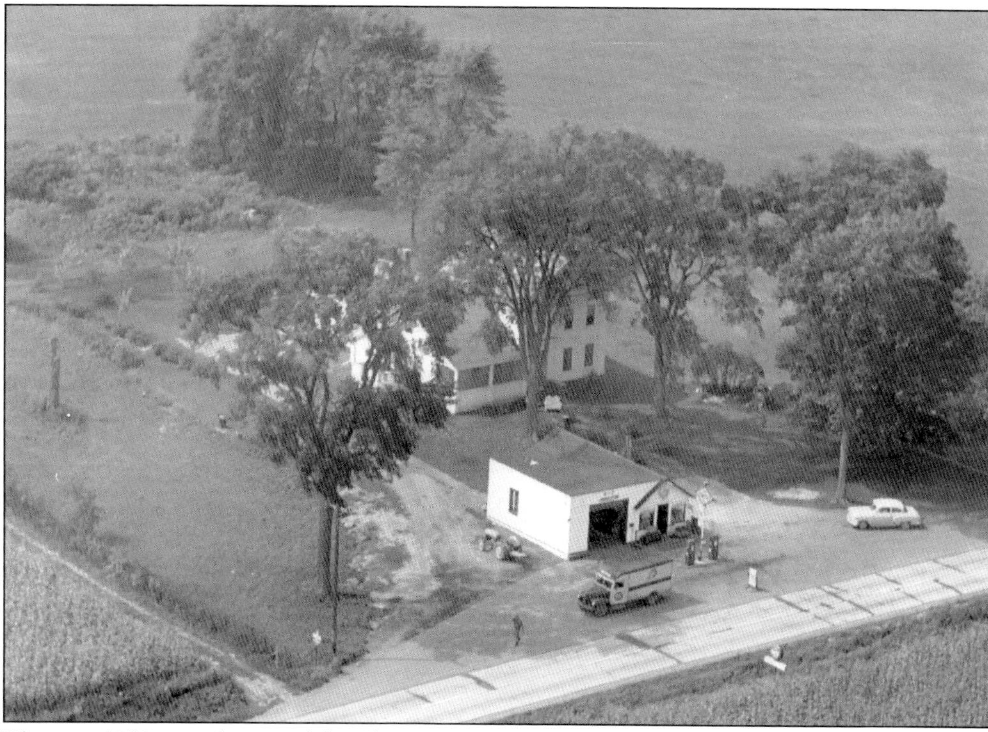

This is a 1950s aerial view of the Elmwood Sunoco Service Station, which was in front of the Collins home shown in the previous photograph. Route 4 is still slabs of cement and has not yet been blacktopped. The station operated until sometime in the 1980s, and then it was torn down by the Collins family.

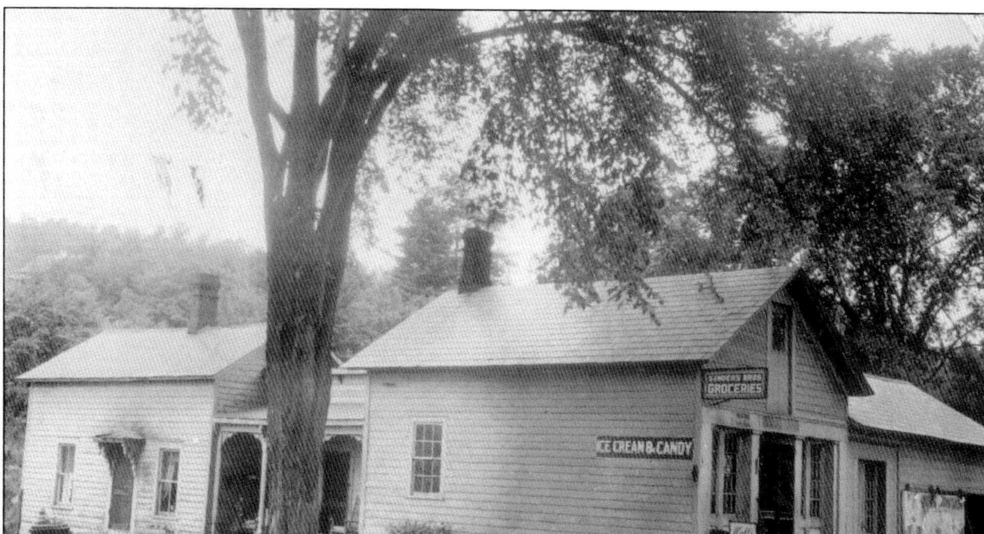

This 1925 picture shows the Pattens Mills store owned by Edward Saunders. The store was located right in the middle of the hamlet, not too far from Halfway Brook. Small general stores such as this one served most all of the needs of the residents of these rural hamlets.

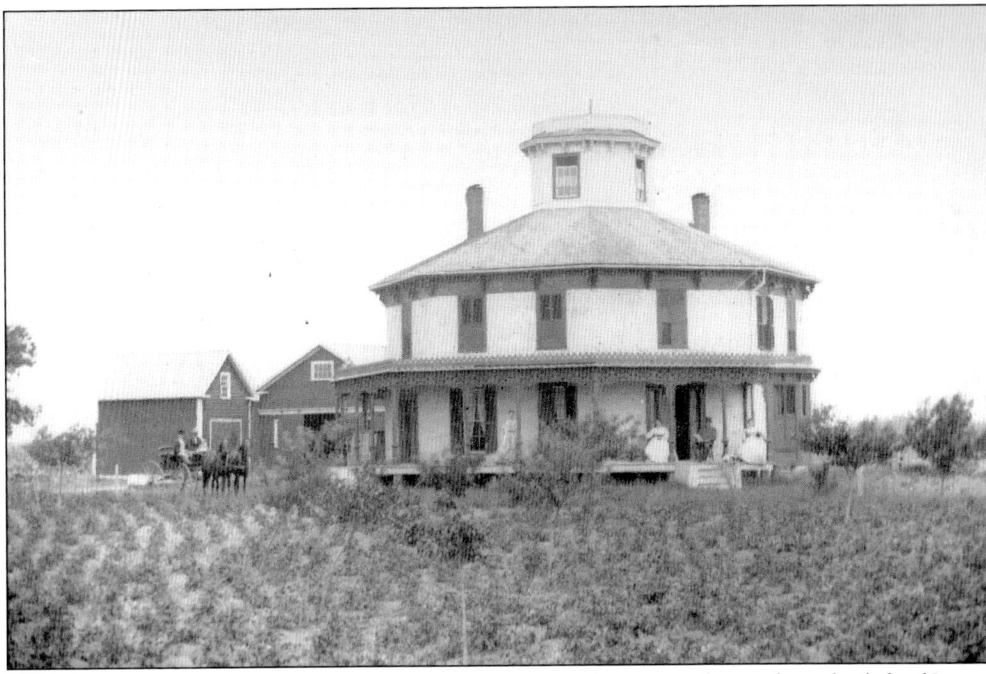

This is the Kingsbury round house *c.* 1880. This unique home was located on the left of Lower Maple Street, at the crest of the hill. It may have been built as early as the 1820s. When this photograph was taken, a Mrs. Goodson owned the house.

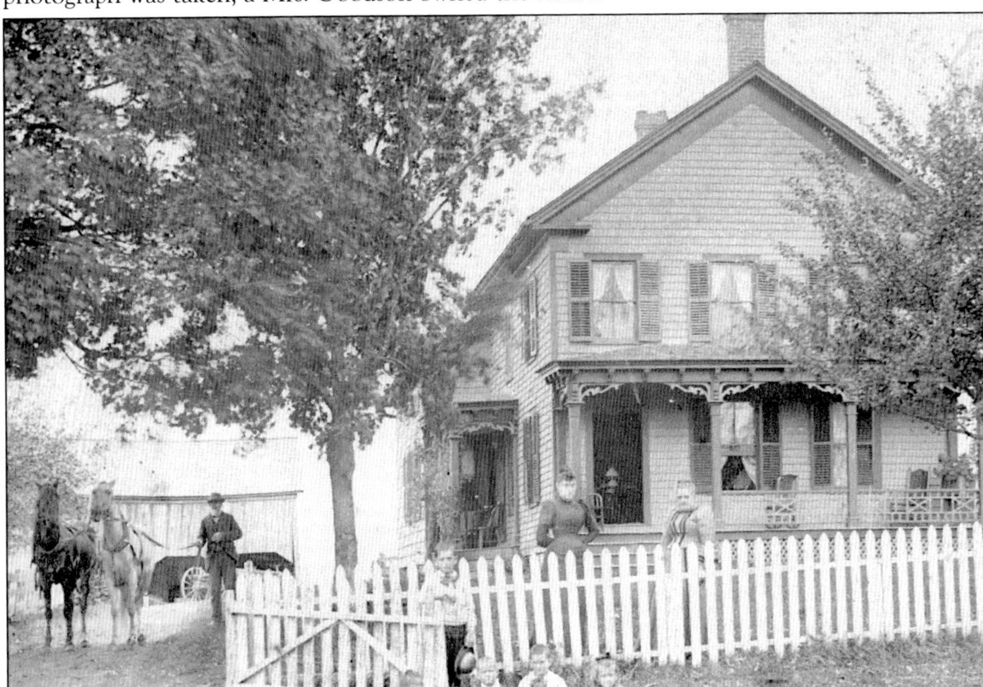

This farm is located on Notre Dame Street Extension, or Mud Street, as it used to be called. The children in front of the fence attended the one-room school at the intersection of Hartman Road, pictured on page 28.

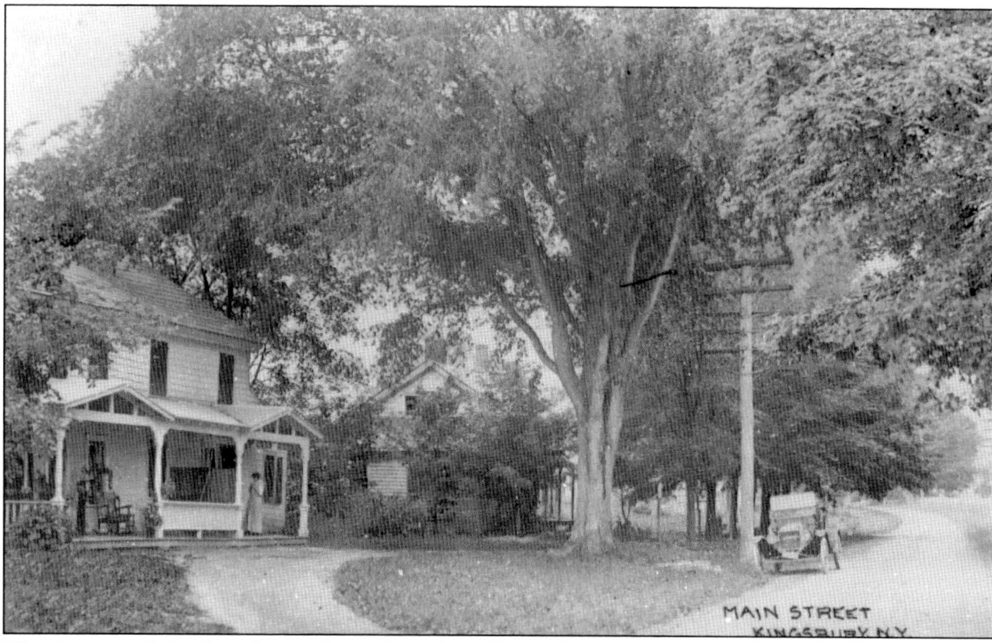

The largest of the hamlets in Kingsbury has always been Kingsbury, itself. Located on Route 4 about halfway between Hudson Falls and Fort Ann, Kingsbury at one time had a cemetery, two churches, a school, a small hotel, a post office, and a couple of stores. This is a Kingsbury store, in the 1920s.

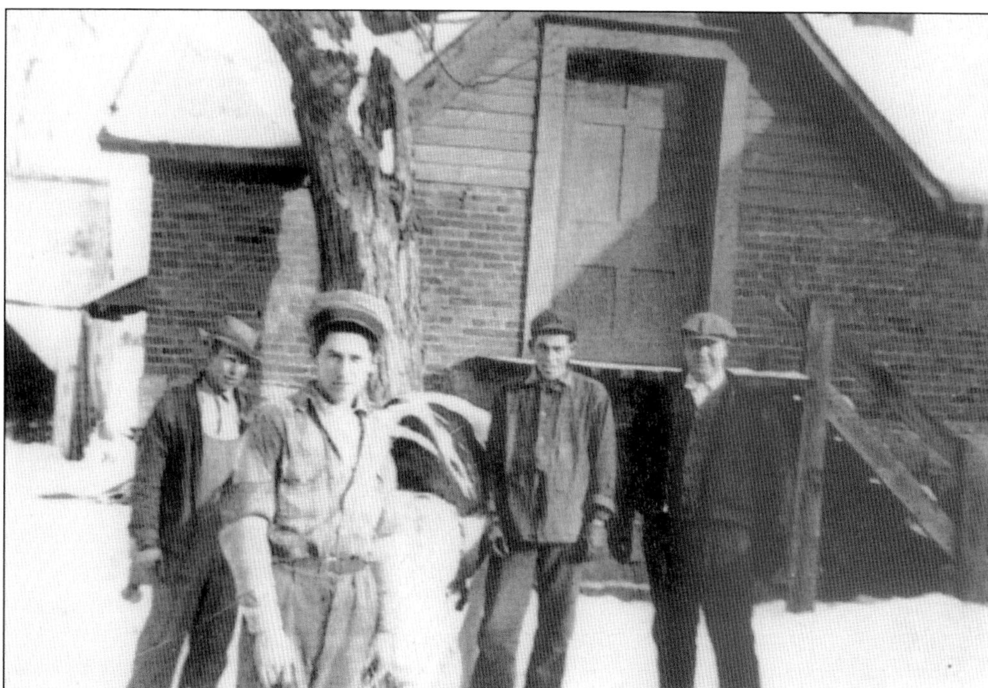

These young men are trying to get this large bull onto a truck to ship it to market. This 1930s picture is at the Fitzgerald farm on Vaughn Road near the Pattens Mills Cemetery.

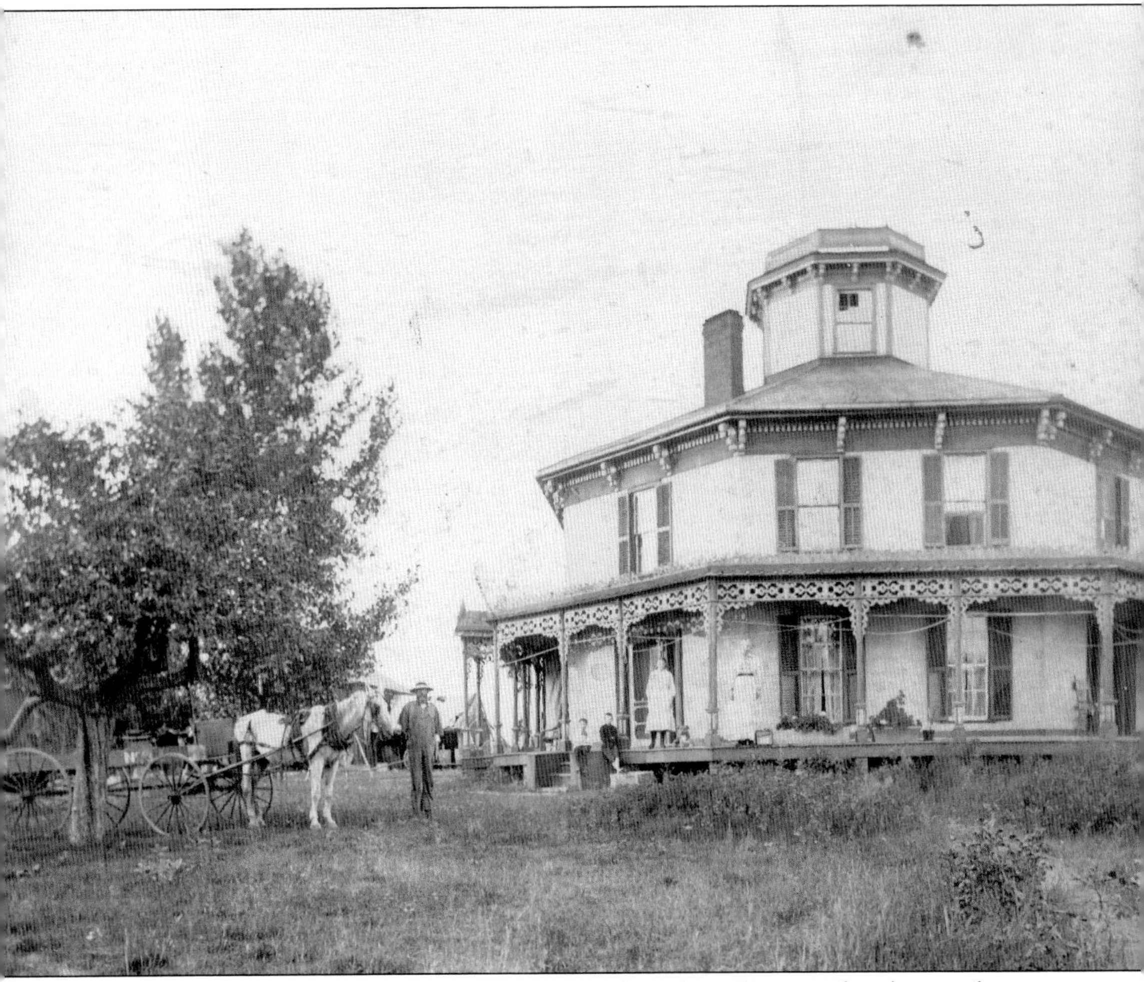

This picture of the Kingsbury round house was taken about 50 years after the one that appears on page 68. The house was demolished in the 1940s. Jeanne Matthews of Fort Edward was born in this house, several years before it was torn down.

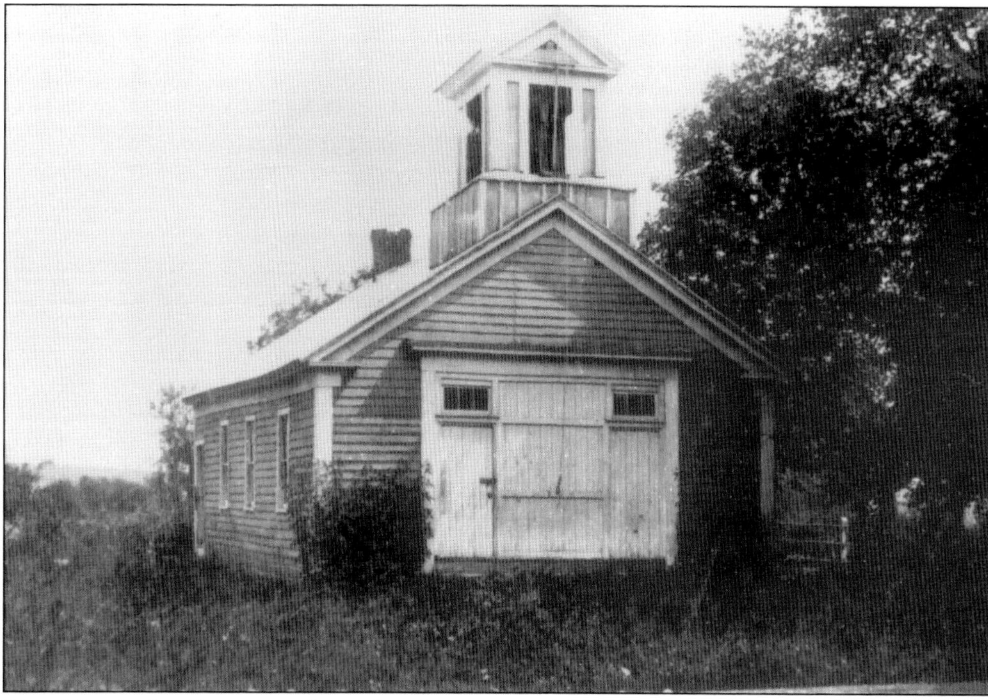

The old red schoolhouse was located at the corner of Dean and Tracy Roads and is typical of all of the small one-room schools in the town. Today it is used as a private residence.

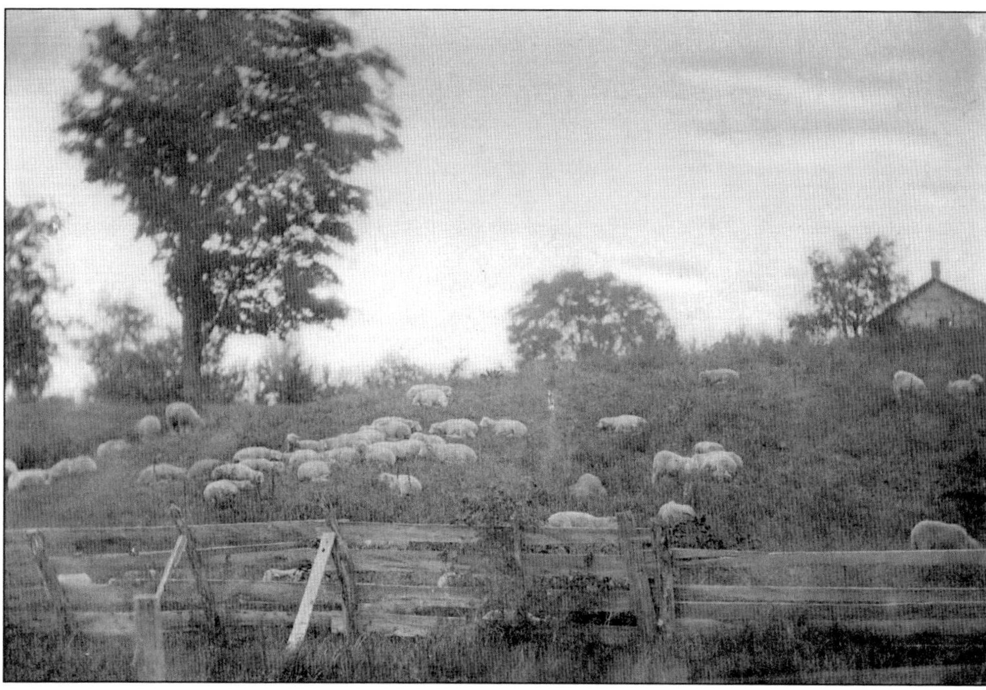

This view shows an active sheep business in Kingsbury in the 1870s. Today, there may be one farm left in town that still raises sheep. However, a farm on Farley Road raises llamas and another farm on Dean Road raises emus. Times do change.

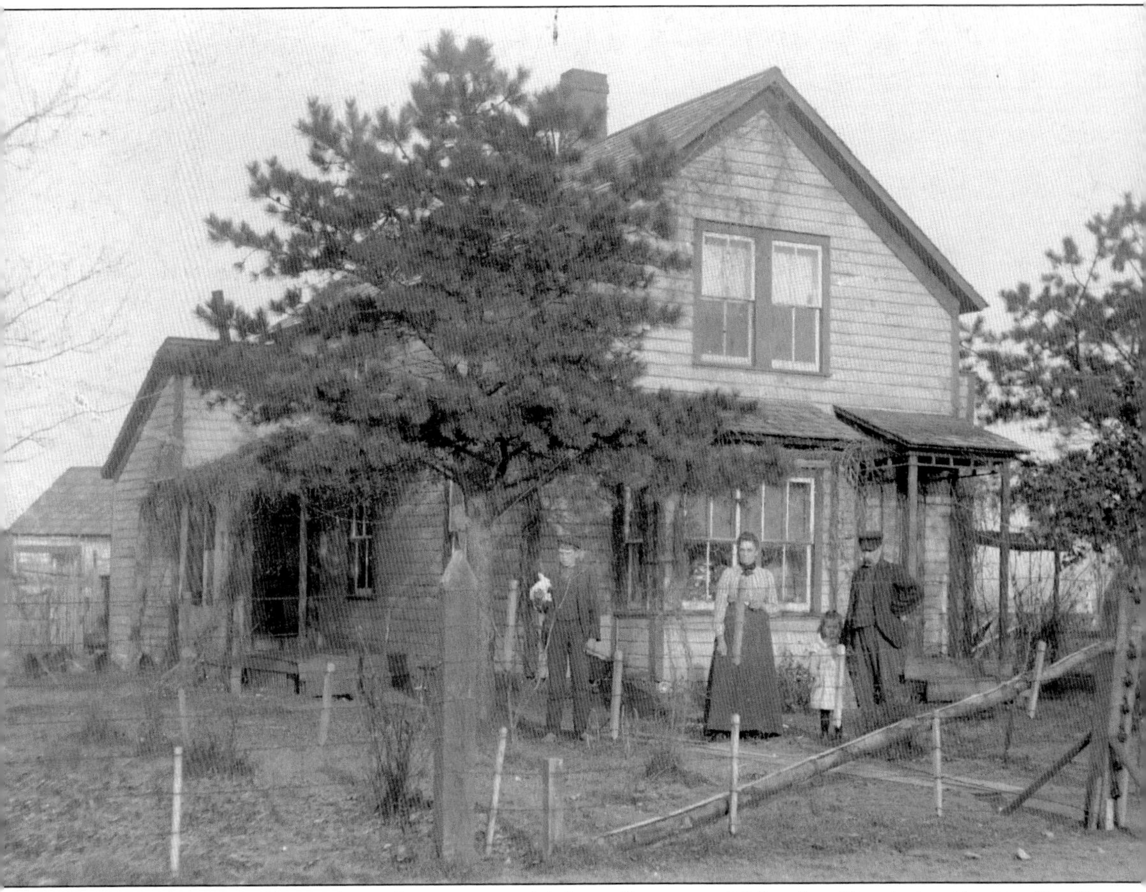

This house is located at the corner of Main Street and Vaughn Road, beside St. Paul's Cemetery. The man and woman are Mr. and Mrs. Otis Chadwick (the author's great great-grandparents). The girl standing between them is Beatrice (the author's grandmother), who was raised by the Chadwicks after her mother died in childbirth. This photograph dates from c. 1905.

Five

EMERGENCY SERVICES

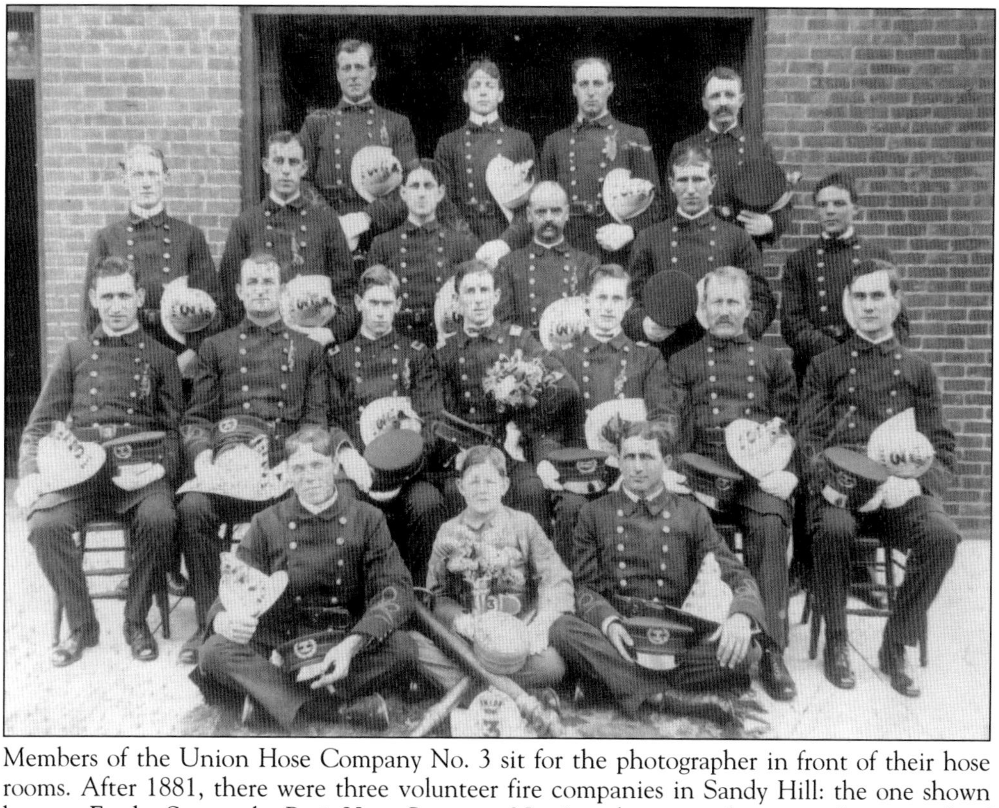

Members of the Union Hose Company No. 3 sit for the photographer in front of their hose rooms. After 1881, there were three volunteer fire companies in Sandy Hill: the one shown here on Feeder Street, the Paris Hose Company No. 1 at the engine house on the west side of the village park, and the Wait Hose Company No. 2 on Main Street across from Willow Street. In 1924, Union Hose was disbanded by the village and was replaced by the Carpenter Hose Company No. 3 at the same location on Feeder Street. In the 1980s, the three groups combined into the Hudson Falls Volunteer Fire Department.

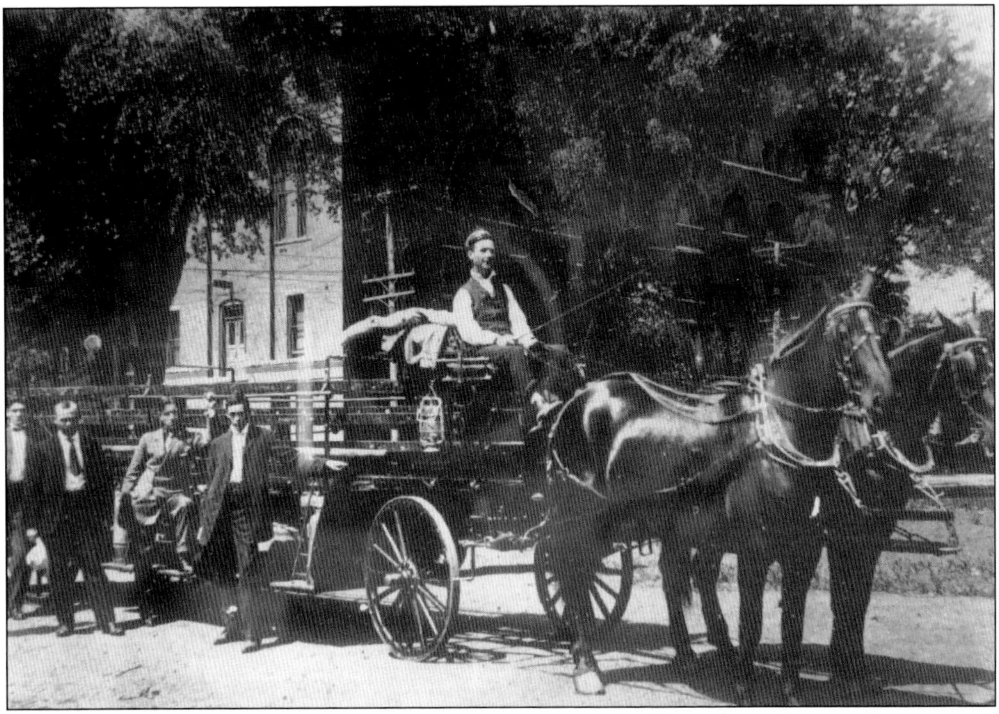

Besides the volunteer fire companies, the village had a small number of men whom it paid to care for the fire horses (and later the motorized trucks) and to drive the equipment to the alarms. This excellent photograph shows one of the teamsters with the village hook and ladder truck in front of the old fire barn, with the Masonic Temple in the background.

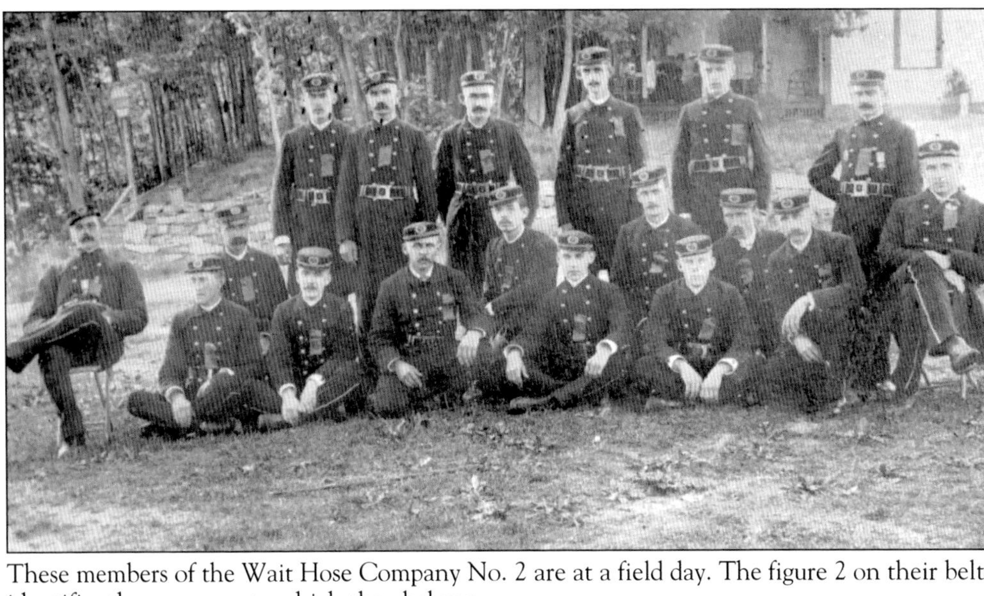

These members of the Wait Hose Company No. 2 are at a field day. The figure 2 on their belts identifies the company to which they belong.

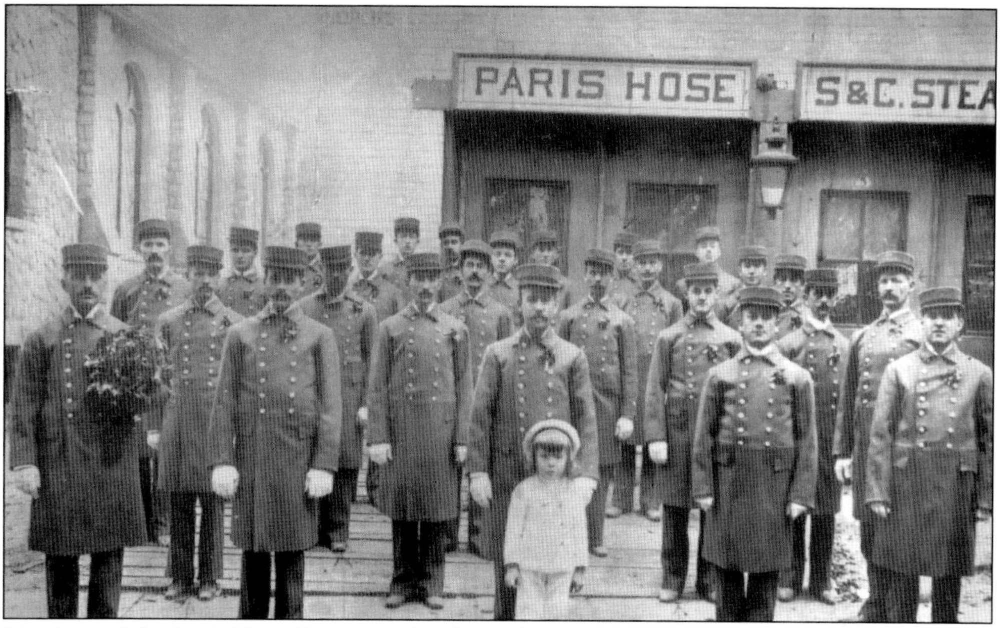

Members of the Paris Hose Company No. 1 stand in front of the old engine house, located on River Street. The village steamer S & C, which was used from the 1880s until the 1920s, was stored on the right side. The hose cart for Paris Hose was kept on the left side. The building on the left is the First Presbyterian Church.

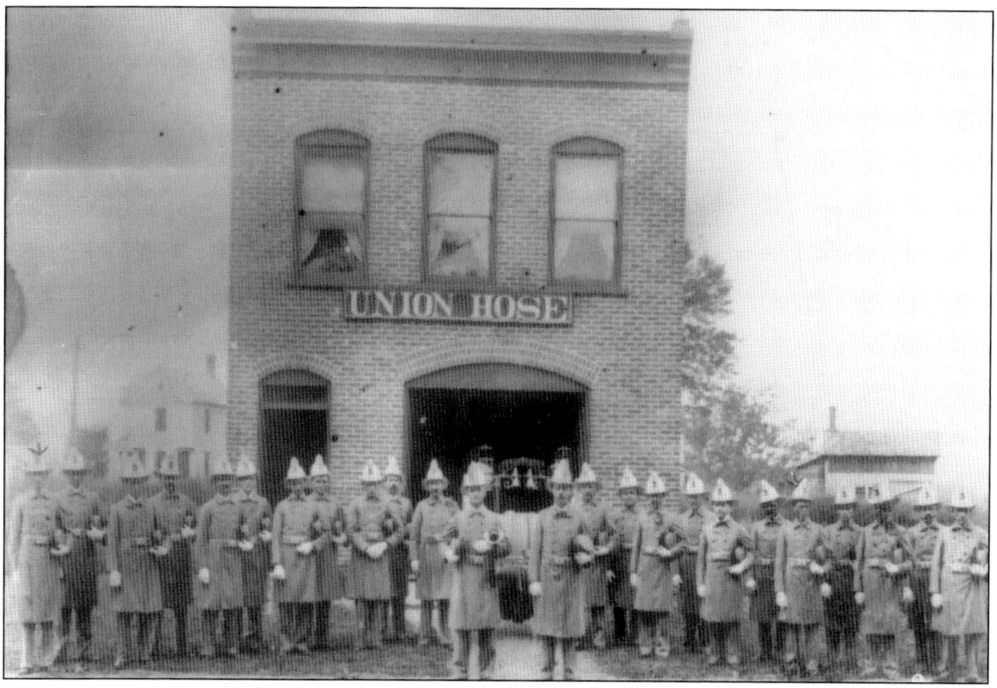

This early photograph shows members of the Union Hose Company No. 3 in front of their hose rooms. They are decked out in their finest, with beautiful leather helmets. Their hose cart has small bells on it. This building is used today as a private residence. The buildings in the background are on Melbourne Avenue.

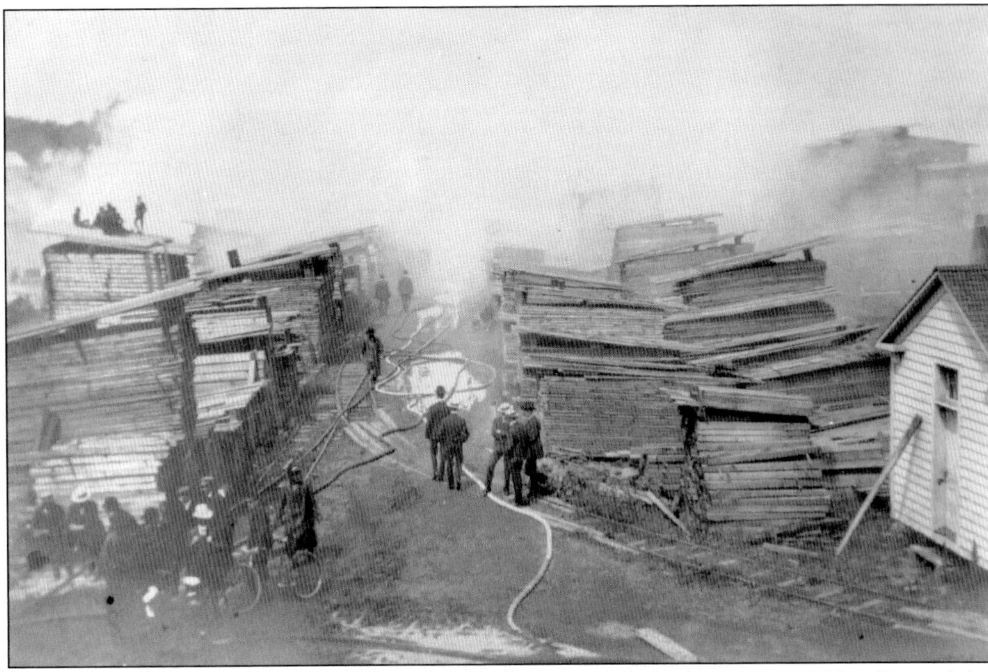

This photograph shows the Griffin lumber mills and woodpiles burning in 1904. Several fire hoses are visible, snaking through the piles of lumber. Also in view are the railroad tracks that were used by a small train to move the sawn lumber around the property.

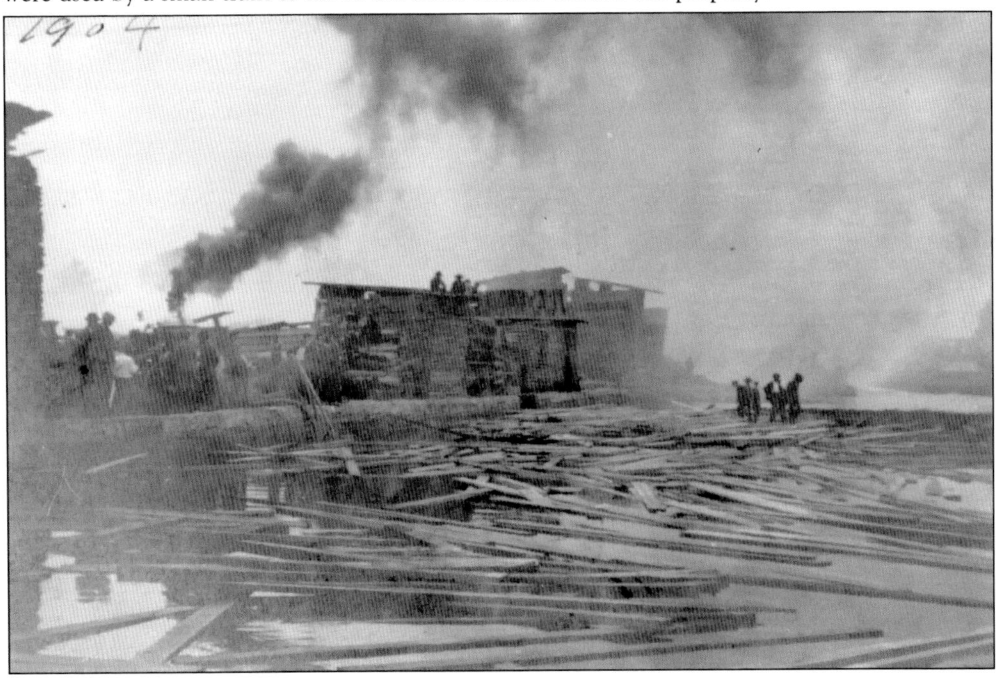

This is the same fire as above, in 1904. What is unique is that this may be the only picture of the S & C steamer in actual operation (it is, in the author's experience). The steamer stands beside the log pond, drafting water from it. The dark plume of smoke is not from the fire but from the fire engine.

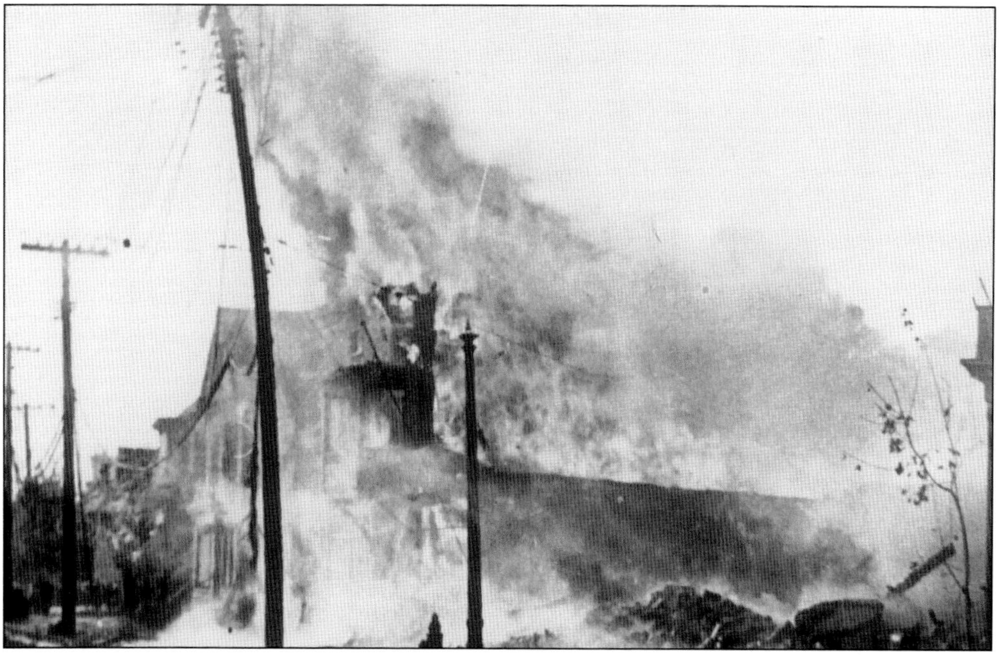

In late October 1940, one of the most spectacular fires in the history of the village took place. One man died in the fire, and several people were injured after jumping out of windows. The fire began around 9:00 a.m. after an explosion occurred in the old Pierson's Hotel. It spread so rapidly that the phone and fire alarm lines were burned through before anyone could contact the fire department. By the time it was over, four buildings had been reduced to ashes. The top picture shows the ferocity of the flames burning the telephone poles. Pictured below are the police and fire chiefs, as well as the coroner and the district attorney examining the remains of the fire's victim, Irvin Rung.

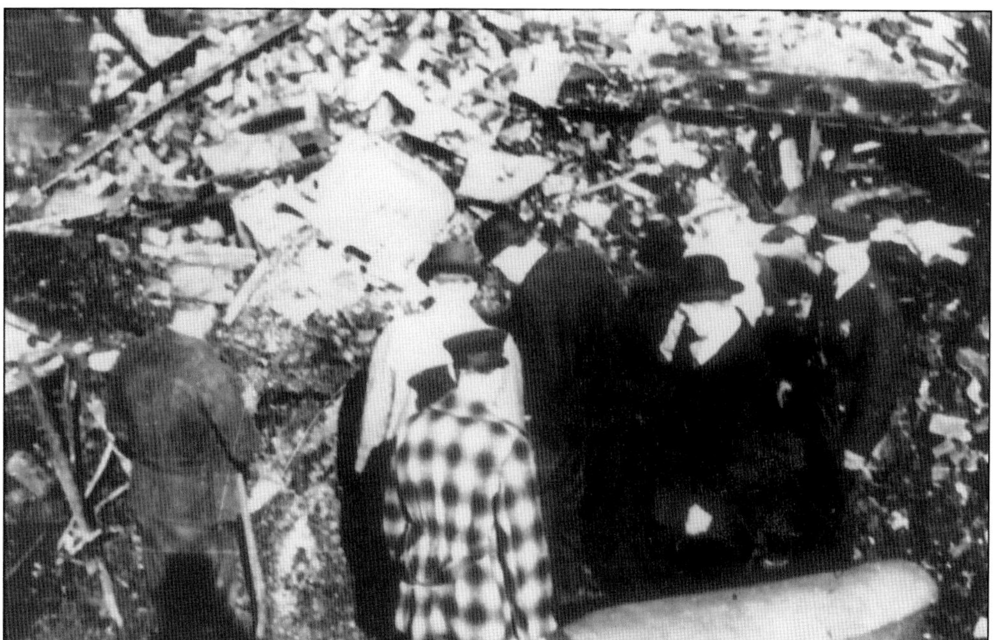

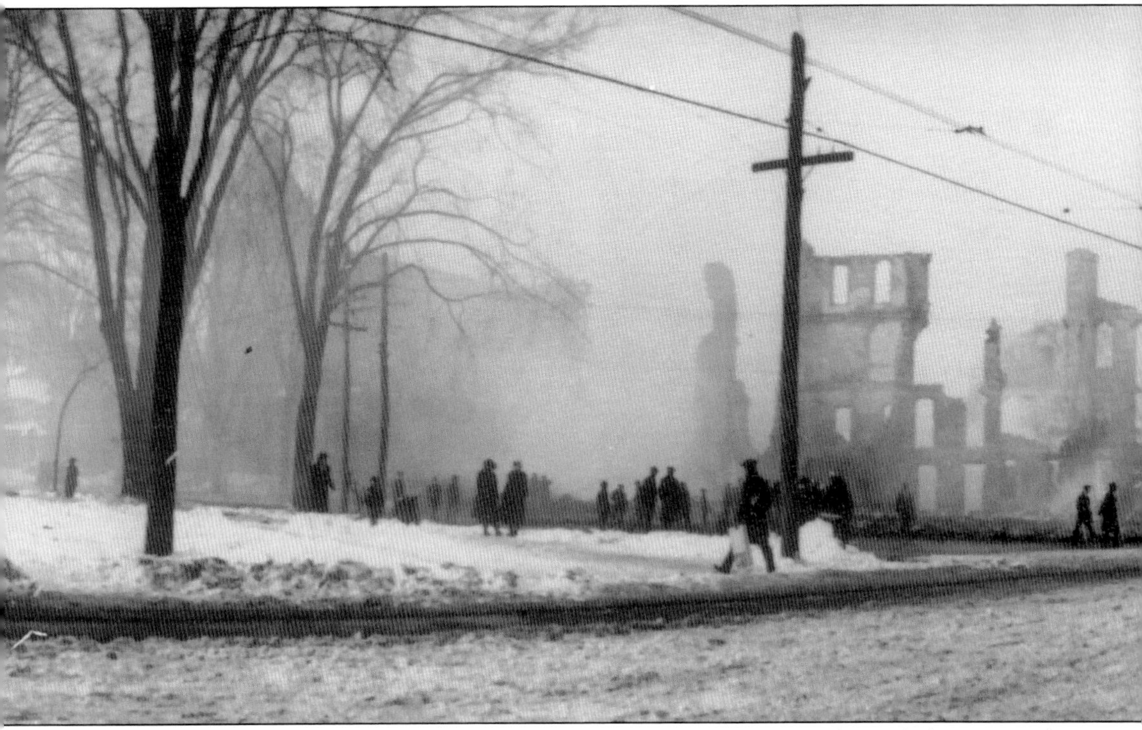

The Middleworth House was built in 1863. In February 1920, it burned down in a huge conflagration which, before being extinguished, destroyed eight buildings and displaced more than 100 people and some 20 businesses. Fortunately, no one was even hurt during this fire. The top photograph, taken on the afternoon of the fire, shows the scene with the fire still smoldering. The destruction was total. The fire began in a diner to the right side of the smoking

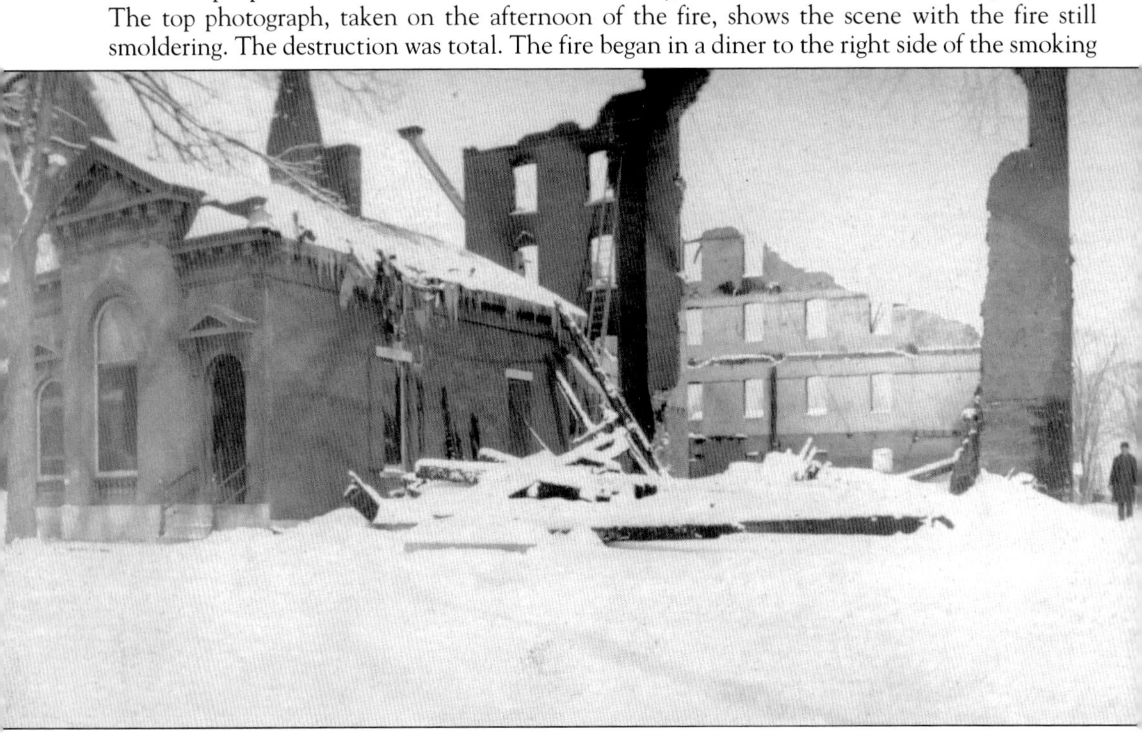

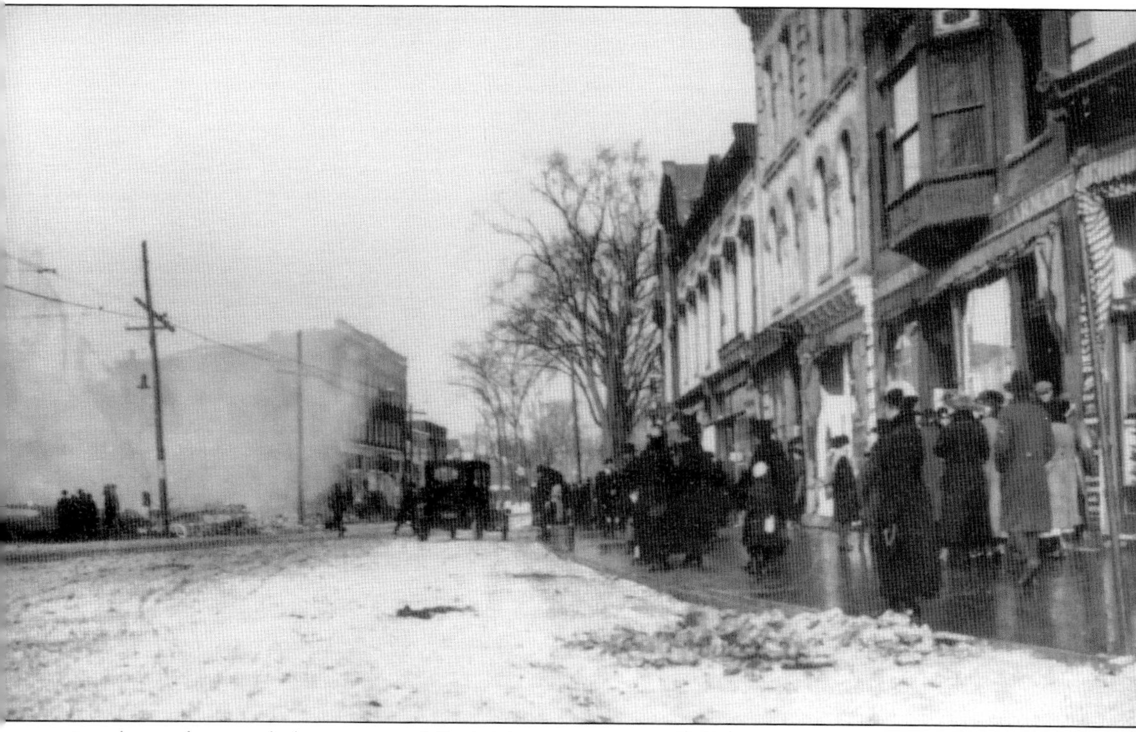

ruins, burned around the corner of Park Place, went up Wall Street, jumped across to Park Place, and burned four buildings there, including the second St. Mary's Church. The bottom picture was taken a little later that winter, looking up Wall Street, where a man is standing. The total area that burned covered about 10 acres.

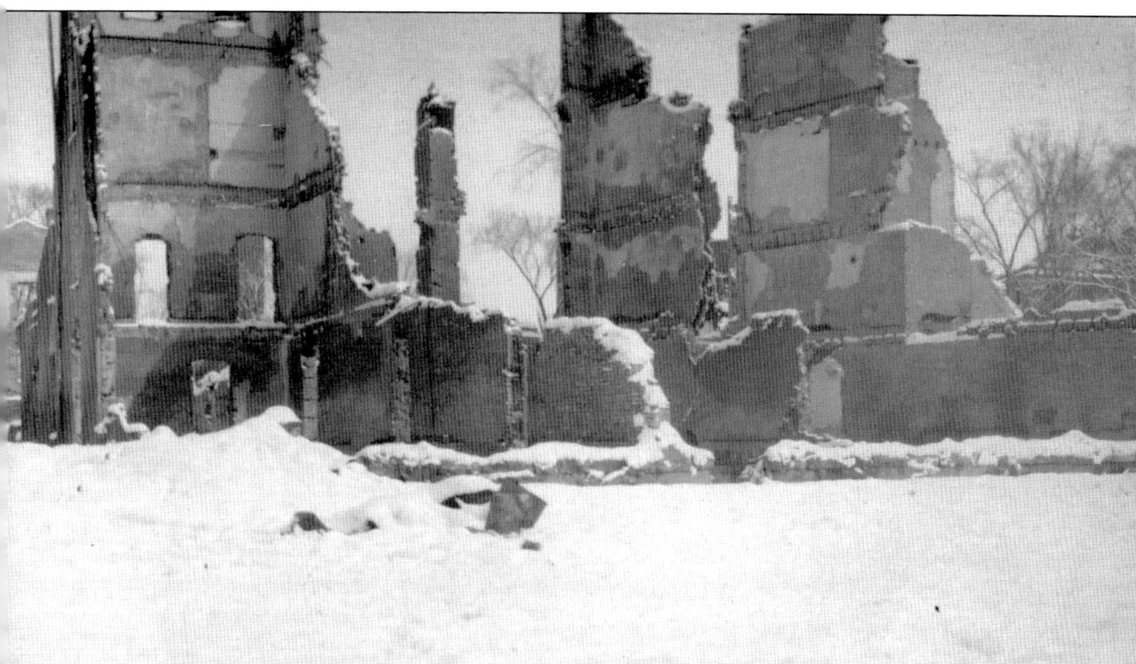

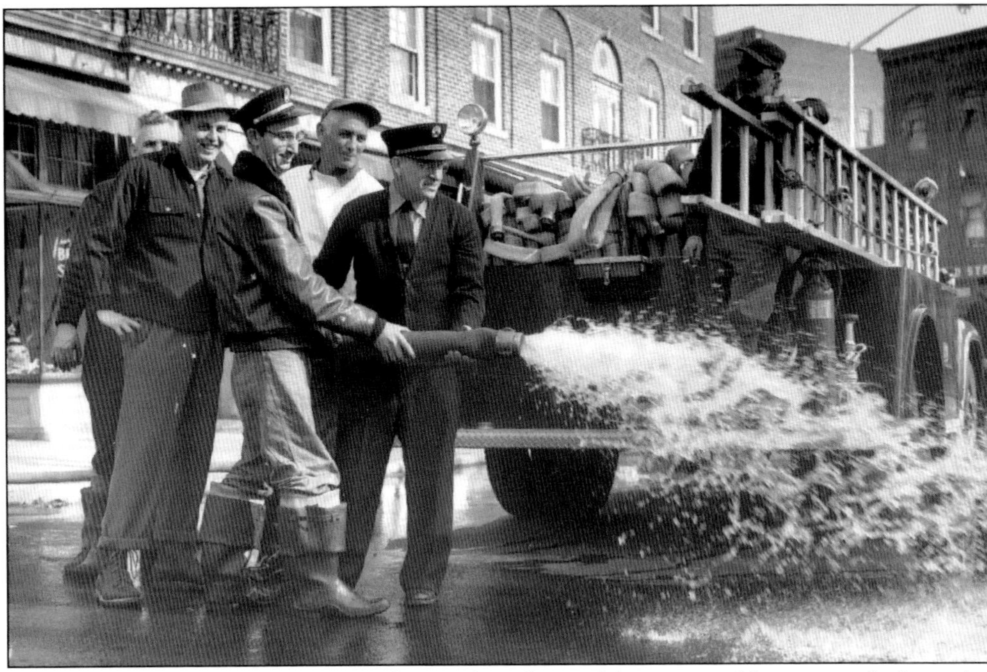

Hudson Falls Fire Chief Leo J. La Belle stands in front of this group of firemen with the end of the hose. The truck is the fire department's 1946 Mack pumper, Engine 19. The picture was taken on Park Place, just in from Main Street, *c.* the late 1950s or early 1960s.

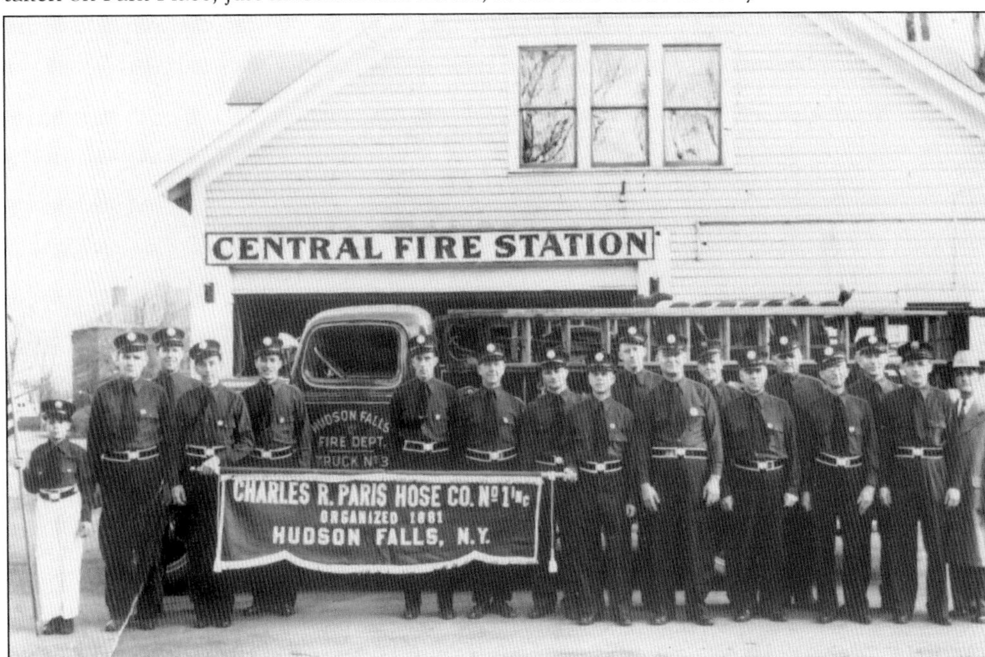

Members of the Paris Hose Company pose in front of Engine 19 in the early 1950s. They are at the Central Fire Station on Locust Street. This building was an old carriage barn that was converted into the fire station *c.* 1900. It had little marks on its ceiling where the harnesses were suspended for the old fire horses. The building was torn down in the 1980s.

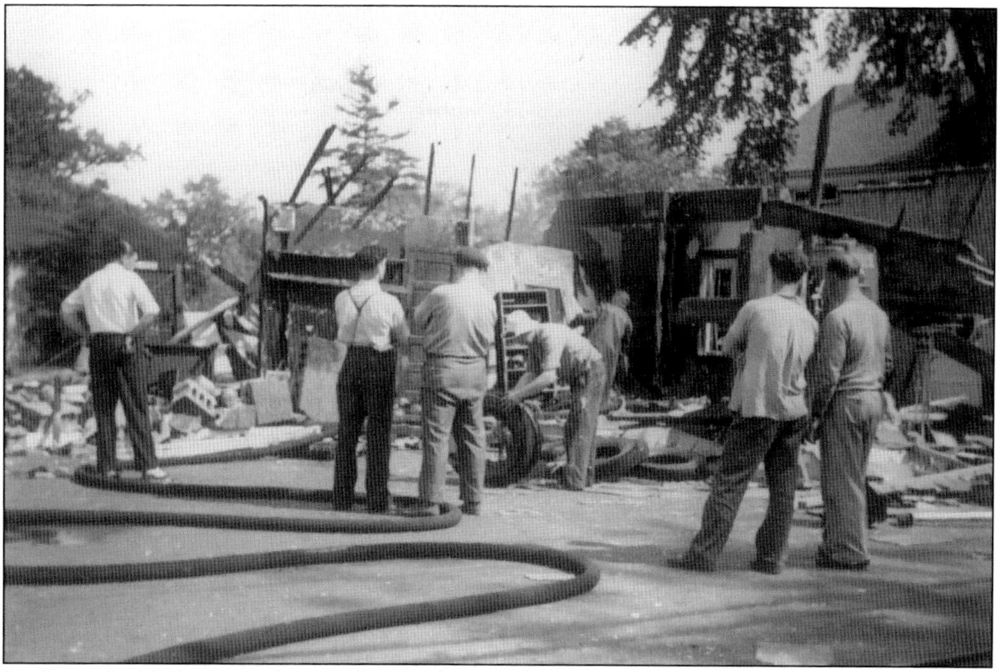

In the early 1940s, a gasoline explosion destroyed this building located at the corner of Main and Beech Streets. The business was Dickinson's Service Station. No one was hurt, and the explosion did not result in much fire, but it blew the whole building apart.

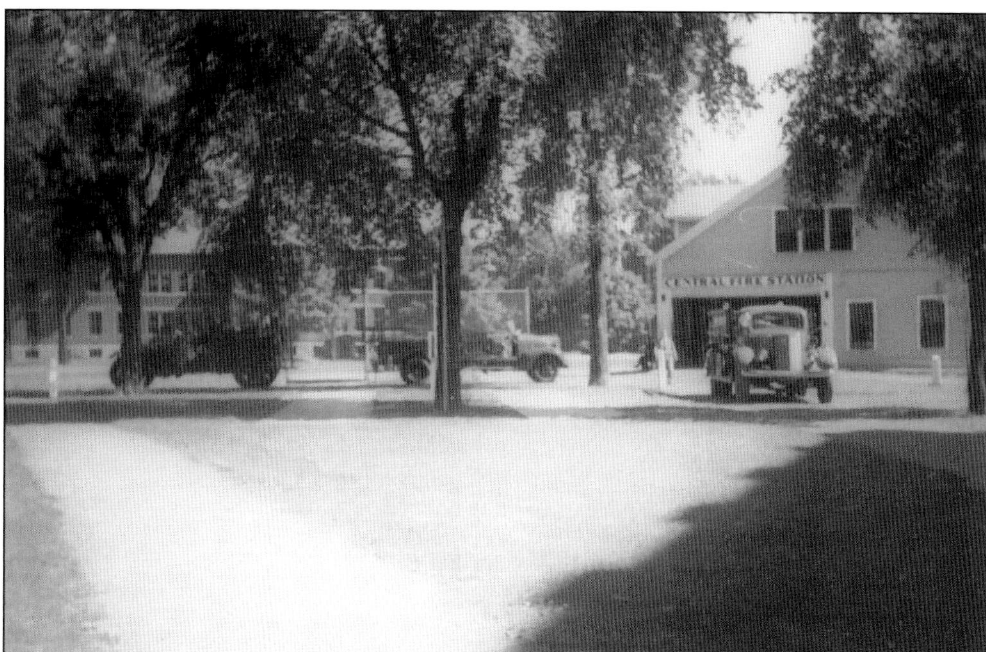

In front of the old Central Fire Station are the three fire trucks the village had in the late 1940s. The one on the right is a Mack pumper. The other two are chemical trucks, an American LaFrance and a Dodge.

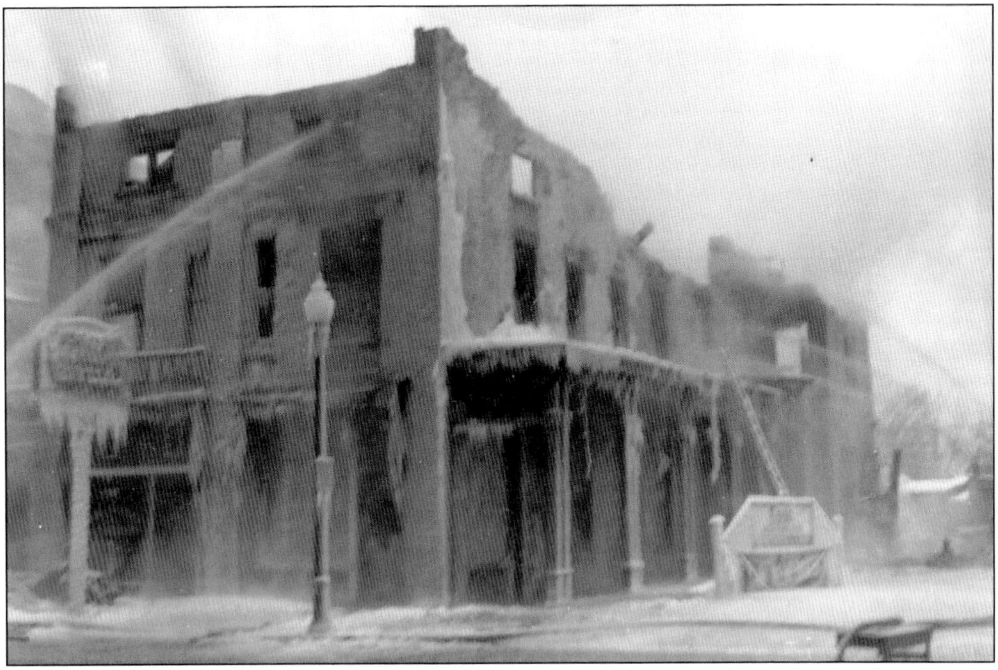

Located next door to the Strand Theatre, this three-story building housed a small restaurant and apartments. It burned in a winter fire in the 1940s. Note the period streetlight in the middle of the picture.

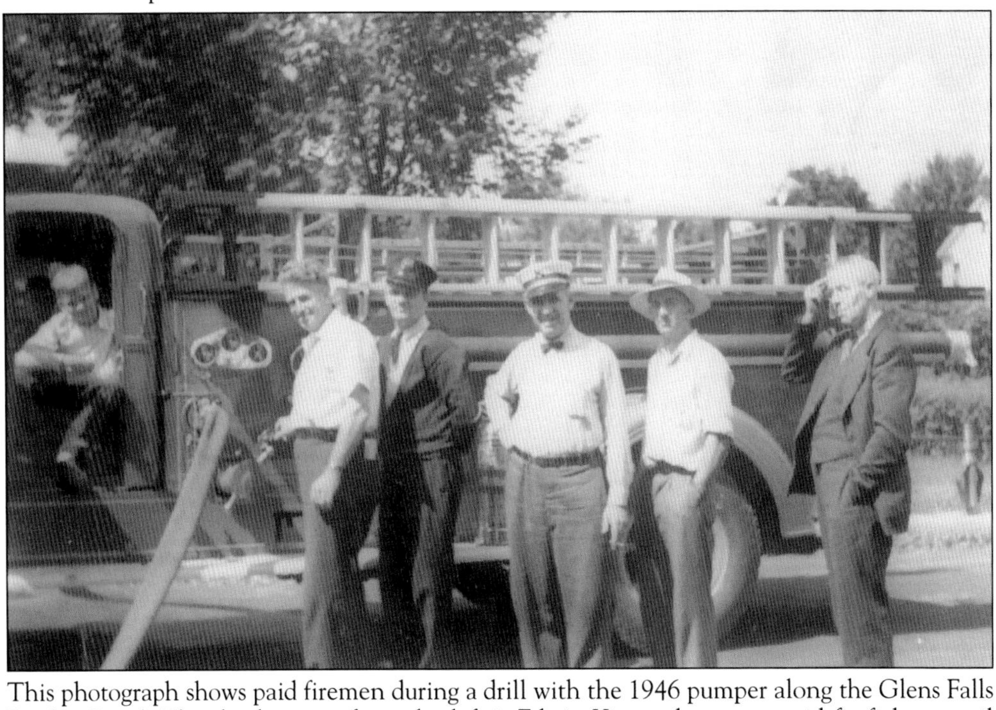

This photograph shows paid firemen during a drill with the 1946 pumper along the Glens Falls Feeder Canal. The third person from the left is Edwin King, who was a paid firefighter until the 1970s. Wearing the white cap is the first paid fire chief, Cap Rivers. Leo La Belle was the second paid chief.

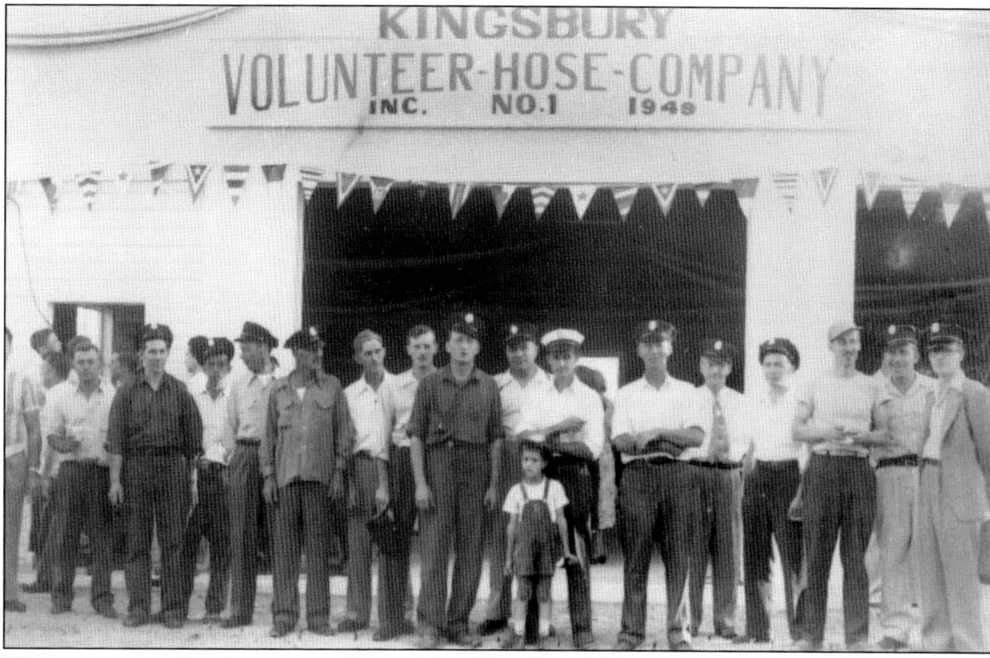

These men are the charter members of the Kingsbury Volunteer Hose Company No. 1. The company was formed in 1949, and the Village of Hudson Falls provided the first truck, an old American LaFrance. The volunteers began in a garage on Burgoyne Avenue and later built this station, which is still in use today as Station No. 1.

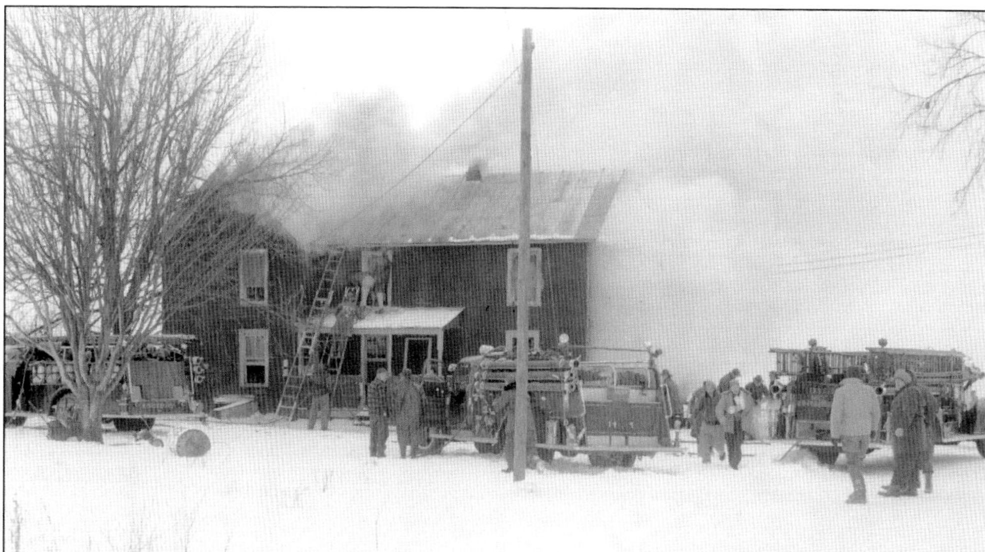

Fire damaged this Kingsbury home in January 1957. The three trucks belong to the Kingsbury Hose Company. One of them is the company's first new fire truck, a Studebaker, which still exists and is in line for refurbishing.

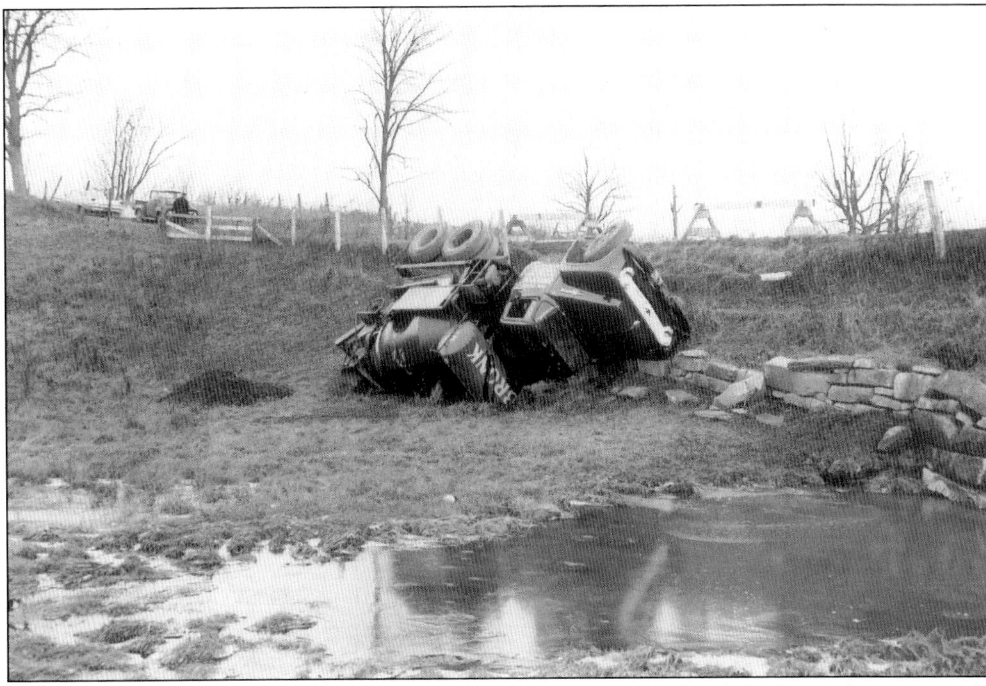

A cement truck rolled over on Stone Schoolhouse Road in December 1960. This is one of a dozen or so pictures that were taken at the accident scene. Remarkably, once it was righted, the truck appeared to have sustained very little damage. Imagine the damage involved in a similar rollover of a modern truck.

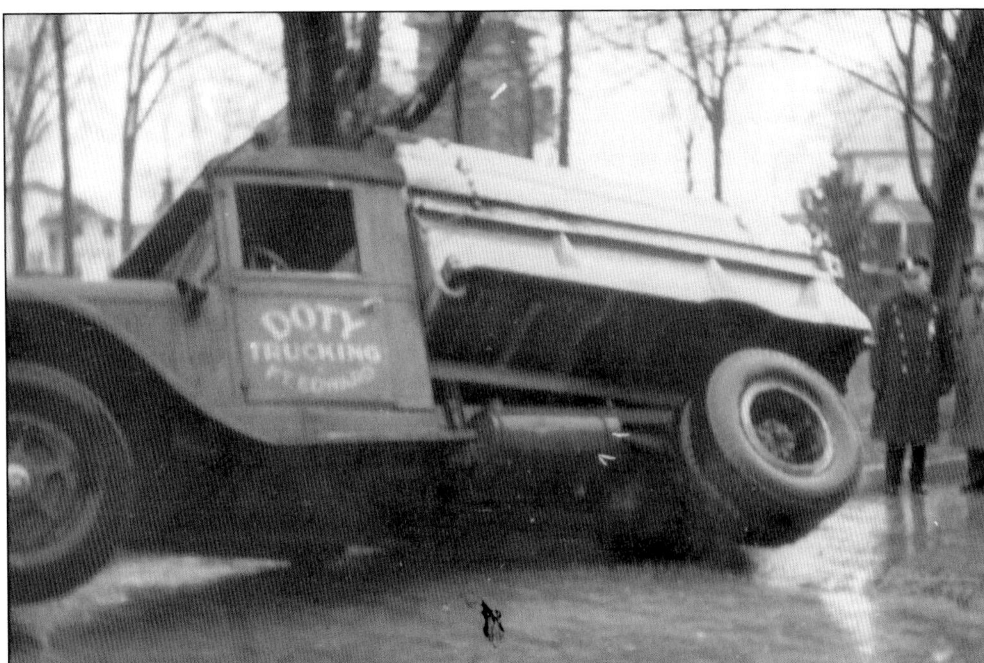

This truck accident occurred at the northeast corner of the village park in the middle of Hudson Falls. Police Chief Mike Usher is at the scene of this 1940s-era crash.

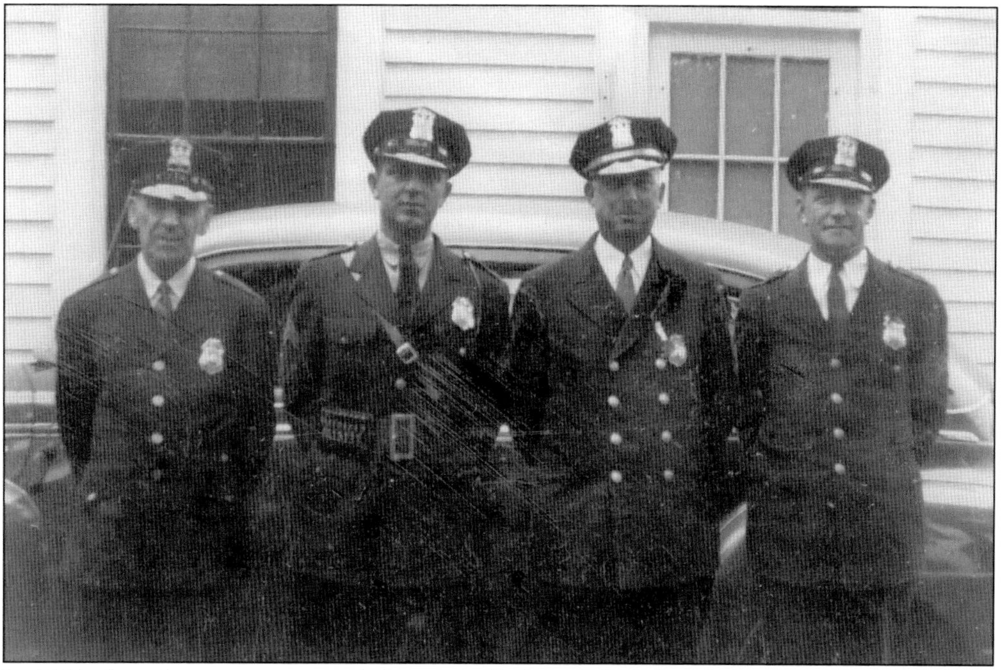

In 1943, these four men comprised the entire Hudson Falls Police Department. They are, from left to right, Charlie Wescott, Sgt. Bing Thompson, Chief Mike Usher, and Sgt. Gerald Rivers. They are standing in front of the village police car.

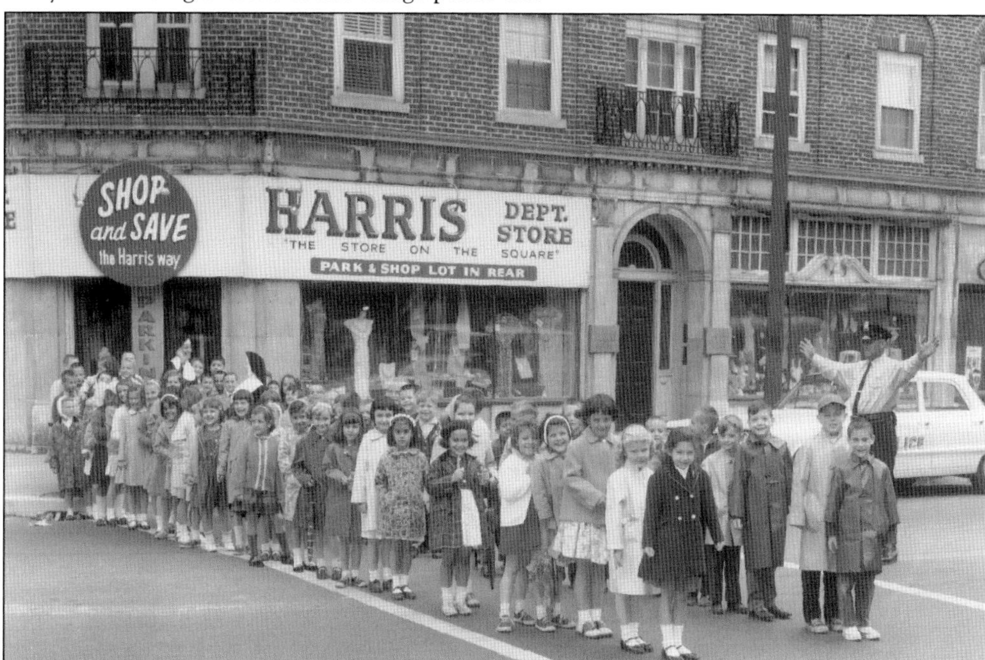

One of the daily duties of the police department was stopping traffic for the schoolchildren who attended the two Catholic schools, St. Mary's and St. Paul's. Most of these children had to cross Main Street by Park Place four times a day. There was always a police officer there. In this 1960 photograph, the officer is Ernie Bercette.

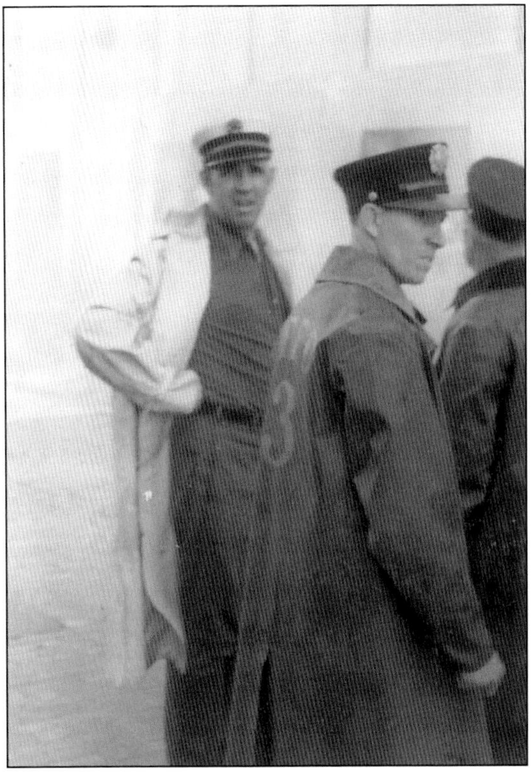

Fire Chief Cap Rivers surveys a smoky fire at a mill site in the 1940s.

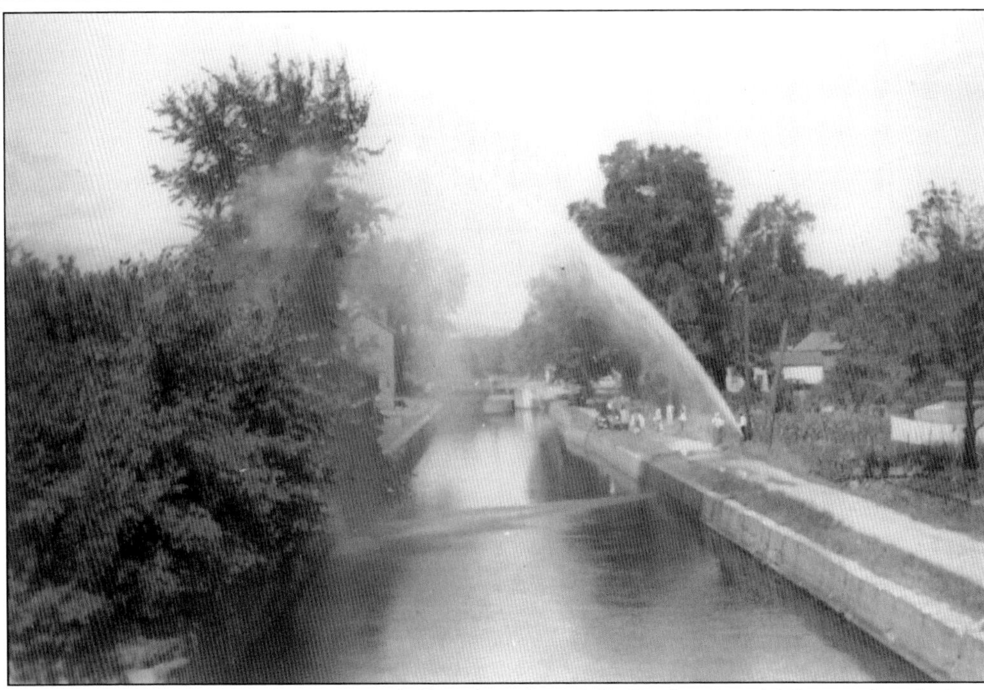

This picture shows a fire department drill at the Glens Falls Feeder Canal. The truck is drafting water from the canal and testing a deluge gun. The photographer is standing on the Martindale Avenue bridge.

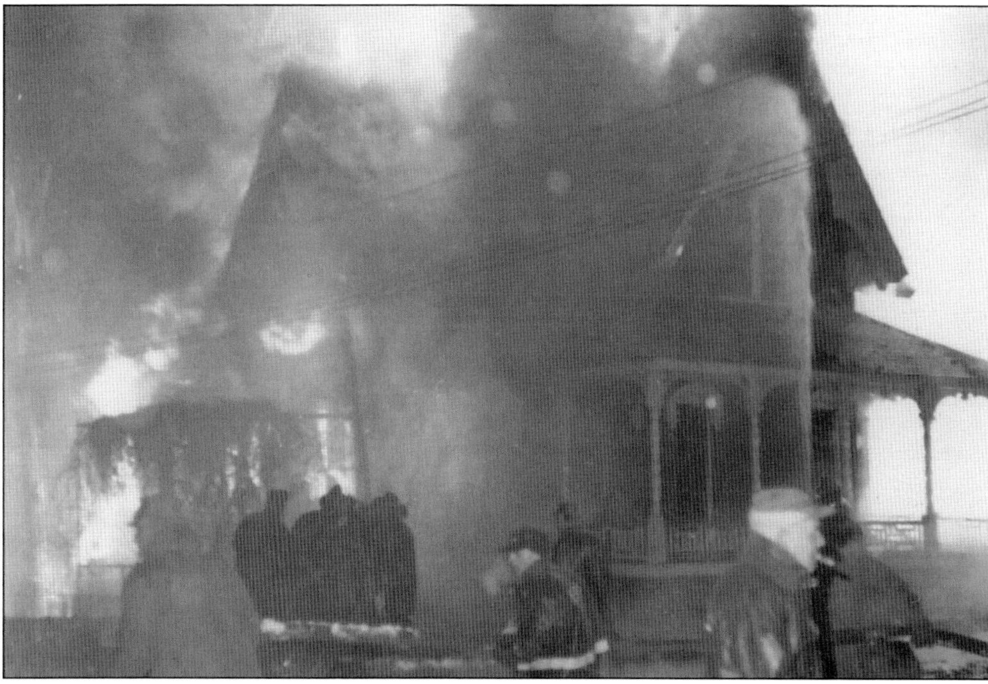

In the winter of 1964, another spectacular fire struck Hudson Falls. It started in a three-story tenement house located across from the Carleton Funeral Home. Before it was extinguished, it burned down seven or eight buildings. The last one to be destroyed was the old Wait Hose building. Some 30 people were left homeless. These two pictures show the ferocity of the fire, which was so hot that it melted the lights of one of the fire trucks.

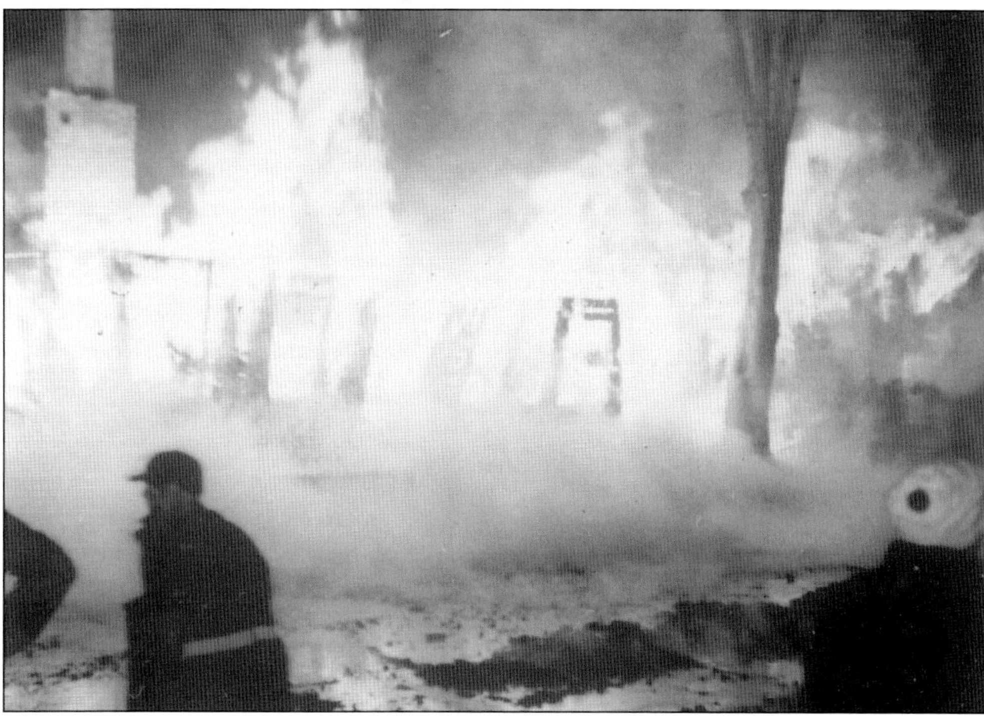

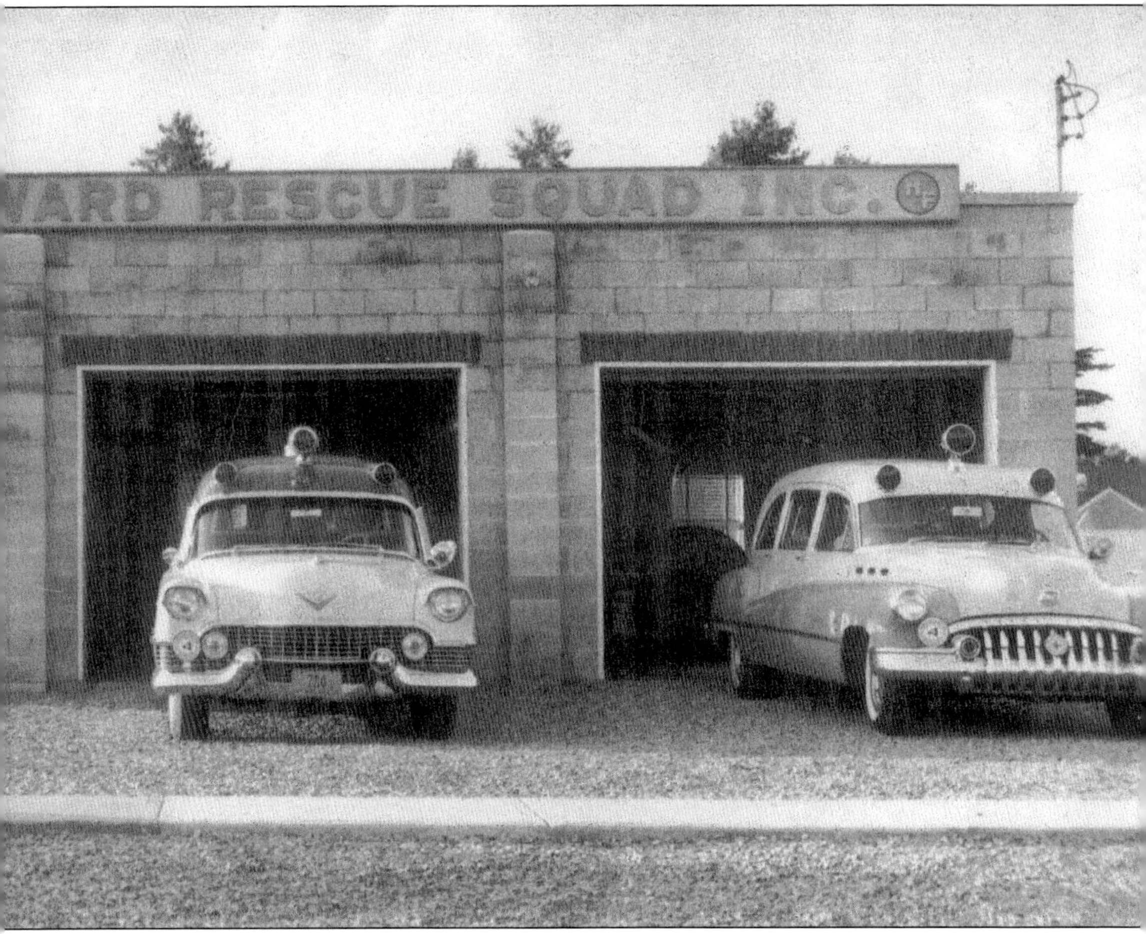

Until the mid-1950s, the only ambulance service in small towns was often supplied by a funeral home. In the case of Hudson Falls, that service was supplied by the Riley Funeral Home. A group of men got together in the 1950s and formed the Fort Edward Rescue Squad. The squad, which always included Hudson Falls and Kingsbury, built rooms on Schuyler Street beside the Union Cemetery. This was a central location with good access to all areas of the towns of Kingsbury and Fort Edward. This photograph shows the new cement block rooms and the first two ambulances. The one on the left, the first, was a Cadillac that was donated to the squad.

Six

Industry and Transportation

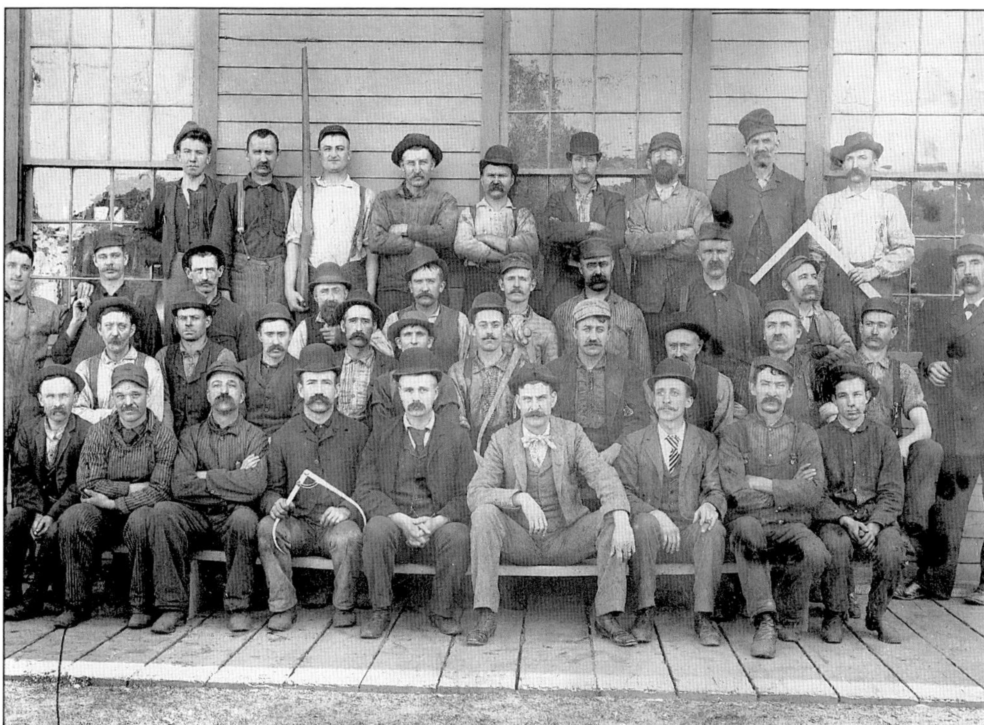

This is a group of workers from the Union Bag mill in Sandy Hill *c.* 1900. Several of the men hold tools of their trade—for example, the carpenter is holding a carpenter's square. At one time, Union Bag had several mills on both sides of the Hudson River near Bakers Falls. The reason the company built the Fenimore Bridge was to have easy railroad access to all of its mills.

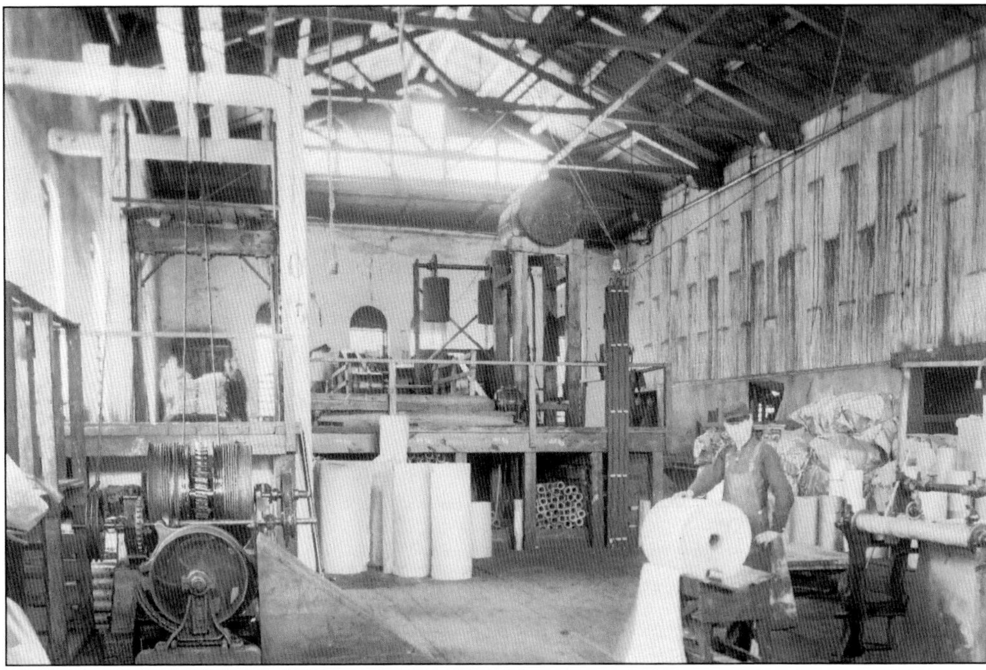

This view shows the inside of the Union Bag building at the bottom of John Street hill. It is one of a series of *c.* 1915 photographs that Union Bag had taken to show all aspects of the paper mill operations. This particular picture shows the north room of the Bakers Falls mill.

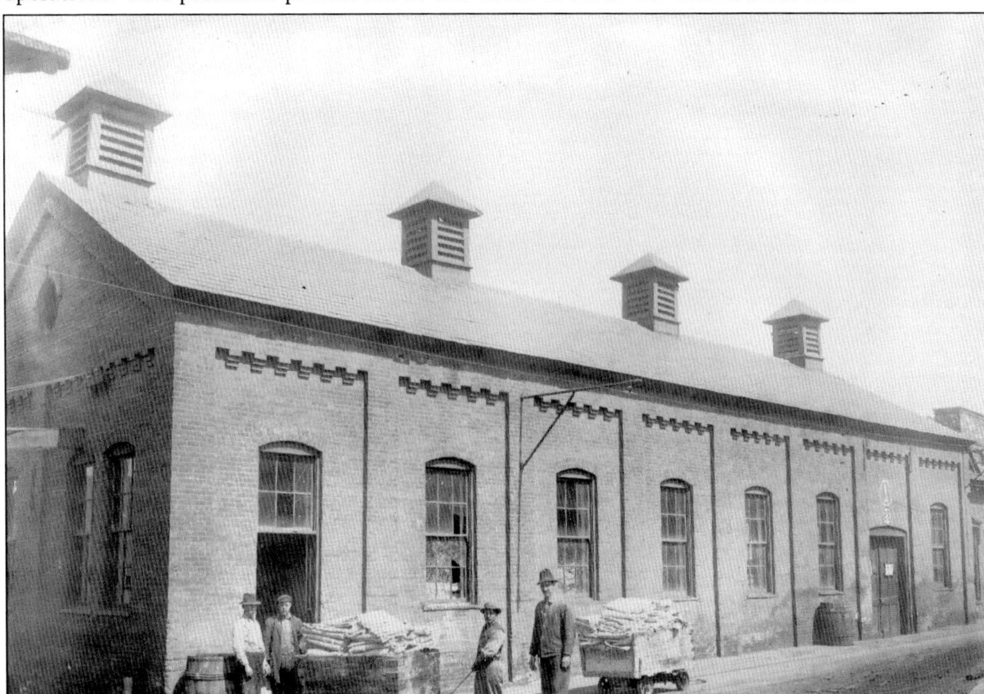

This is the fiberboard mill of Union Bag's Bakers Falls mill *c.* 1915. For such ordinary type of work, the architecture of this building appears to be of the highest quality.

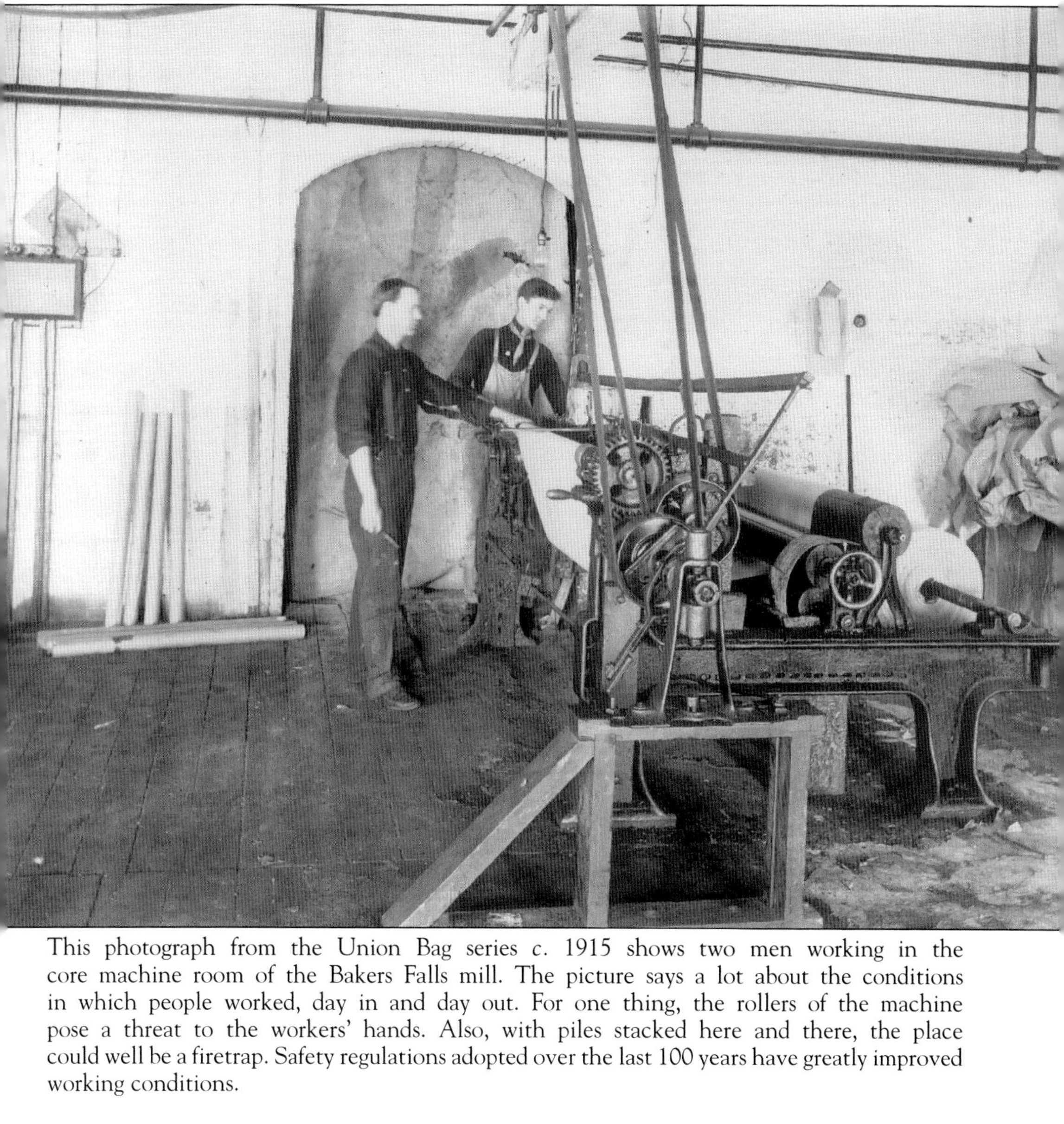

This photograph from the Union Bag series *c.* 1915 shows two men working in the core machine room of the Bakers Falls mill. The picture says a lot about the conditions in which people worked, day in and day out. For one thing, the rollers of the machine pose a threat to the workers' hands. Also, with piles stacked here and there, the place could well be a firetrap. Safety regulations adopted over the last 100 years have greatly improved working conditions.

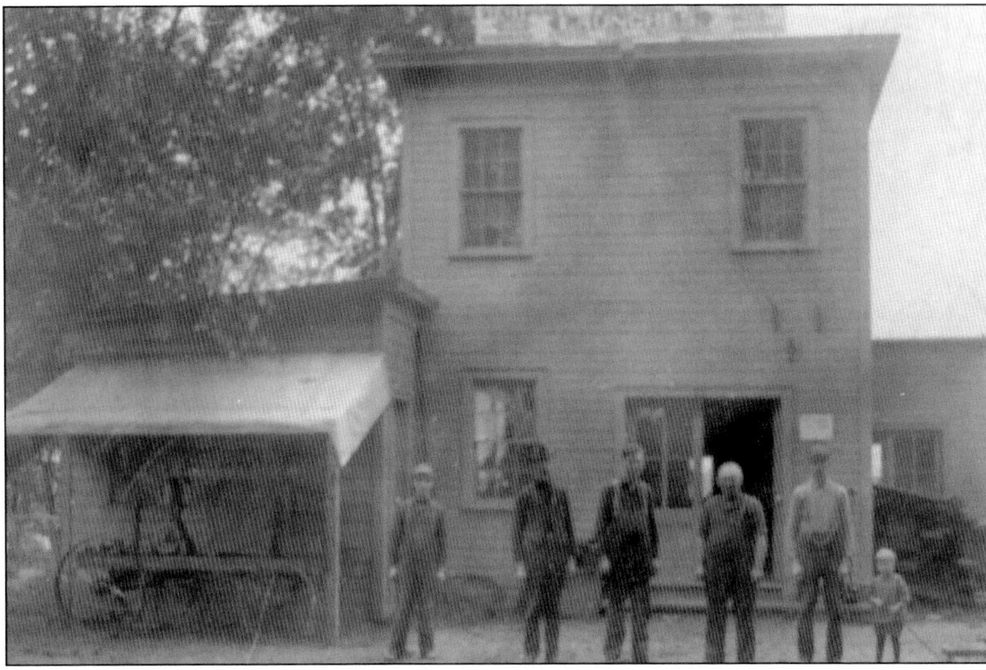

This is the Hubbard Gasoline Engine Company, located on Main Street across from Beech Street. It was in business *c.* 1910, manufacturing a specialized gasoline engine, which had particular patents that were highly innovative for the time.

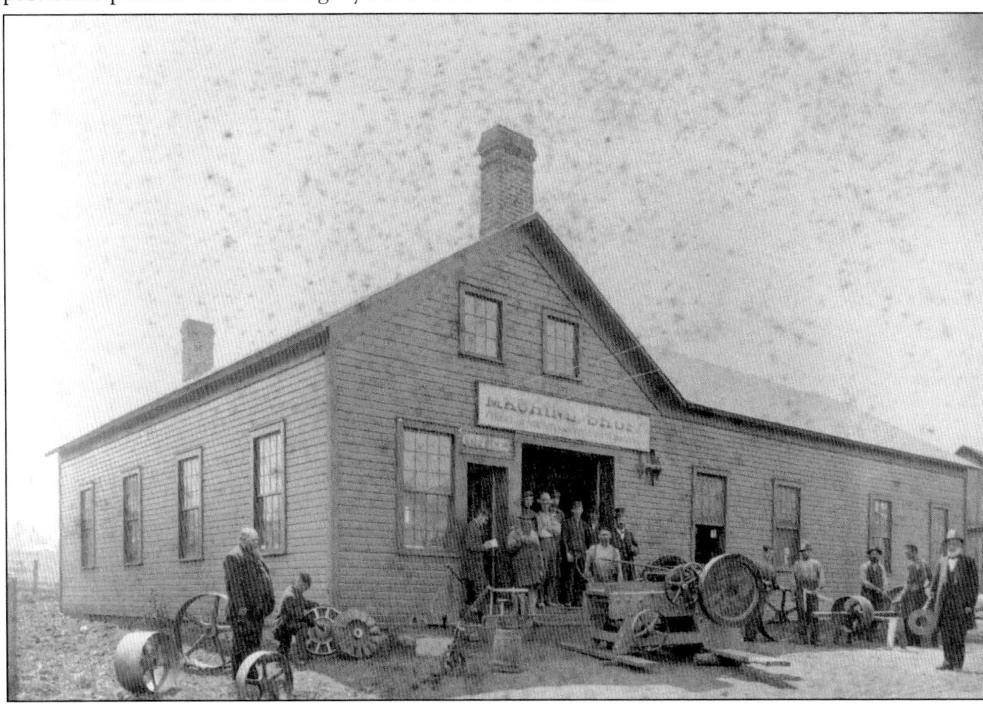

This machine shop was located at the bottom of John Street across from Sumpter Street. It manufactured various types of wheels used in the mills that surrounded the business. This photograph was taken in the 1890s.

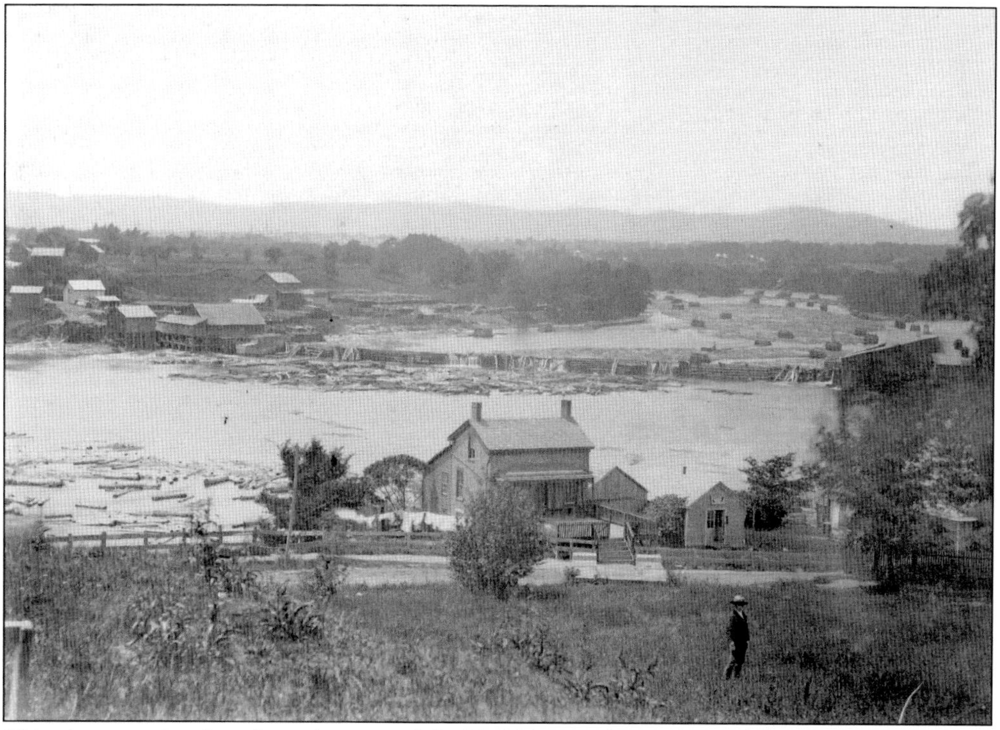

This photograph taken from the area of the Earl Towers shows the middle of River Street hill. The house perched on the edge of the hill that goes down to the river is somewhat startling. The railroad tracks ran along the hill, below the house. In plain view are the so-called Upper Dam and the mills, located on both sides of the river.

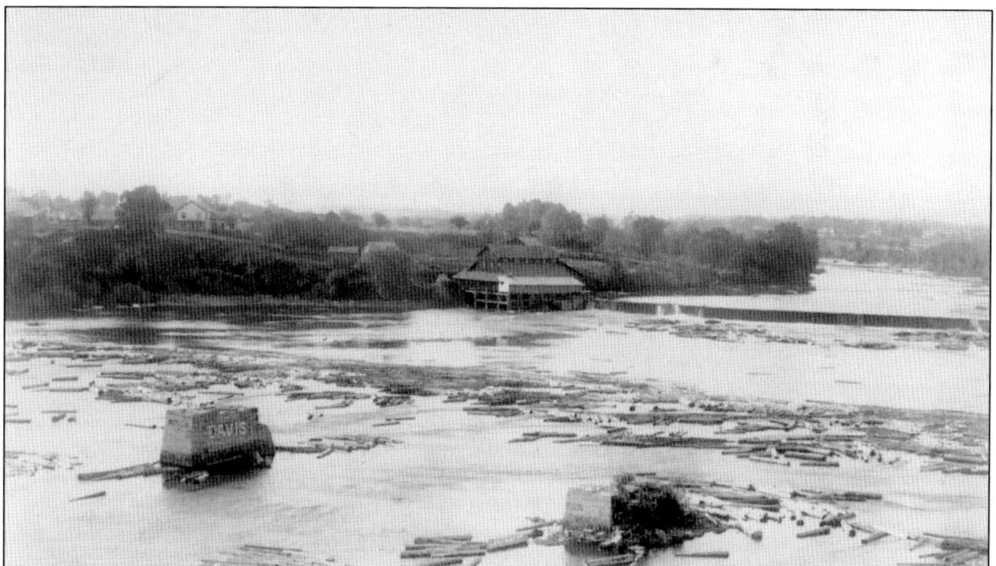

These stone piers are located in the Hudson River about in the middle of where River Street hill is. This is an 1880s photograph, and at that time the piers were over 50 years old. They were built to hold a railroad bridge in the 1830s. However, the company ran out of funds and the project folded. Still existing, the piers are all that remain of the project.

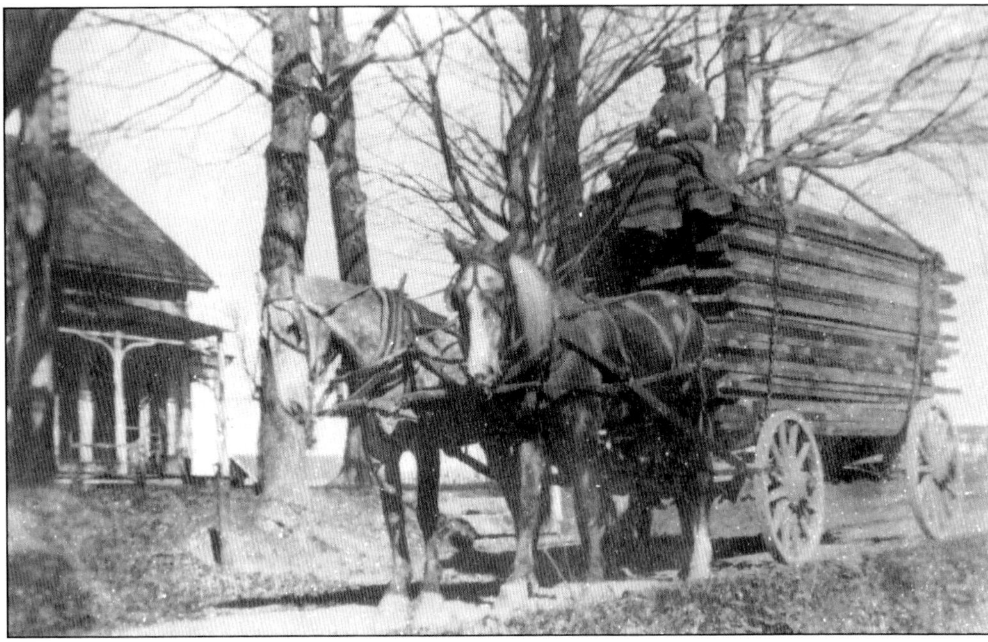

This load of large planks, probably from the nearby Kenyon Lumber Company, is being hauled along Burgoyne Avenue. On the way back, without the load of lumber to sit on, the teamster had to stand up on the wagon.

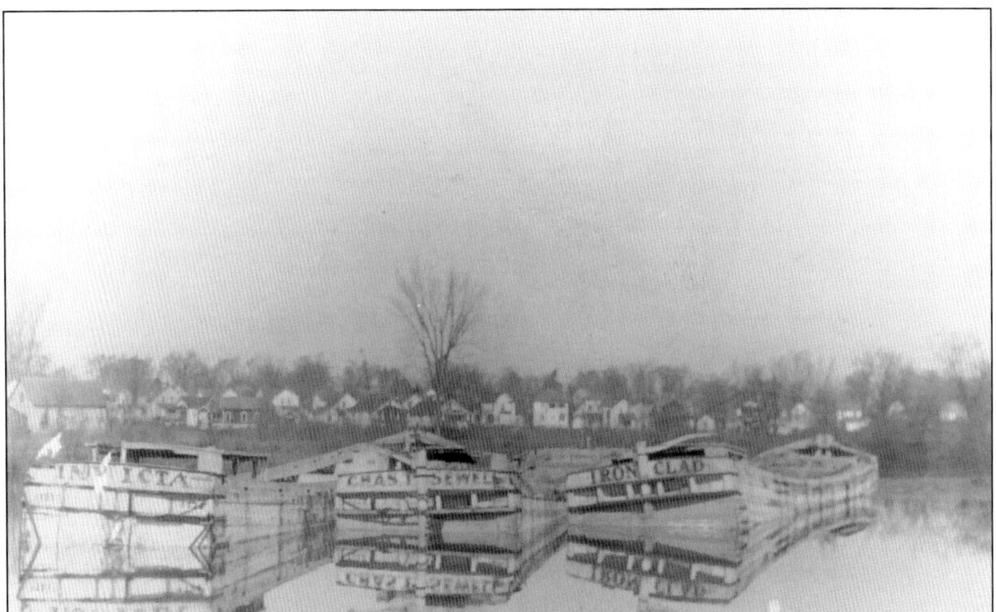

These three canal boats sit in one of the three log ponds of the Kenyon Lumber Company, on Maple Street. The houses in the background are on School Street. In the late 1960s, the ponds were filled in so that the site could hold the Hudson Falls Department of Public Works storehouse. At that time the remains of the three boats were still there, and so they were buried on the spot.

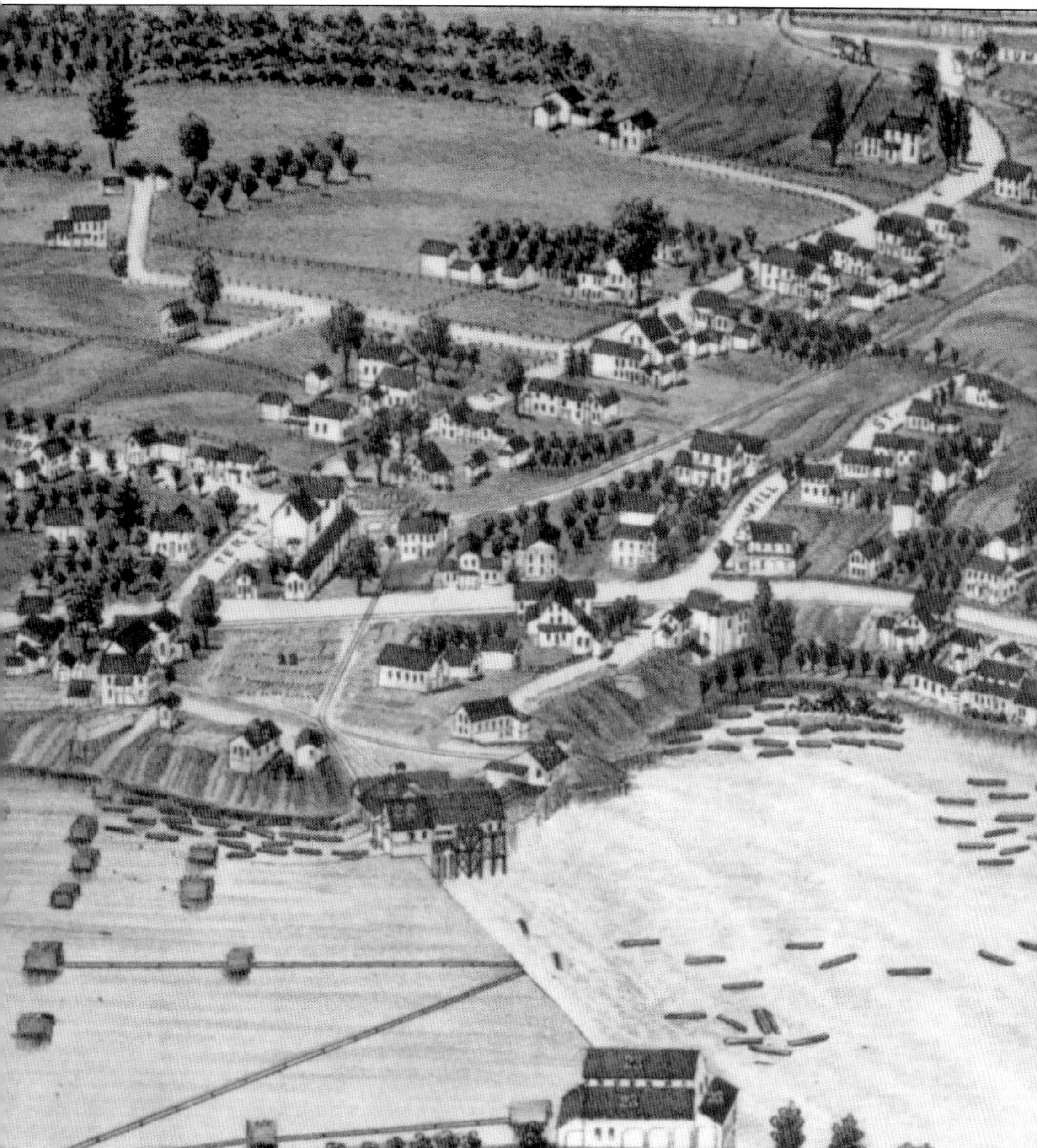

This enlarged section from an 1880s map of Sandy Hill shows a bird's-eye view of the Richards sawmill complex on River Street. The interesting sight in this picture is the little railroad that connected the mill to the Glens Falls Feeder Canal. The engine that operated on this railroad, called "the Fred" for Orson Richard's son Fred, is visible at the top right.

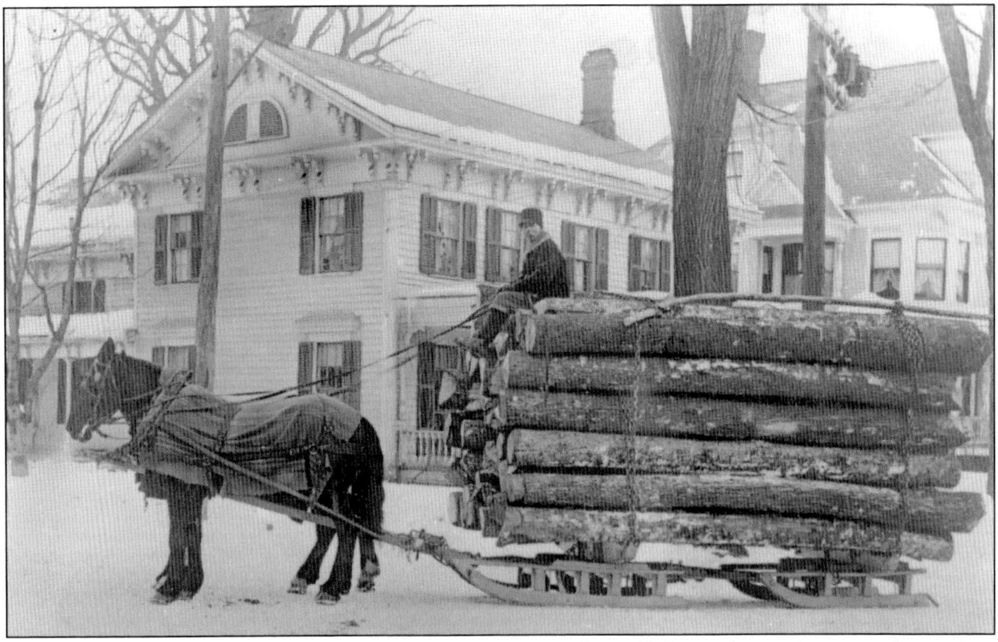

The lumber industry was extremely important to Sandy Hill from the 1850s into the 1930s. When Albert Baker's sawmill opened in the 1860s, it probably seemed impressive. However, compared to the huge mills that operated here 100 years later, it was quite small. This load of logs is being skidded through the winter streets of Sandy Hill.

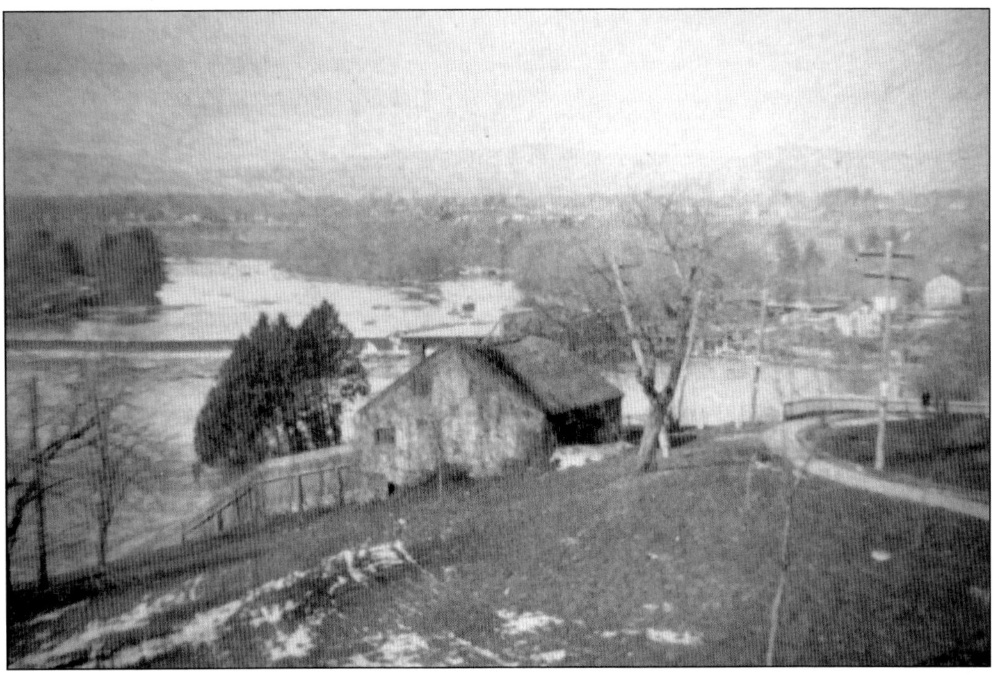

Every small 19th-century village had a blacksmith shop. In Sandy Hill it was not under the "spreading chestnut tree" but right in the middle of town. This small blacksmith shop was located at the top of River Street hill across from the Baptist church (later St. Paul's).

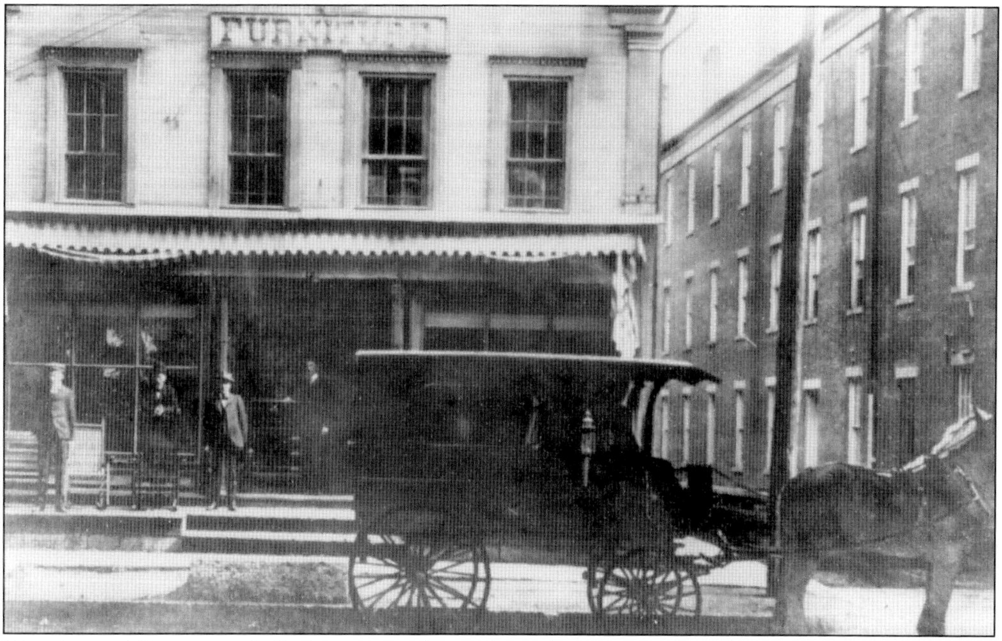

The firm of Rogers and Carleton was located at the corner of Park Place and Wall Street. In front of the business is an early hearse. The company operated a furniture store and undertaking business. Today, it might seem odd that these two businesses were combined. However, while the workers were making furniture, they could also make coffins. This building burned to the ground in the 1920 fire that destroyed the Middleworth House, the large building on the right, up Wall Street.

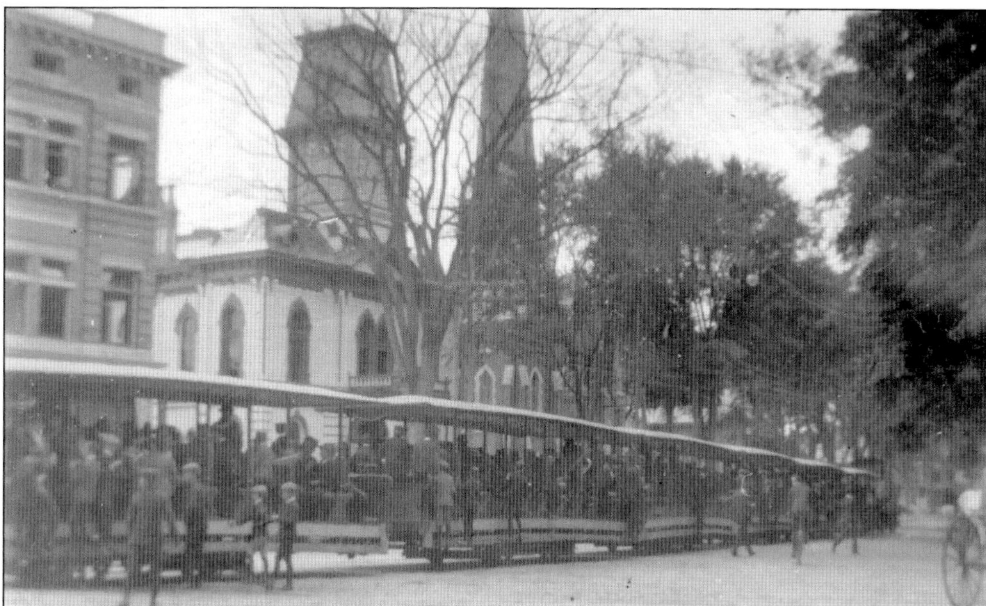

This odd view shows what appears to be an extremely long set of trolley cars in front of the courthouse on Main Street in Sandy Hill. Perhaps this "train" is taking many people out of town for some sort of special occasion—maybe the Washington County Fair in Fort Edward.

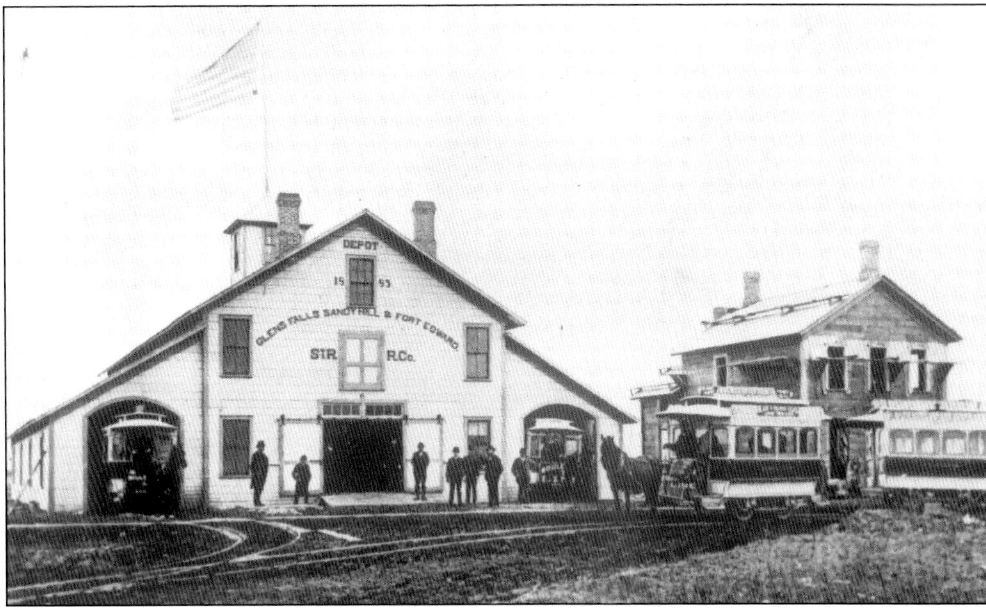

This building was pictured on page 45 as a used car dealership. It was originally the headquarters of the first trolley system in the area. The Glens Falls, Sandy Hill, and Fort Edward Street Railway Company began in 1895 and ran horse-drawn trolleys between the three named communities. The building is located on Feeder Street near the Boulevard. The horses were stabled in the main part of the barn, and the railway cars were kept in the two wings.

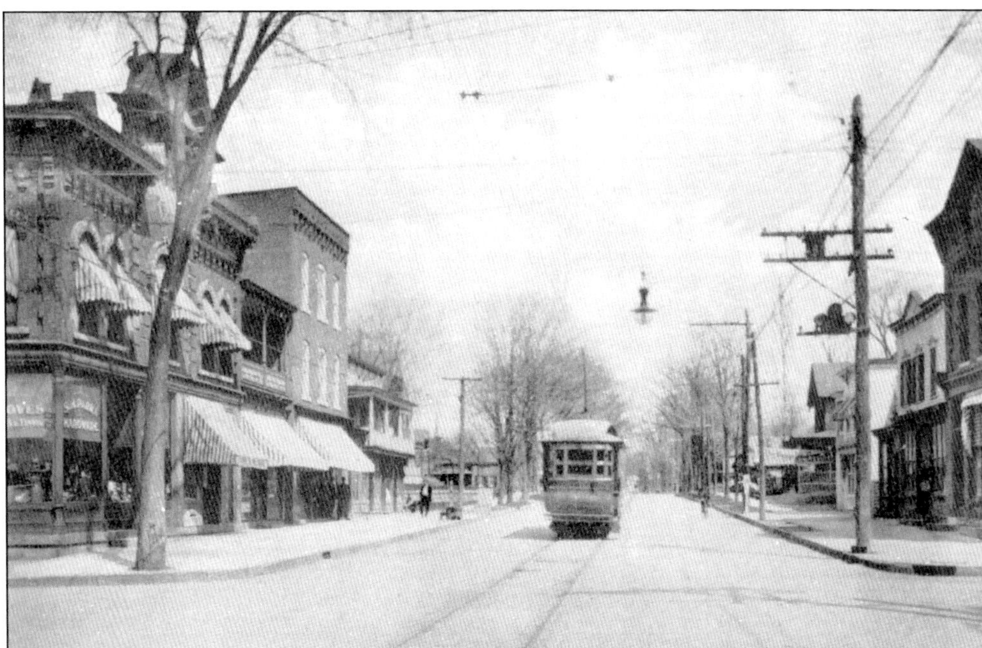

This picture shows one of the later-model electric railway cars on Main Street just north of John Street. Note the lack of any other type of traffic on what is today a very busy street corner.

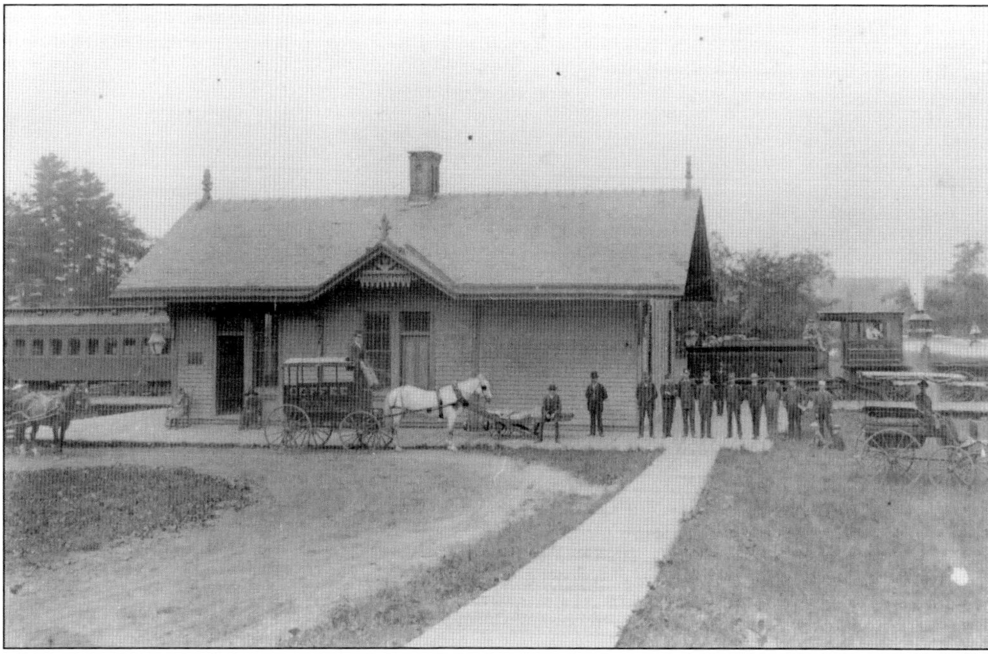

Located at the bottom of Depot Street hill is the Sandy Hill depot of the Delaware and Hudson Railroad. Waiting outside the wooden station is a coach for the Coffee House Hotel, ready to pick up guests who were getting off the train. Pictured here in the 1880s, the station was later replaced with a brick depot, which today houses a small factory.

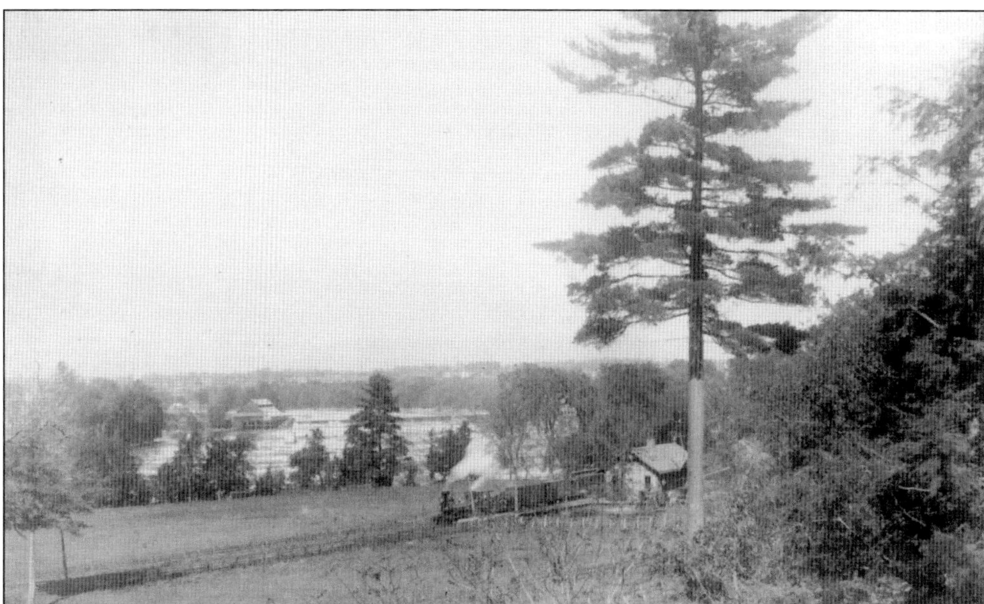

A passenger train pulls out of the Sandy Hill depot, on its way to Fort Edward in the 1880s. Cattle graze in the field beside the tracks. This photograph was taken from the top of the hill along Main Street near Elm Street.

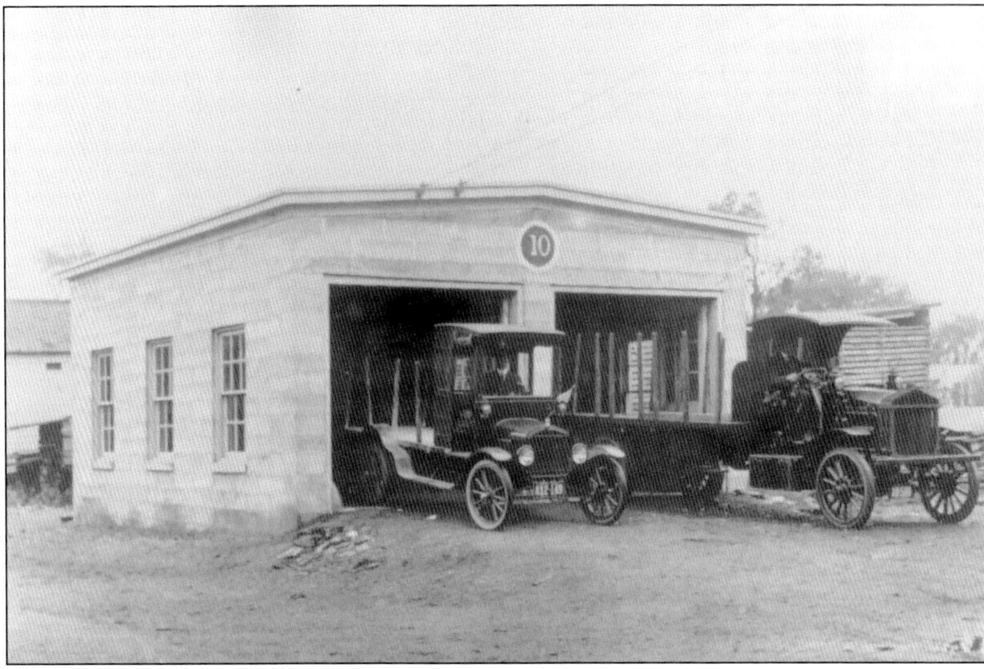

Sometime following World War I, this truck garage became part of the Griffin Lumber Company. It was located in the Griffin lumberyard between Maple and Pearl Streets. Griffin purchased several military trucks and many supply wagons after the war and used them for many years.

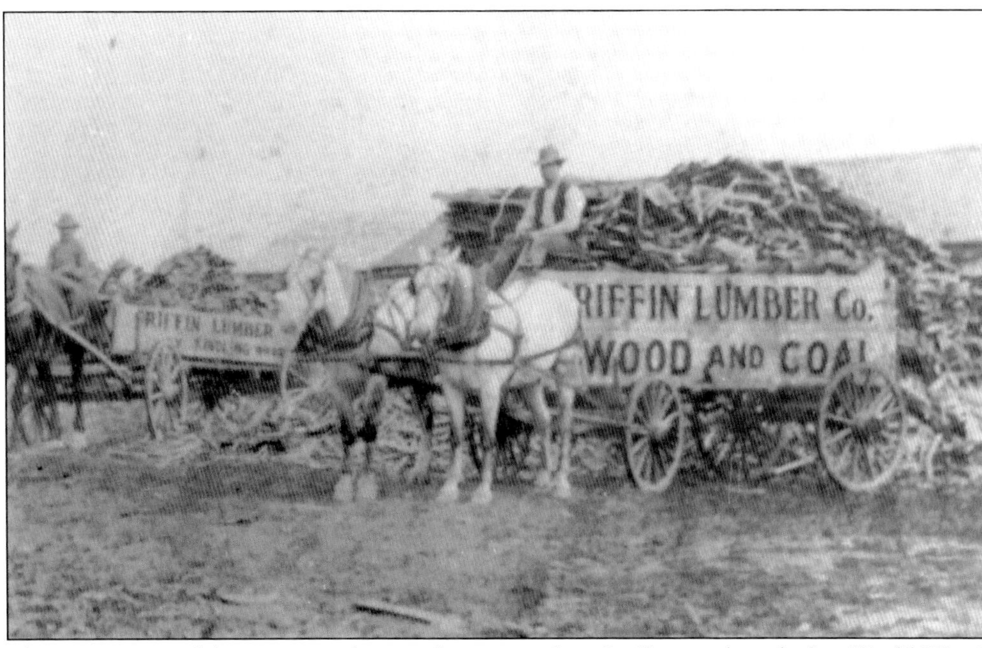

These are some of the army surplus supply wagons that Griffin purchased after World War I. They are loaded with kindling, which was sold to homeowners in and around the village.

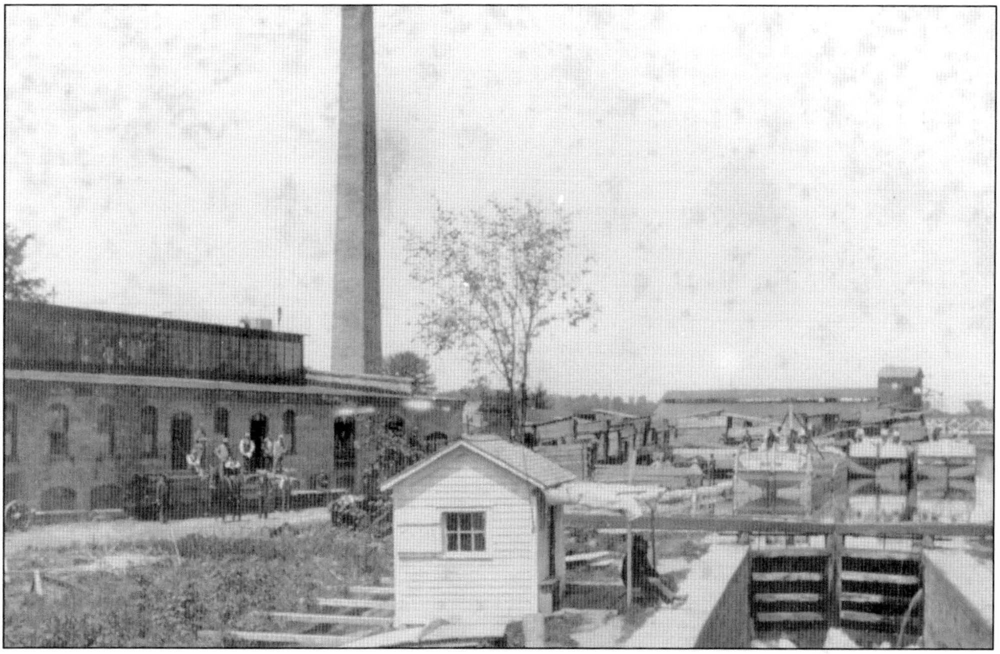

This is a view of Lock 13 of the Glens Falls Feeder Canal. The buildings are part of the Griffin Lumber Company. The closest one is the manufacturing facility on Pearl Street. The one in the distance is the coal silo facility on Maple Street. Both of these structures are still in use today.

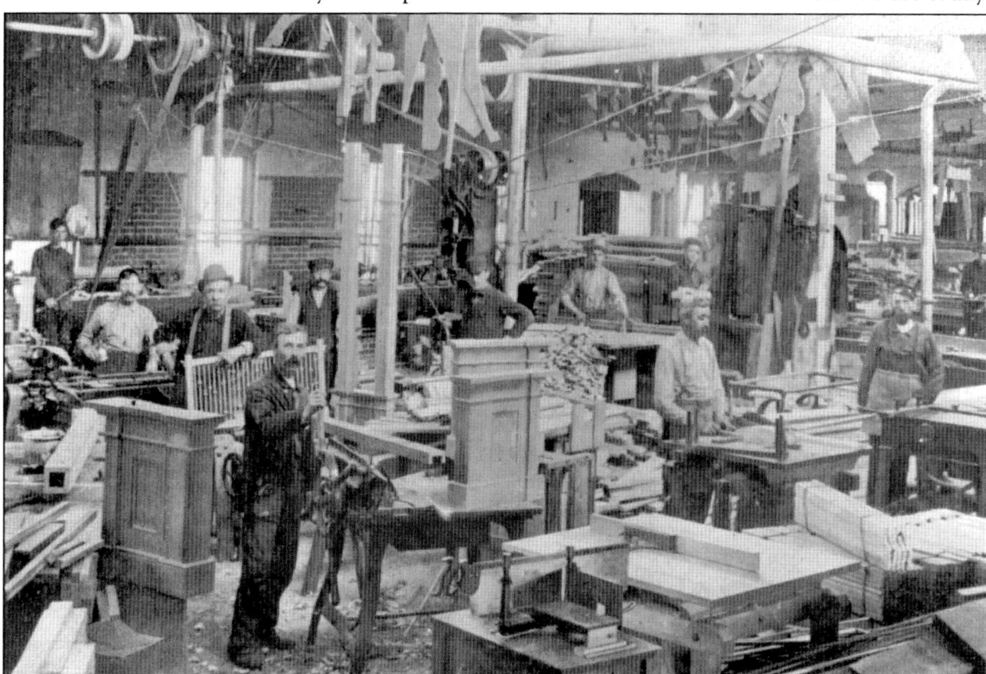

This is an interior picture of Griffin's manufacturing mill on Pearl Street. Taken after World War I, it gives an indication of the bad working conditions that existed in many paper mills of the day. The workers are making decorative interior parts for manufactured homes, which Griffin pioneered in.

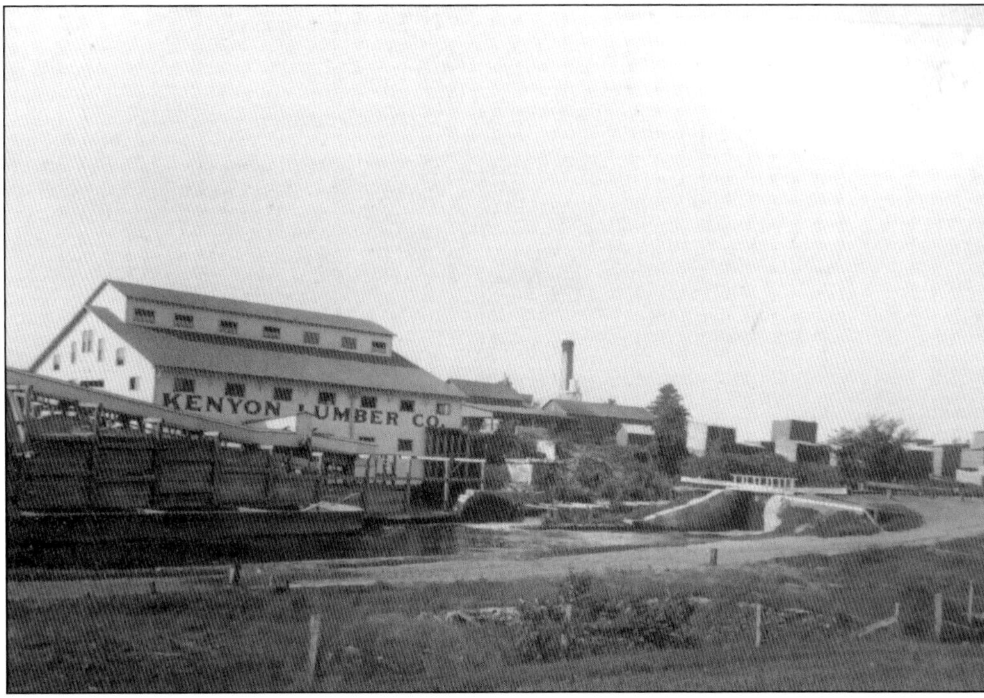

The Kenyon Lumber Company was located on the south side of Pearl Street beside the Glens Falls Feeder Canal. The log ponds were about one-quarter of a mile away on Maple Street and were connected to the Kenyon sawmill by a small canal. Note the lower end of Lock 12, with the gate closed.

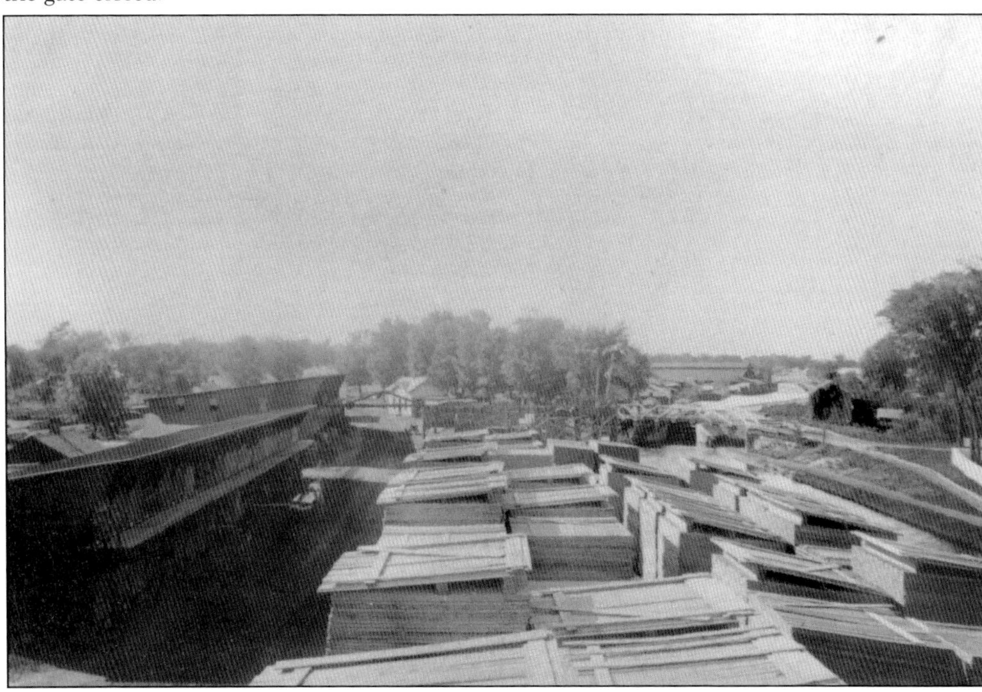

These piles of freshly cut Kenyon lumber are ready to be shipped out of Sandy Hill on canal boats.

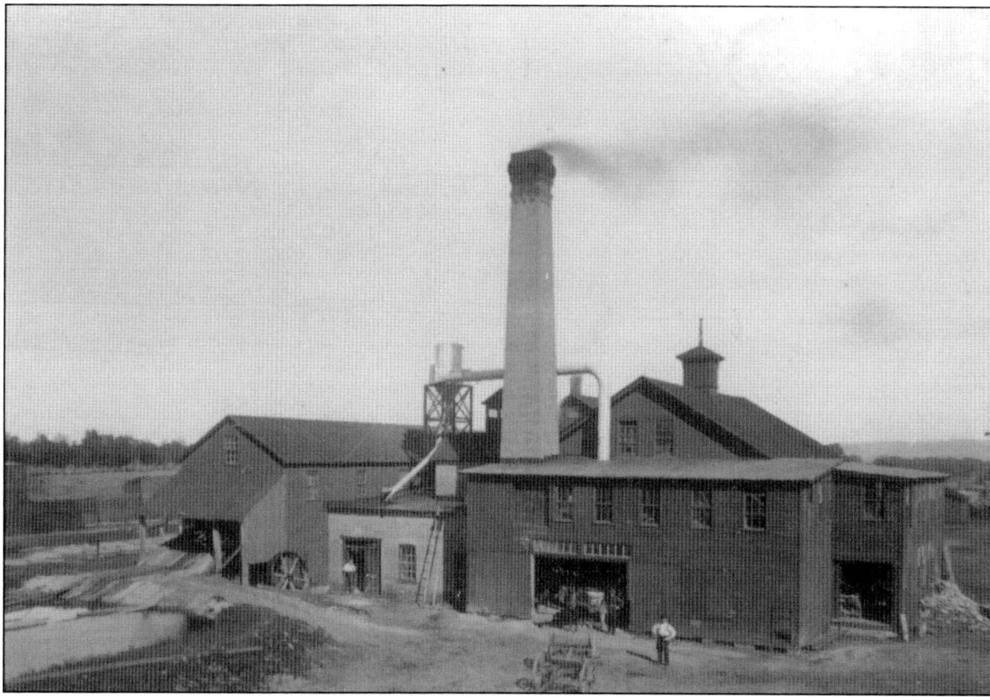

This is the boiler house for Kenyon Lumber. The fuel used to fire the boiler was the sawdust produced in the sawing and planing processes.

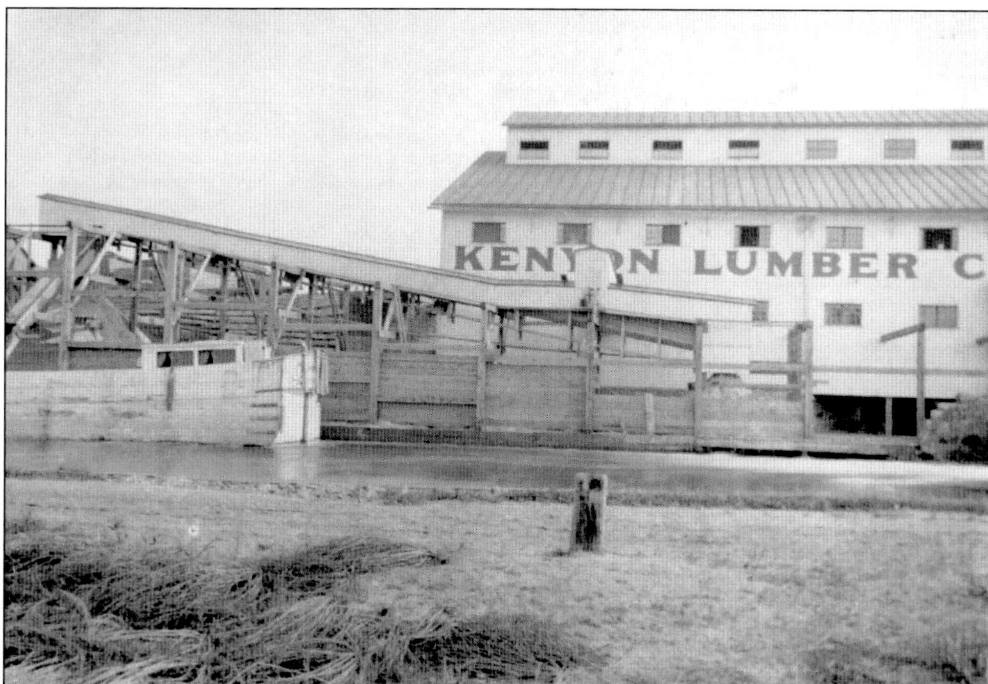

The canal boat alongside Kenyon Lumber is being loaded with some of the excess sawdust from the company's operations. There were many uses for this extra sawdust. Before modern refrigeration, it was used in the storage of ice during the summer.

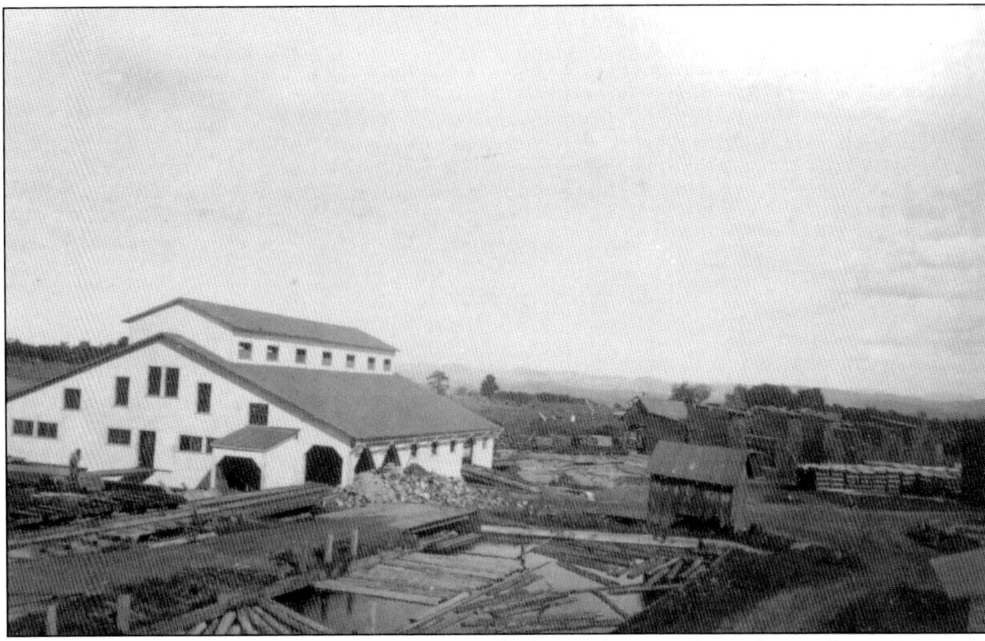

Some of the logs brought over from the Maple Street log ponds are being floated into the Kenyon Lumber sawmill. These logs were cut in the Adirondack Mountains in winter and were floated down the Hudson River to the Glens Falls Feeder Canal and then into their holding ponds. Each large sawmill placed its own mark on the ends of the logs to tell them apart.

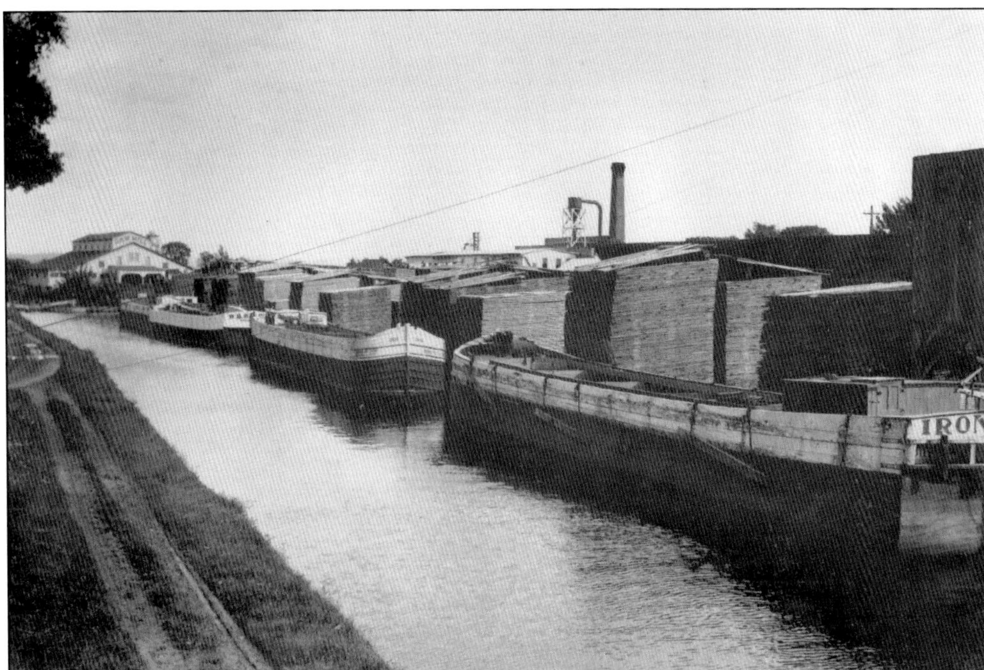

Four canal boats wait to be loaded with Kenyon Lumber. The photographer is standing on the Pearl Street bridge. Today, the Hudson Falls American Legion Post No. 574 has its rooms located here in one of the old Kenyon buildings.

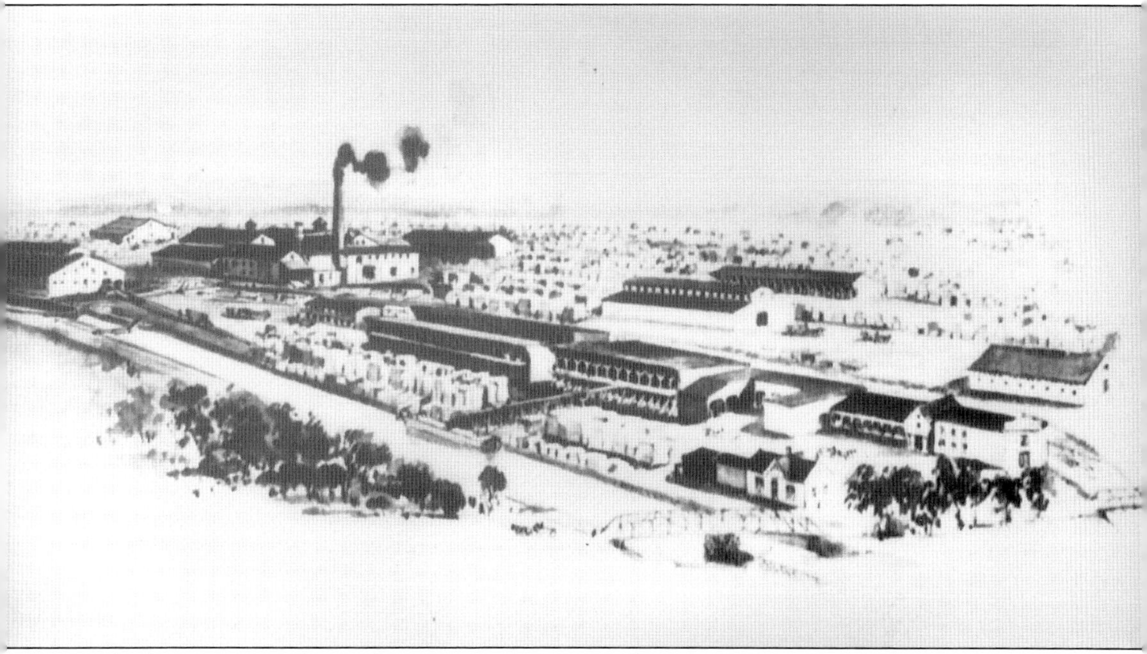

This bird's-eye view shows the entire Kenyon Lumber Company complex. Some of the buildings on the right side of the complex were built where some of the houses on Pine Street stand today. Imagine all of the buildings, both in Hudson Falls and beyond this area, that were constructed with lumber from this huge mill.

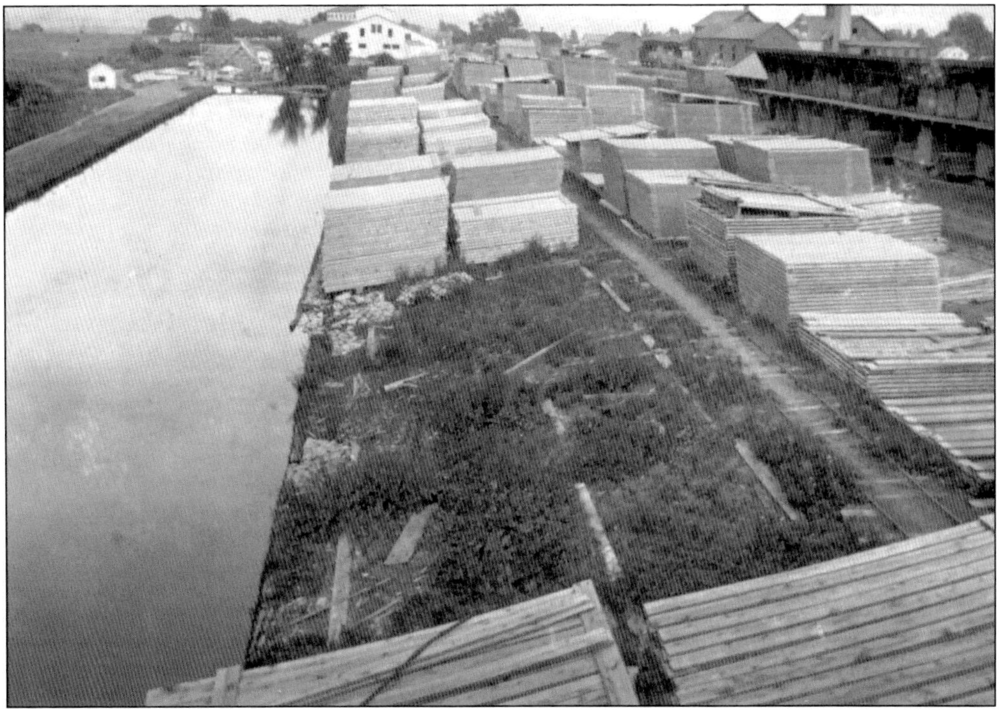

The American Legion rooms are located in the building at the right edge of this picture.

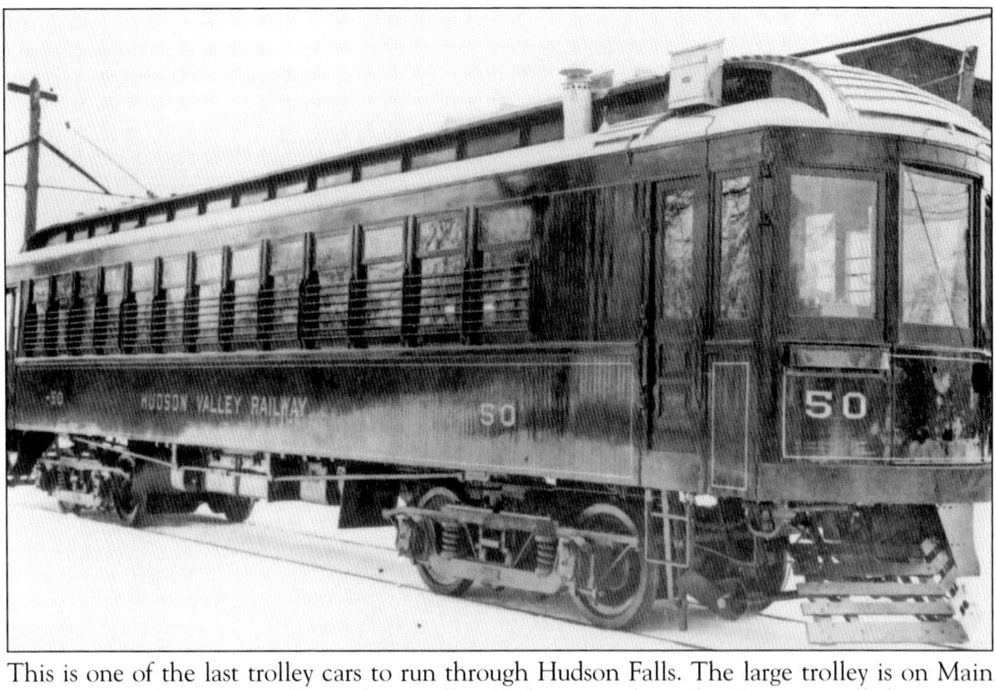

This is one of the last trolley cars to run through Hudson Falls. The large trolley is on Main Street near John Street. The Hudson Valley Railway ran from the Troy area all the way to Warrensburg. These cars ran until the late 1920s, when buses replaced them.

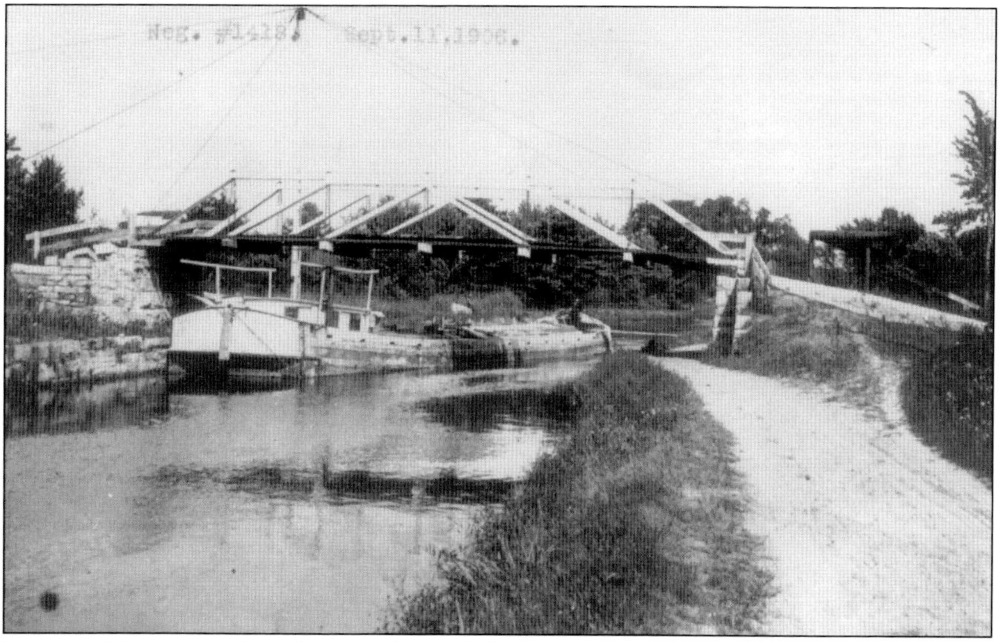

This canal boat is docked along the Glens Falls Feeder Canal at Warren Street in 1906. The gin pole on the left side of the canal was used to load Kingsbury dolomite onto the barges. This street crossed the Boulevard at the point at which it became Quarry Crossing and then continued north to the huge quarry. It was from this point that stone was shipped to New York City for use in the construction of the Brooklyn Bridge.

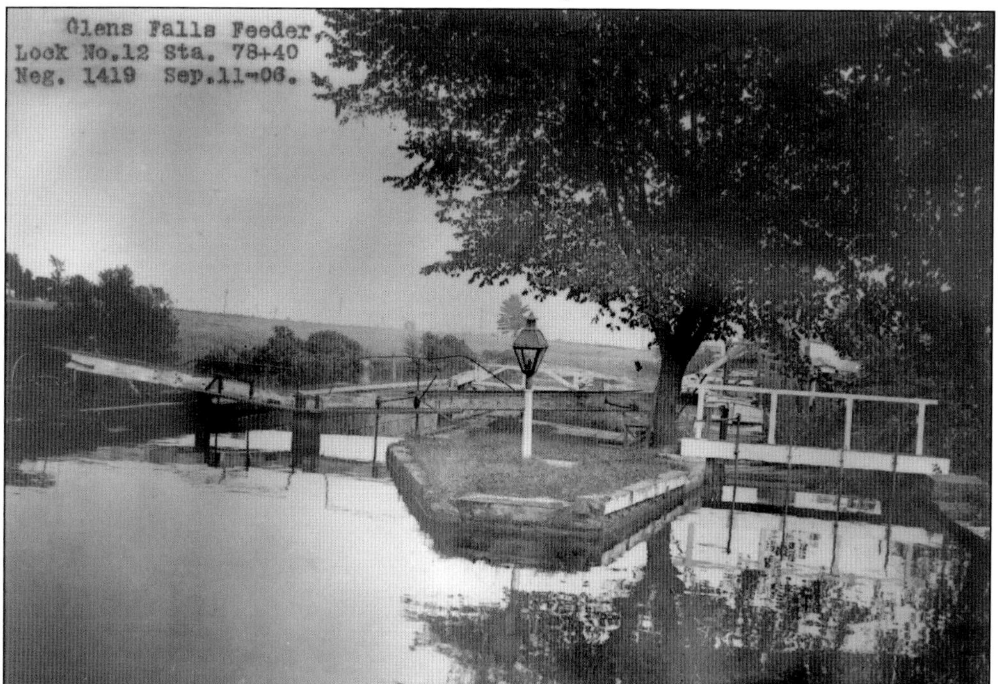

This is the upper end of Lock 12, between Pearl Street and Burgoyne Avenue. This is a New York State photograph from 1906. Note the beautiful lantern on the island.

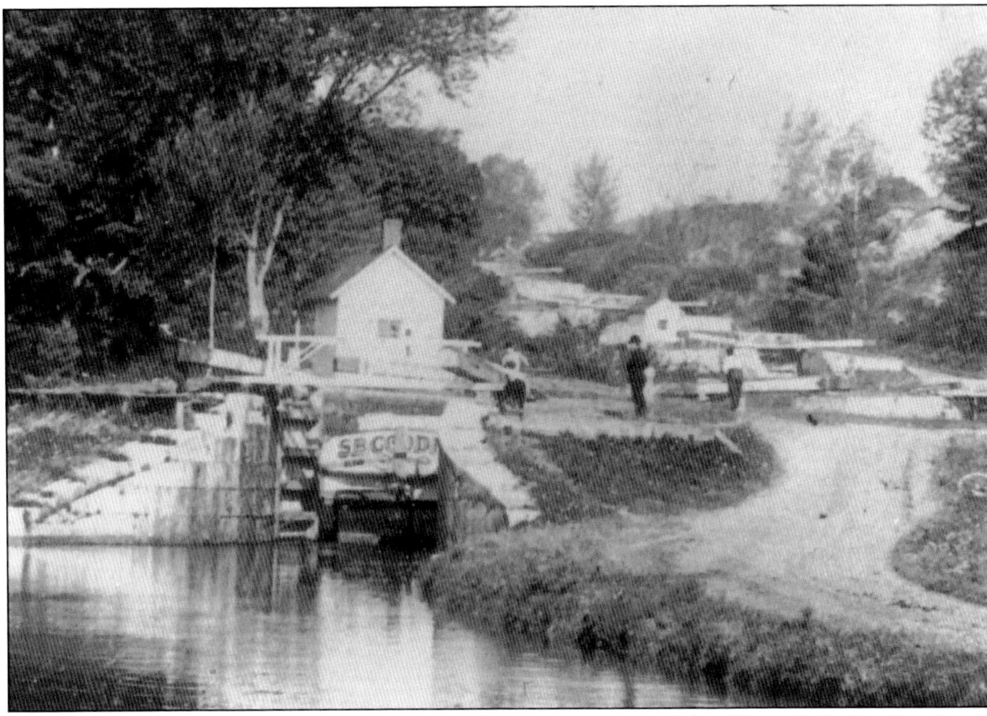

This is a good view of a canal boat being pulled into Lock 5 of the Glens Falls Feeder Canal. The lockkeepers are bending over the poles that close the lock gate once the boat is inside. Just above this lock is the set of locks called the Five Combines, because there were five locks in a series of steps.

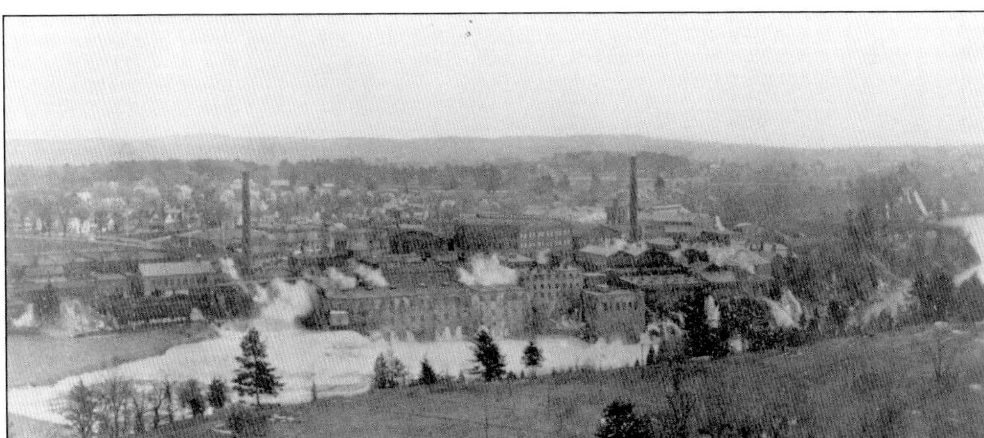

This is an excellent view of Bakers Falls and all of the mills there *c.* 1900. The smokestack on the left was taken down in December 2000. Most of these mill buildings have also been demolished since the 1950s.

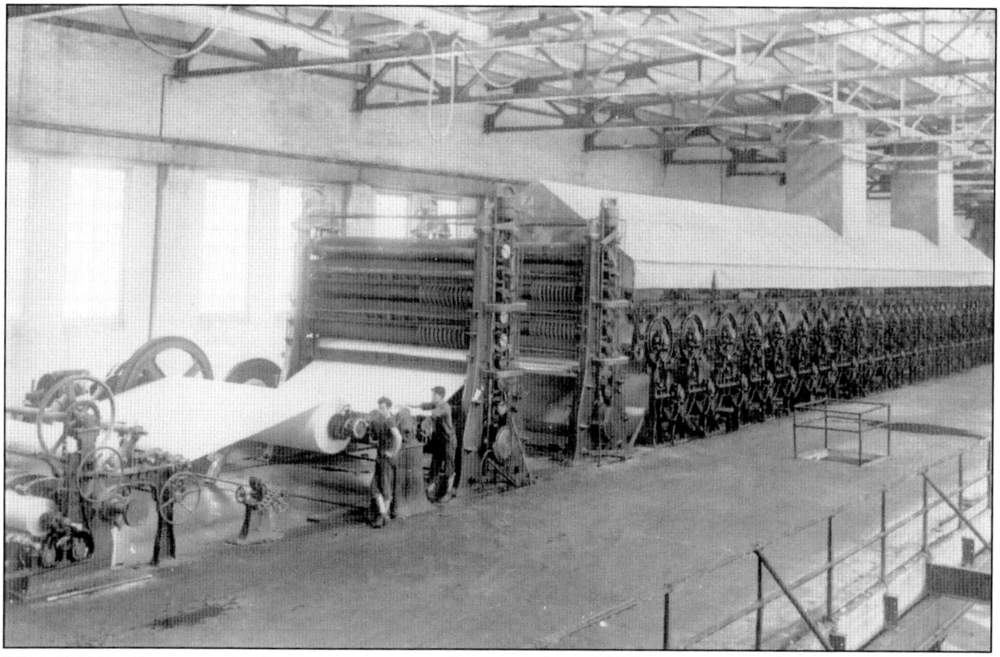

This 1920s photograph shows a paper machine in the old Union Bag mill on Sumpter Street. Although large in its day, it is small compared with a modern paper machine.

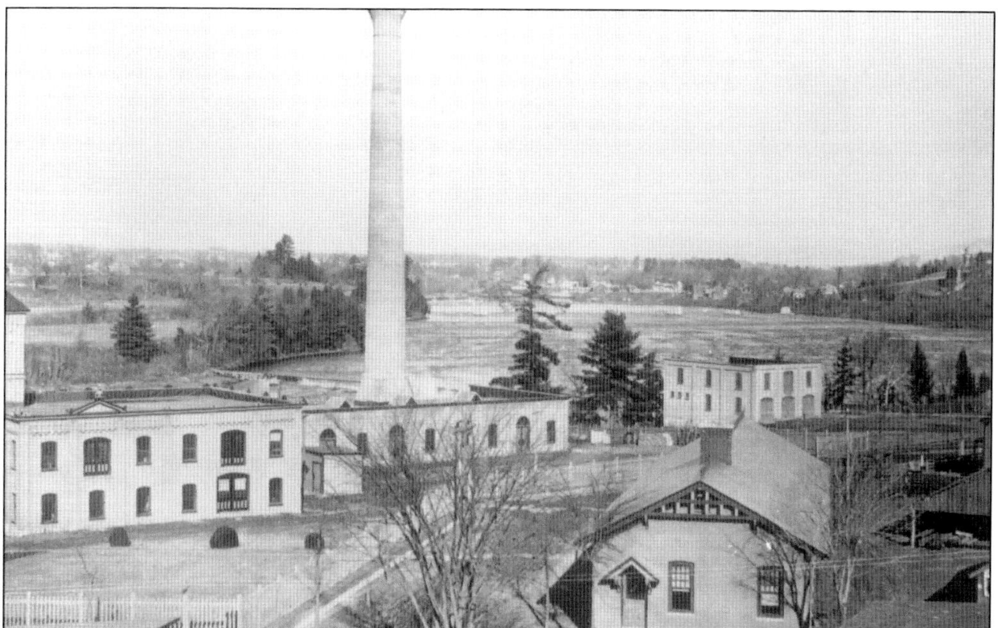

The Howland Paper Company was located at the bottom of John Street hill in the 1870s and 1880s. Union Bag bought this company. The photograph shows the company buildings, which were located on either side of what is today Allen Street.

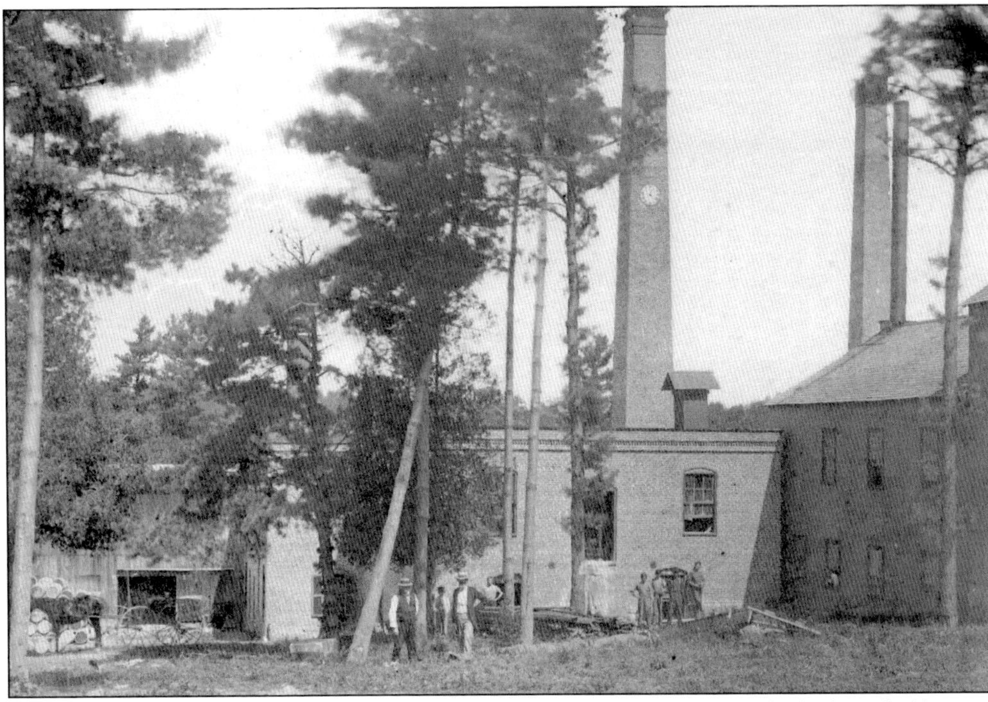

This is likely a *c.* 1870 view of the Howland Paper Company. Note the clock about halfway up the smokestack in the center of the picture.

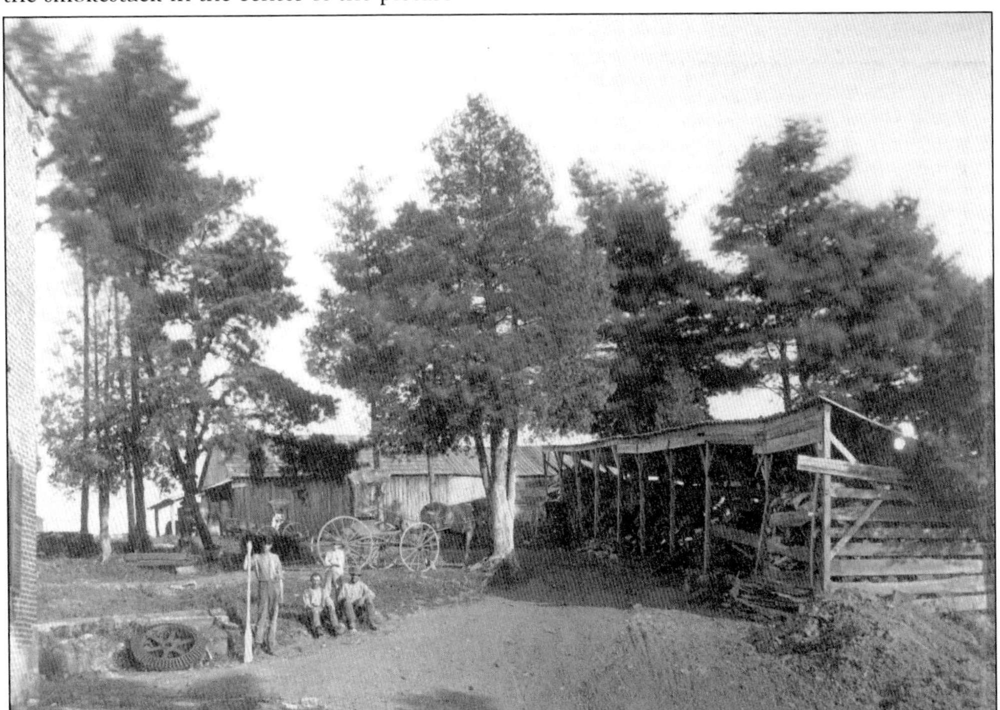

These workmen seem to be on a break someplace in the Bakers Falls mill area in 1870. Photography was a rare art in 1870, and these men were lucky to have their picture taken.

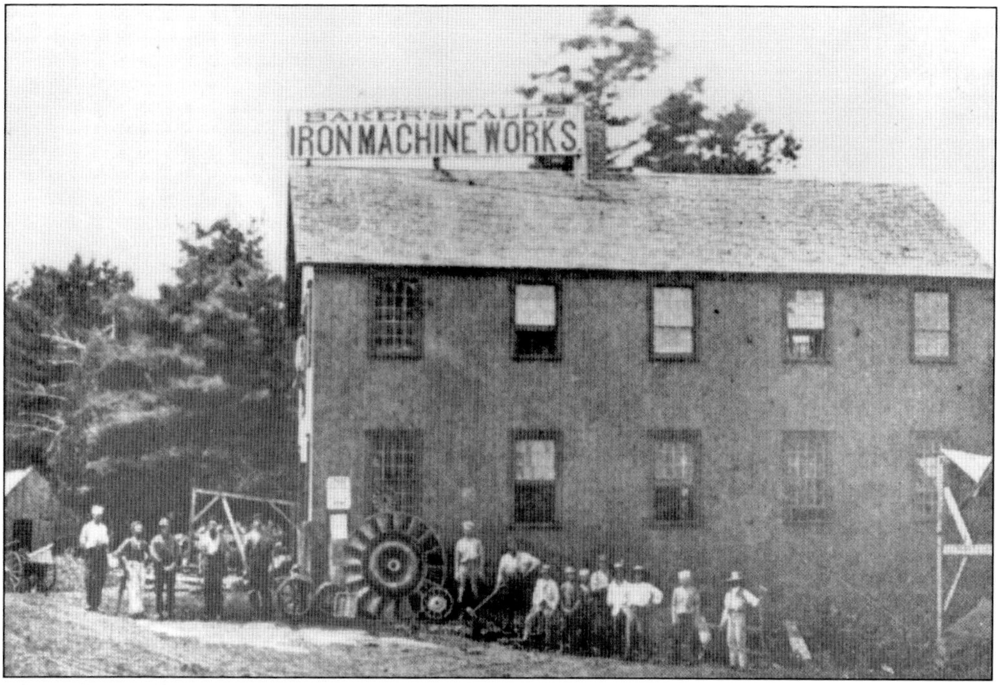

The Bakers Falls Iron and Machine works was started in 1857 on Allen Street. The company later became known as Sandy Hill Iron and Brass and, later, as the Sandy Hill Corporation. In the top photograph, the entire staff gathers on the north side of the building for a picture. The bottom photograph, taken in 1870, shows just a few workers and the back side of the sign on the roof. The business is still in operation today as Valmet, producing parts for the paper manufacturing industry.

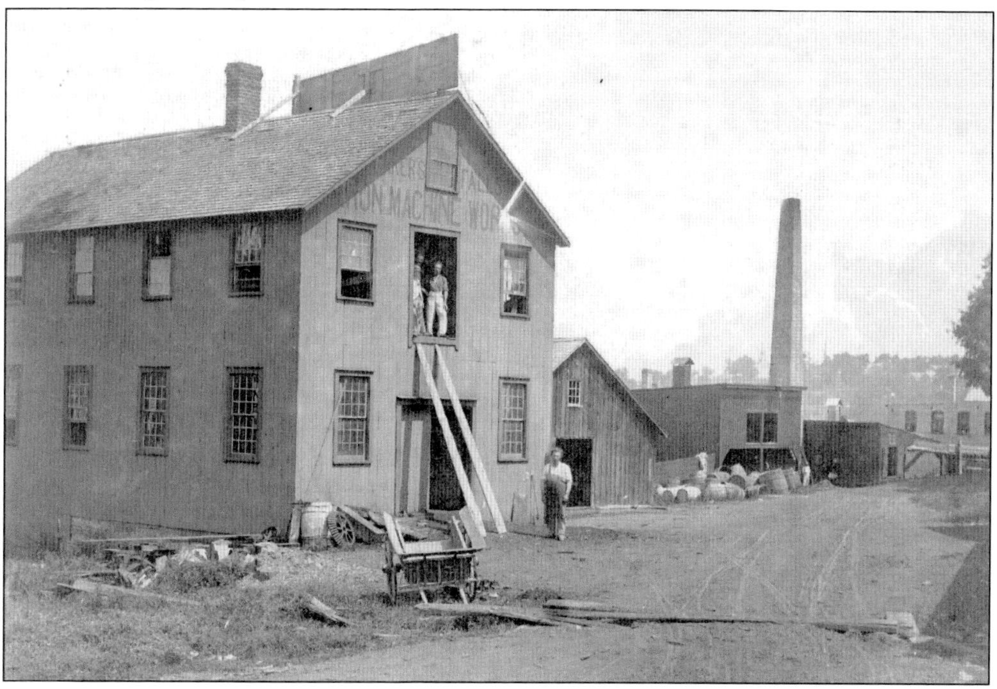

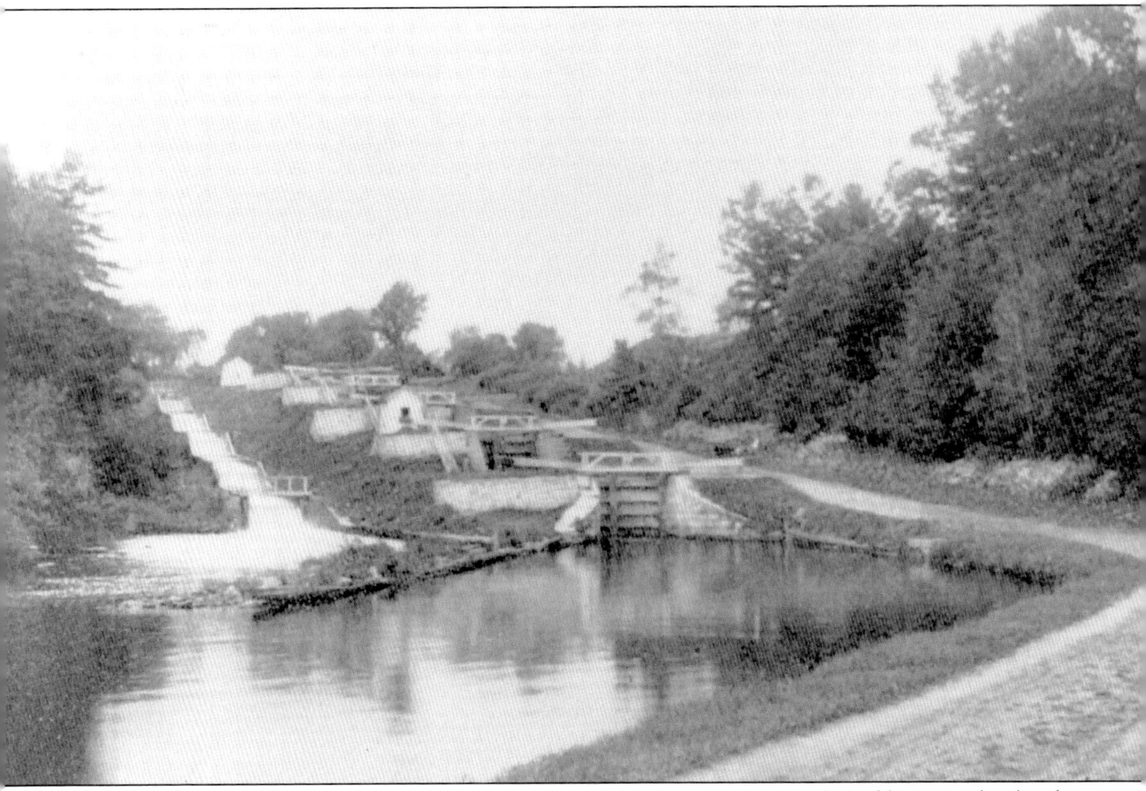

This view has been reproduced many times over the years, on postcards and historical calendars. It shows the Five Combines. The water on the left was a bypass for the flow when the locks were all closed. It took about two hours for one canal boat to be "locked through" all five locks. At either end were located taverns, where canalers could wait their turn.

Seven

People and Military

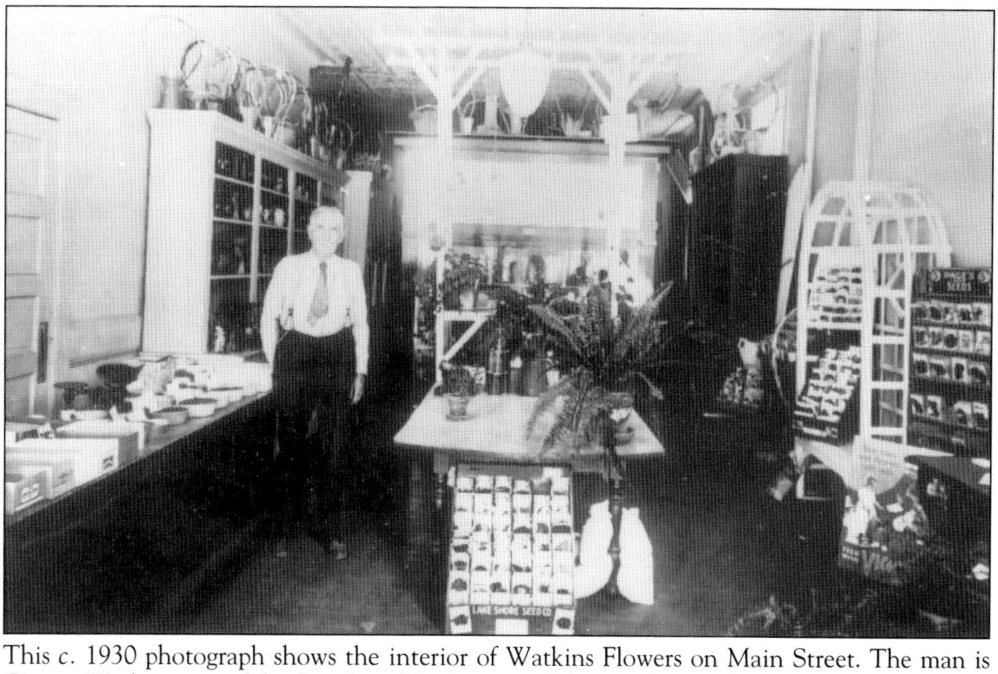

This *c.* 1930 photograph shows the interior of Watkins Flowers on Main Street. The man is George Watkins, son of the founder of the business, John Watkins. John Watkins began with a small greenhouse on Minor Street and later opened this store on Main Street. The store is still a florist shop today, Parkside Flowers.

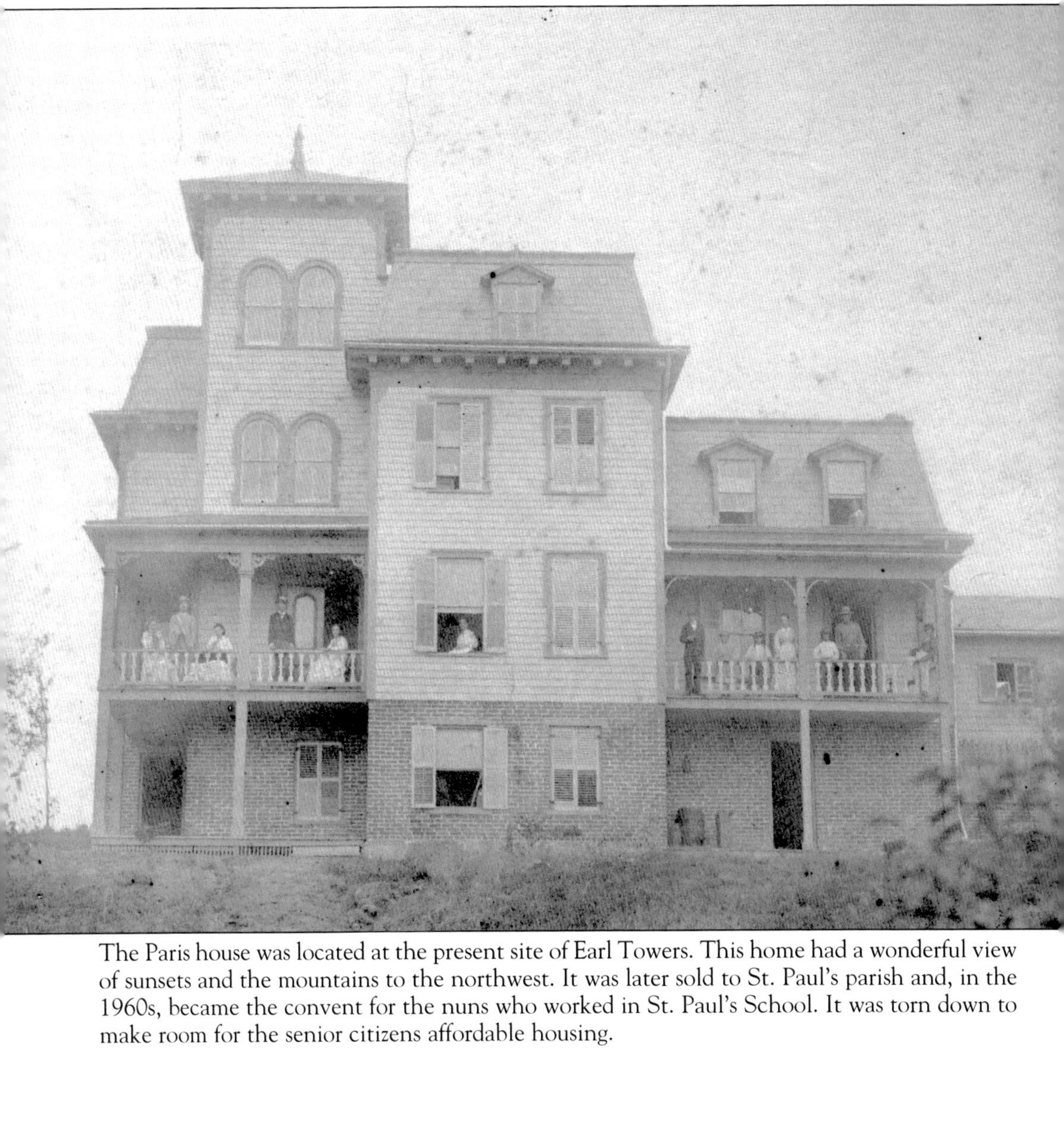

The Paris house was located at the present site of Earl Towers. This home had a wonderful view of sunsets and the mountains to the northwest. It was later sold to St. Paul's parish and, in the 1960s, became the convent for the nuns who worked in St. Paul's School. It was torn down to make room for the senior citizens affordable housing.

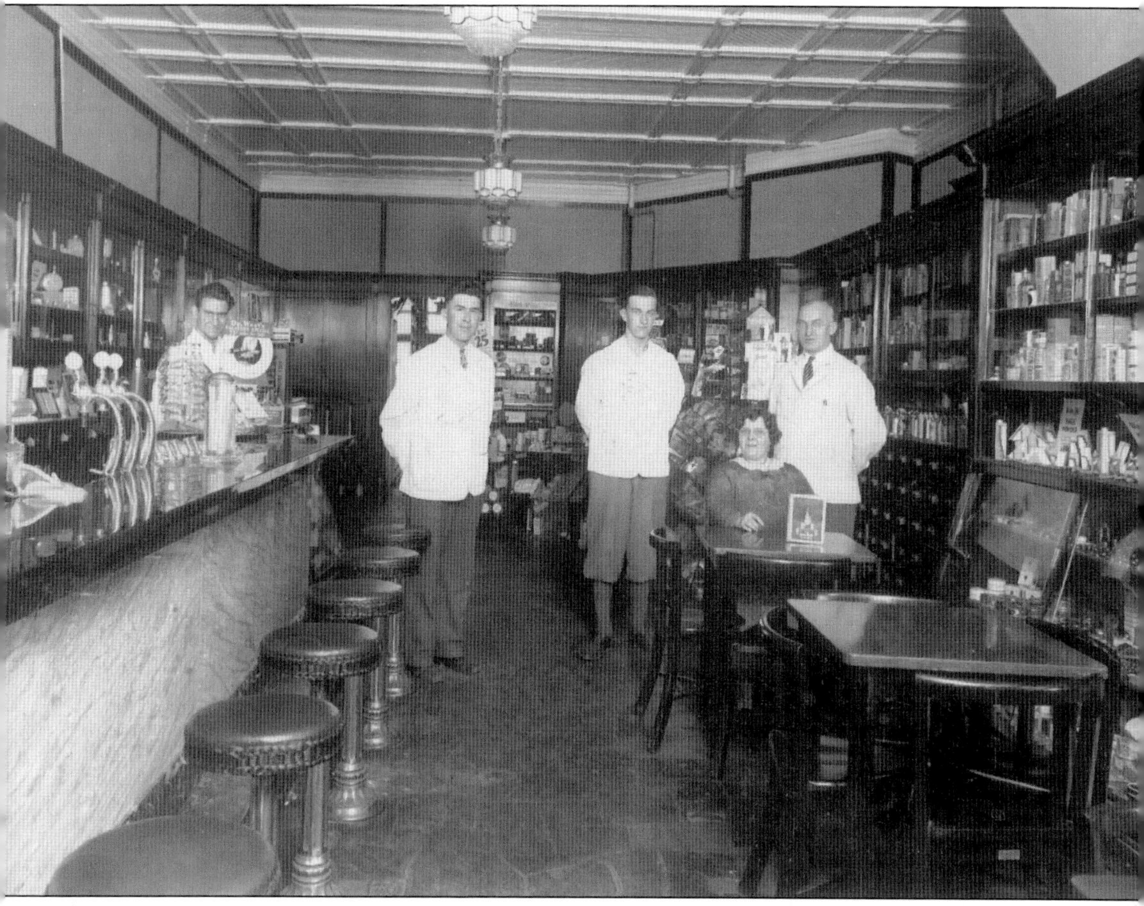

This is a summer 1927 picture of McCann's Pharmacy, which is still in business today. At that time, during Prohibition, most pharmacies had a soda fountain. The three Main Street pharmacies—McCann's, Baker's and Moriarity's—were no exception. A soda fountain was a gathering place where people swapped stories and the gossip of the day. Pictured, from left to right, are George LaPoint, Charles Havens, John McCann, Leona Phelps, and Joseph McCann.

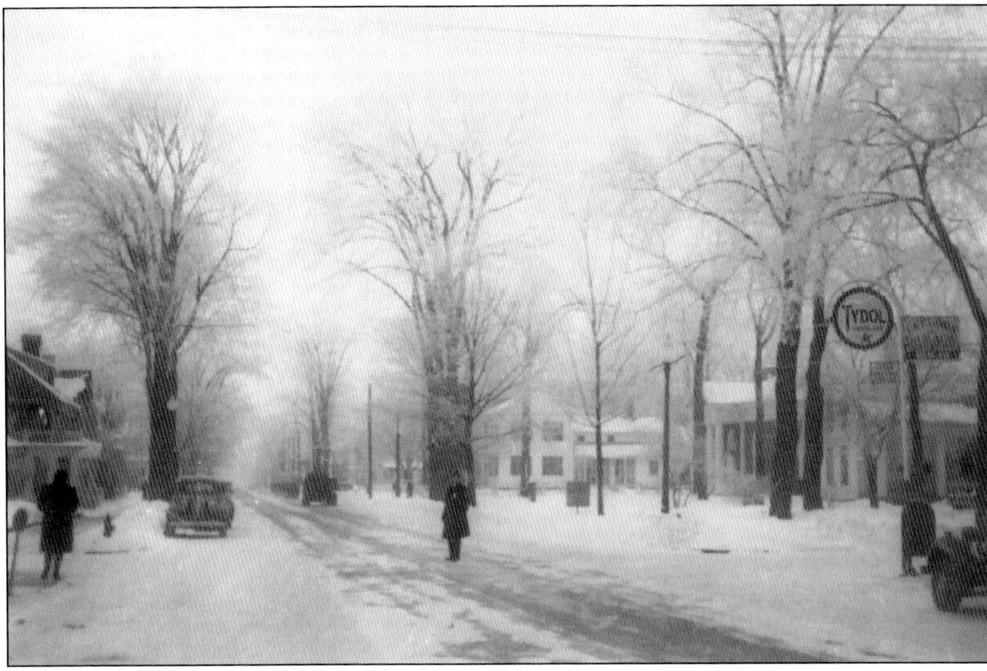

This winter scene shows Police Chief Mike Usher directing what little traffic there is at the corner of Main and Locust Streets c. 1940.

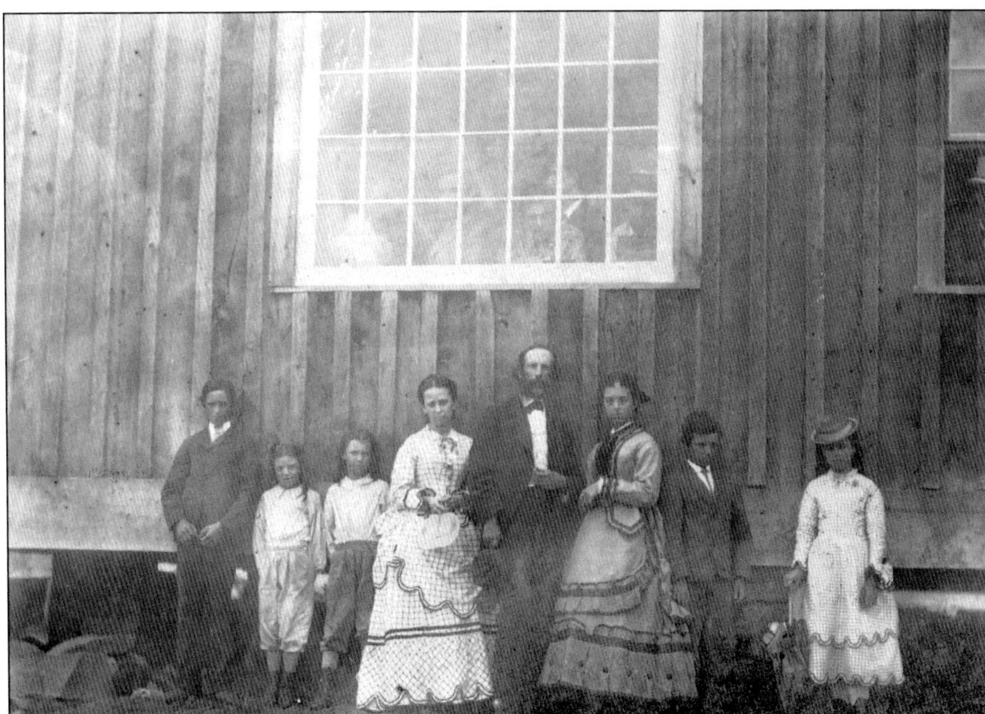

Many of the c. 1870 photographs of Sandy Hill and Kingsbury were taken by John Peoli, pictured here with his family. A friend of the Paris family, Peoli was a photographer from Argentina. He spent the Argentinean winters in Sandy Hill, where it was summer.

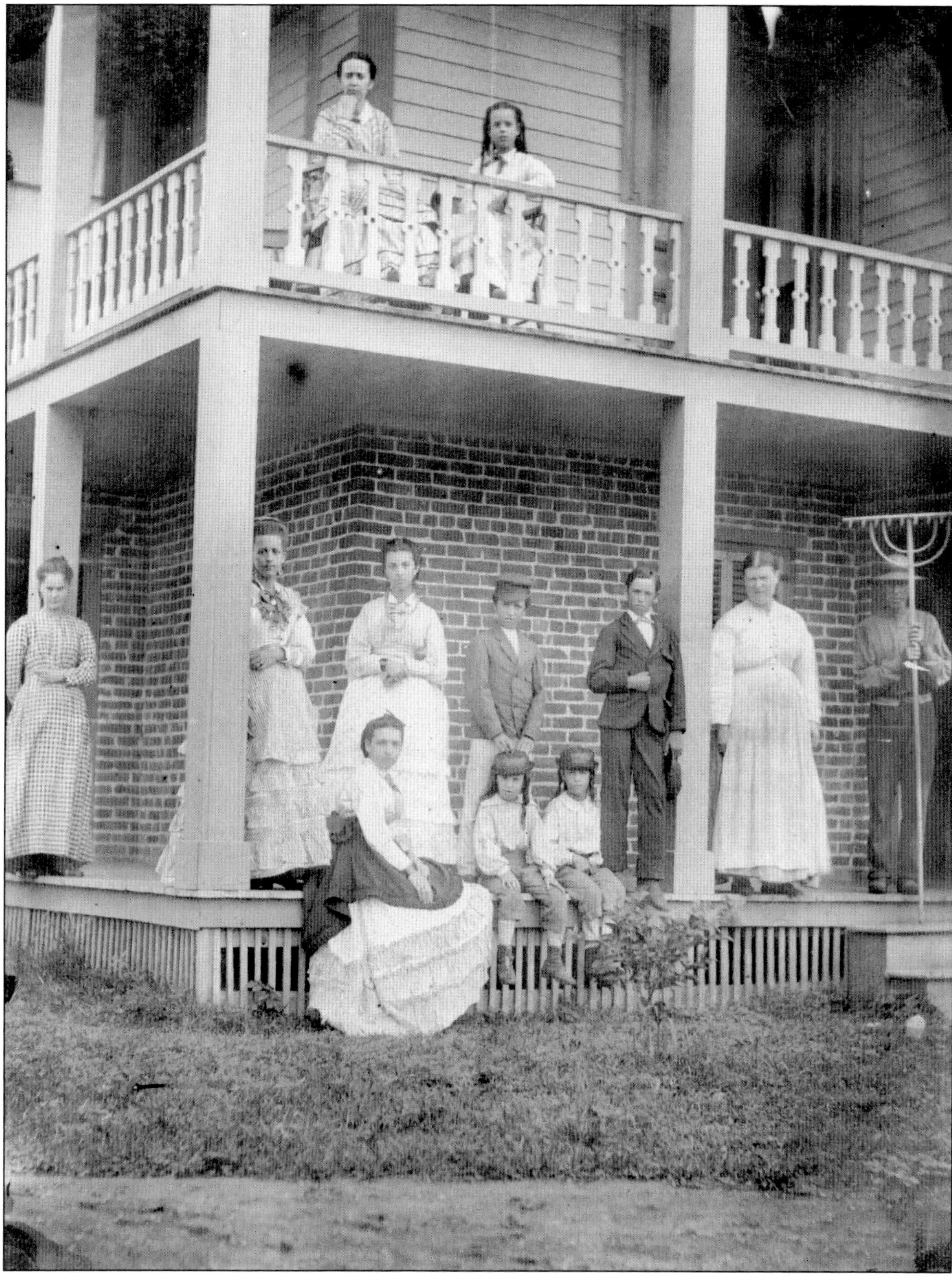

This is a close-up photograph that John Peoli took of members of the Paris family at their house on River Street hill. The detail of the clothing is remarkable. The rake that the man is holding seems to be of an earlier period, indicating that Sandy Hill might have been behind the times in tools in 1870.

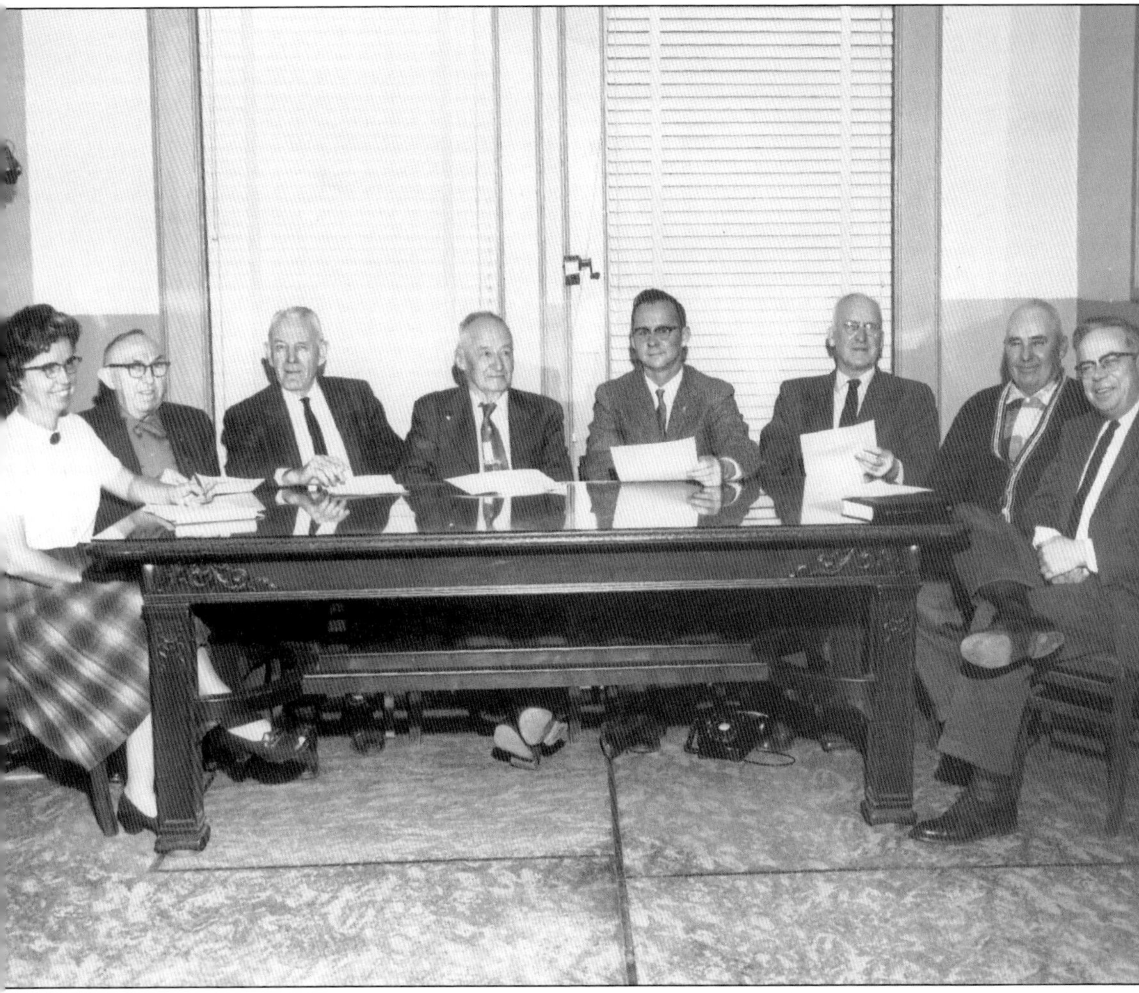

The members of the Kingsbury town government in 1961, from left to right, are Mrs. H. Washer, town clerk; Jerry Moynihan, councilman; Robert Wilber, councilman; Amos Wright, town supervisor; Amos Carpenter, town justice; Roy Stone, town justice; Howard Bromley, highway superintendent; and Thomas Remsen, attorney. It is interesting to note that the table they are sitting at is still used for all town board meetings today.

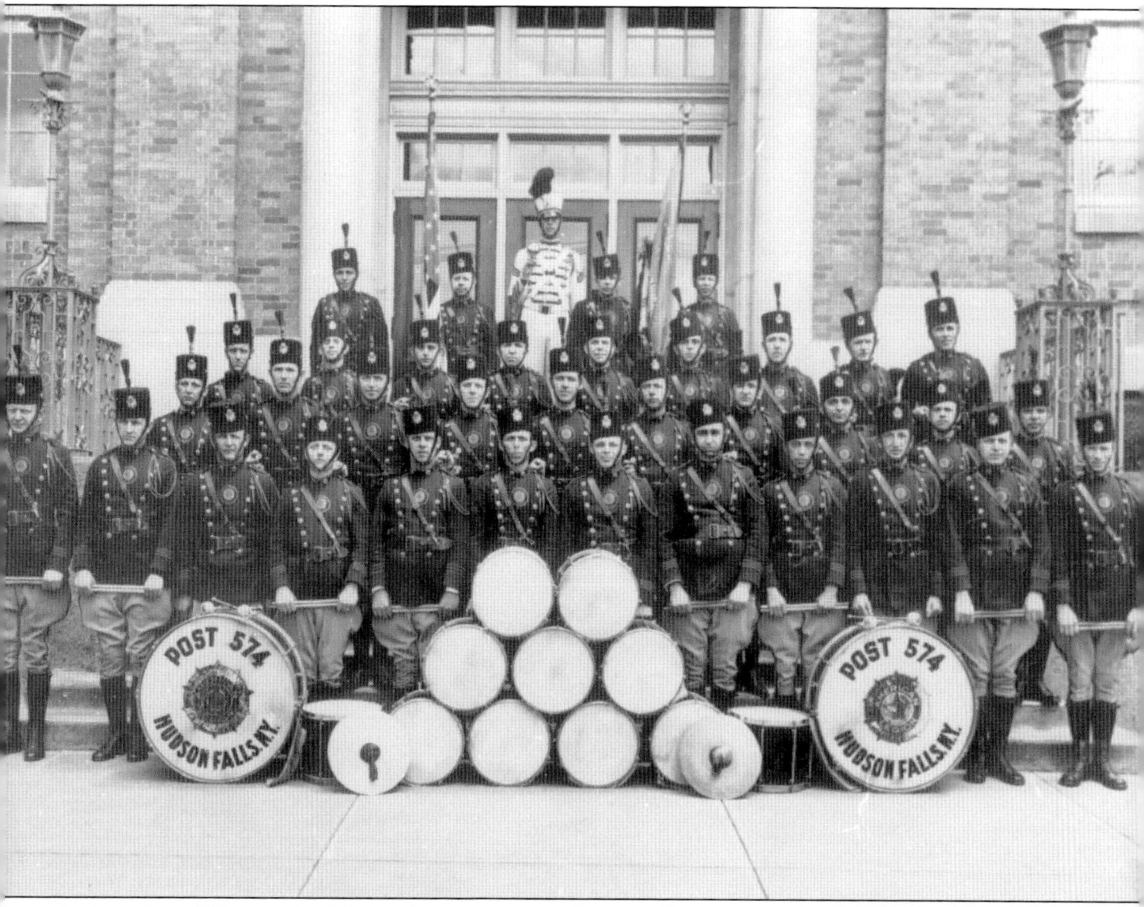

During the 1920s and 1930s, the American Legion Post in Hudson Falls had a fine drum-and-bugle corps. Members of the corps pose are on the steps of the Hudson Falls High School on Main Street. Their snappy uniforms are similar to those of the British army's light infantry bands. It could be that legion members saw the British uniforms when they were in England or France during World War I.

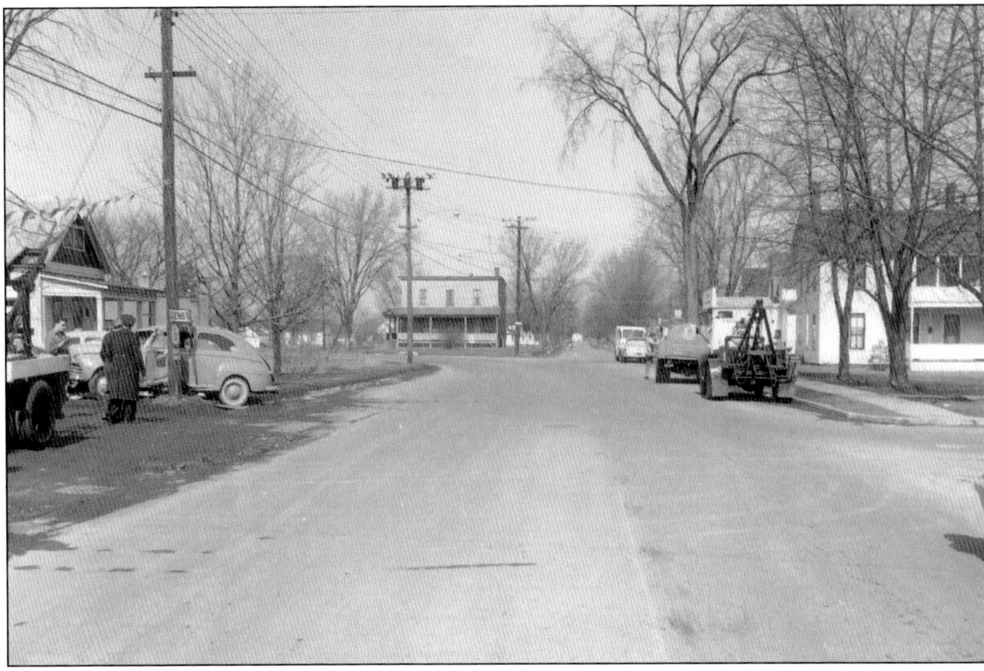

This automobile on the left has struck a telephone pole in front of Goddale's used furniture store on Feeder Street. Police Chief Mike Usher is investigating the crash. This accident took place in March 1957.

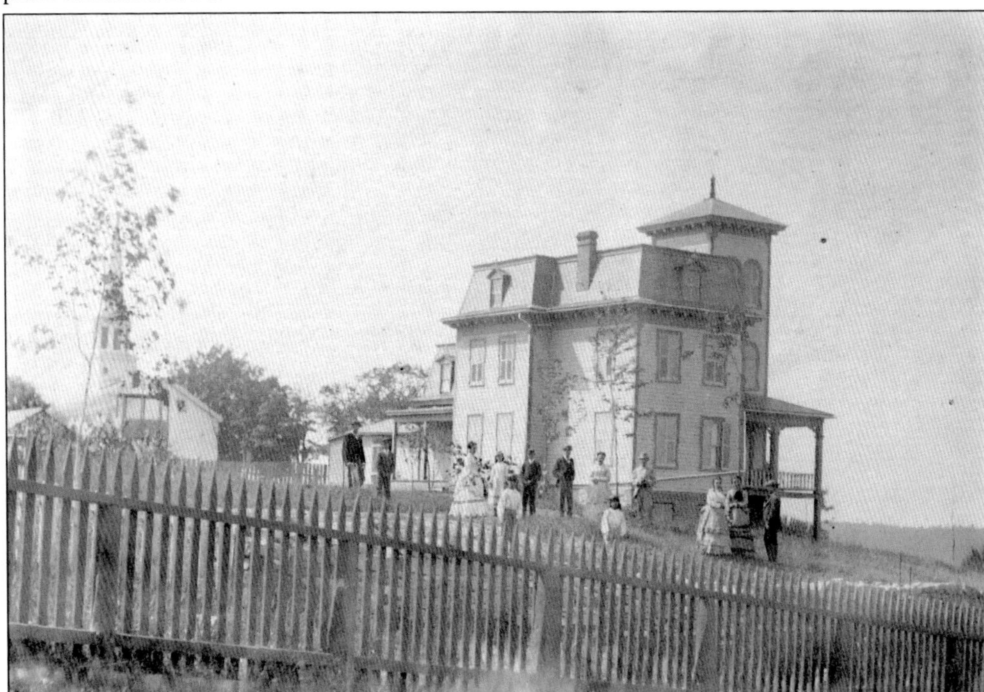

This photograph by John Peoli shows the Paris house. The photograph was taken from Walnut Street, looking south. In the background is the steeple for St. Paul's first church.

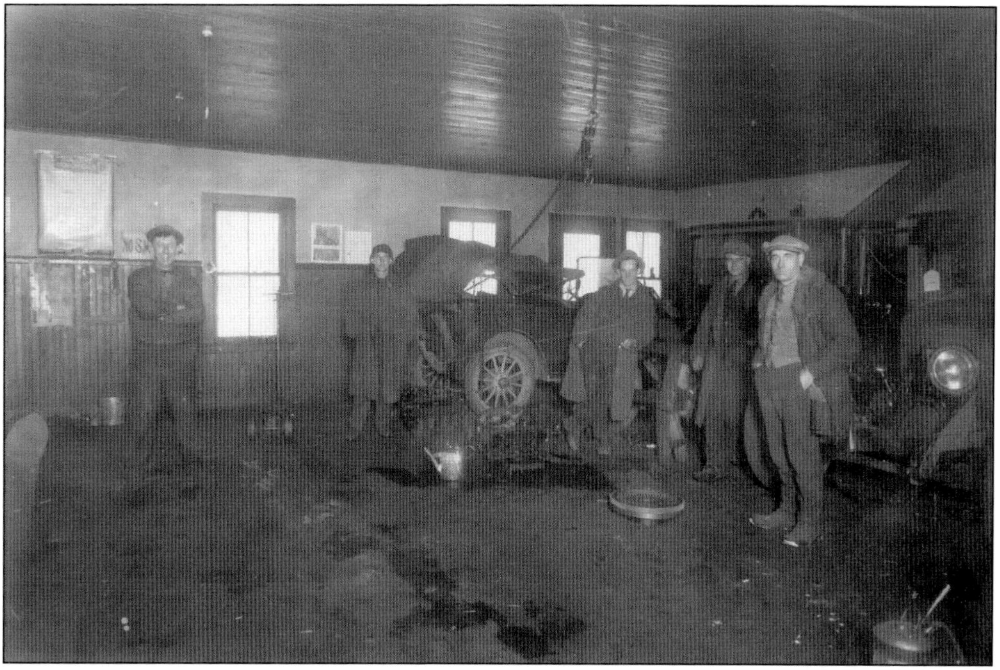

This 1930s picture shows the interior of LaMere's Garage on Maple Street, located behind the courthouse. The man on the left is probably the owner, Stephen LaMere (grandfather of the author).

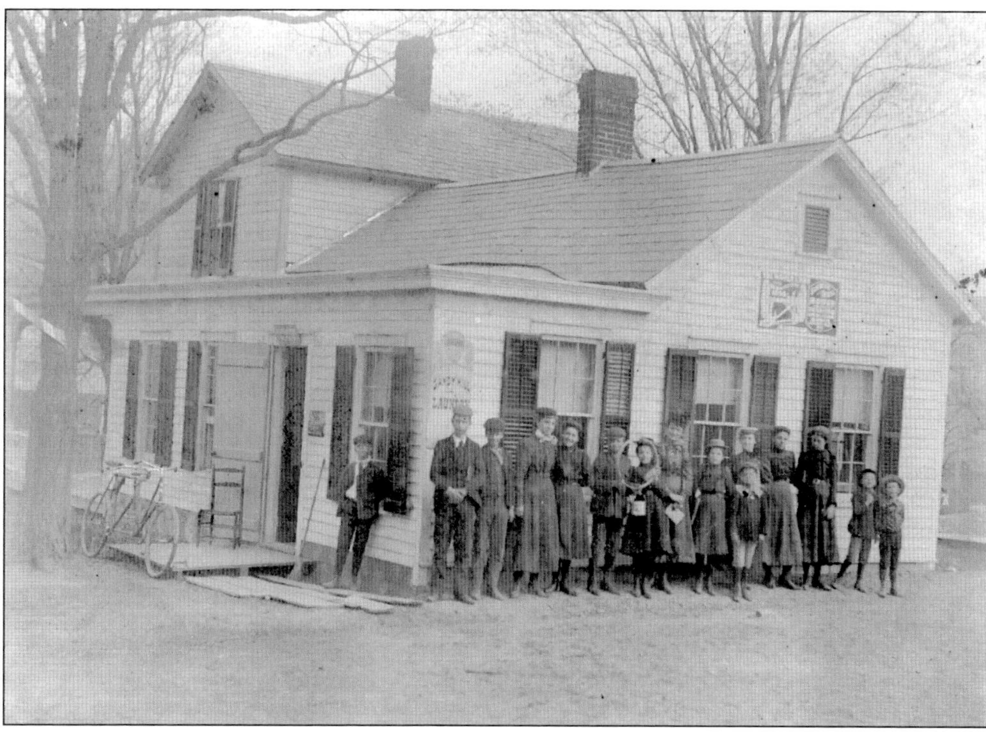

This photograph of the Sandy Hill Laundry was taken shortly before the village name changed to Hudson Falls.

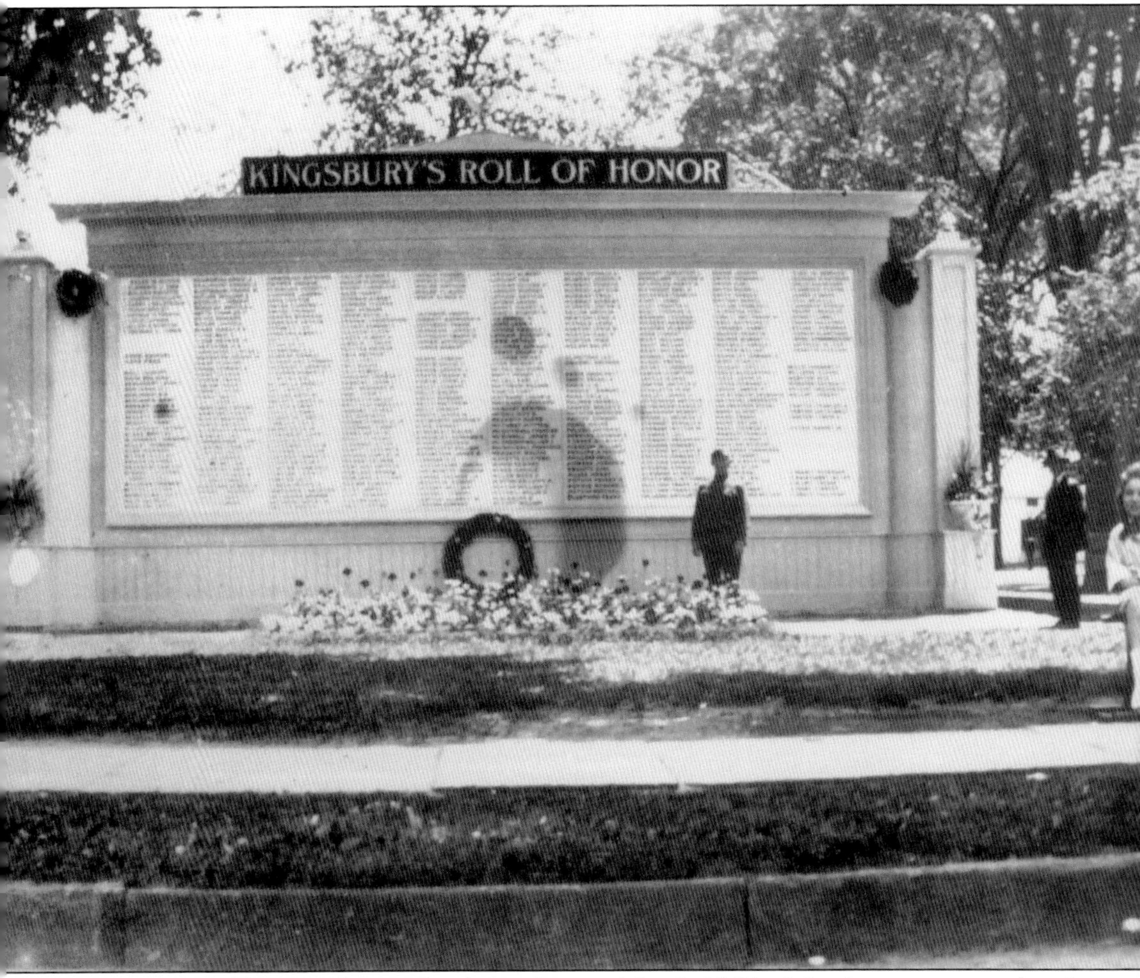

During World War I, the people of Kingsbury and Sandy Hill had this large sign erected at the north end of the village park. On the sign were placed the names of all of the men from the town who went off to serve in the armed forces. For those who were killed in action, a star was placed beside the name. A man who might be one of the returning soldiers stands in front of the sign.

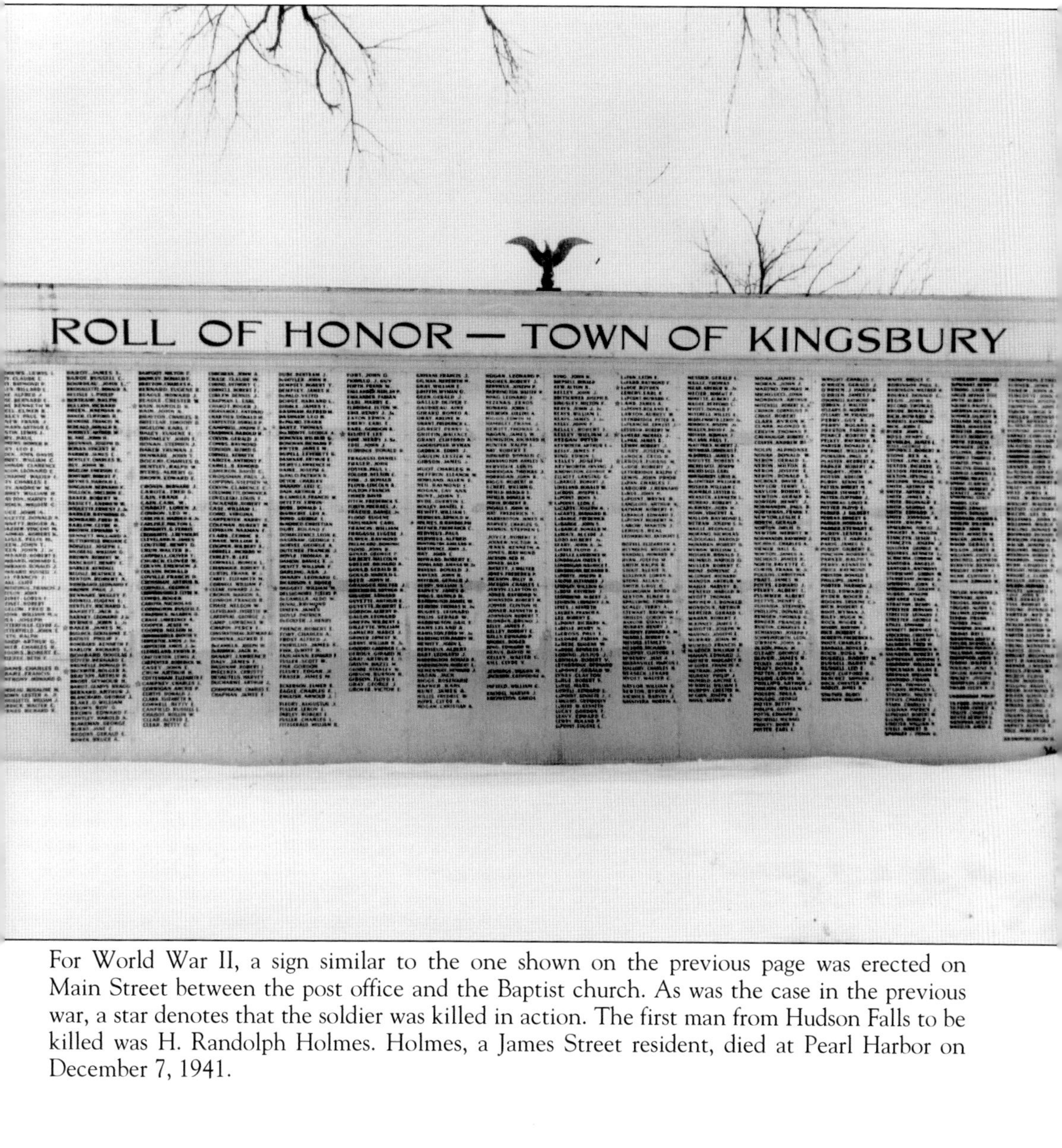

For World War II, a sign similar to the one shown on the previous page was erected on Main Street between the post office and the Baptist church. As was the case in the previous war, a star denotes that the soldier was killed in action. The first man from Hudson Falls to be killed was H. Randolph Holmes. Holmes, a James Street resident, died at Pearl Harbor on December 7, 1941.

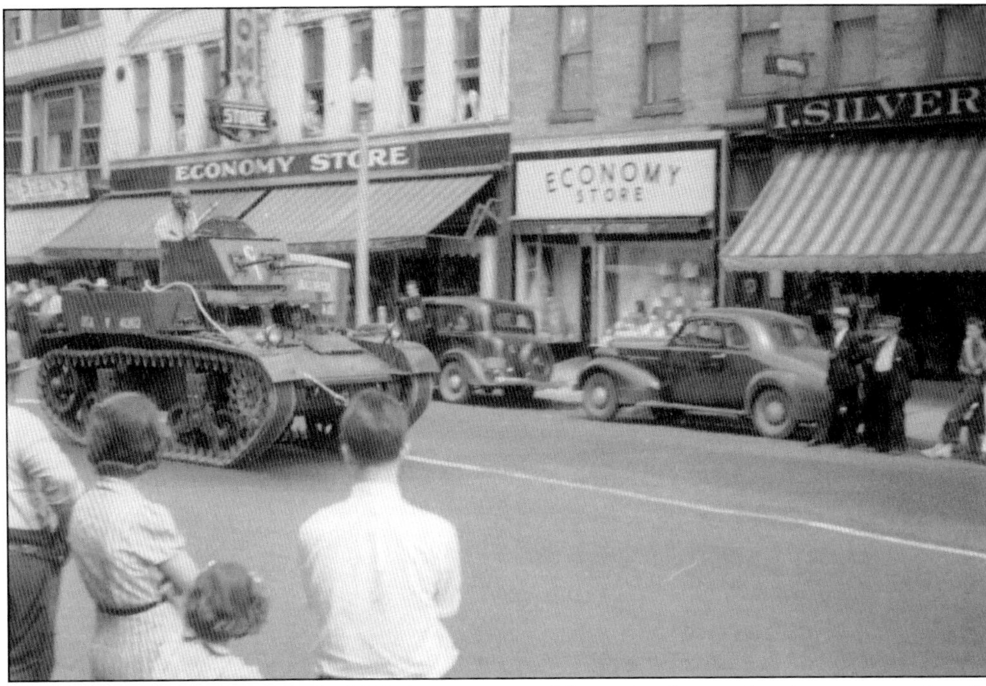

Leading up to World War II, the U.S. Army prepared for action by conducting war exercises. In June 1939, a huge exercise was held in the Plattsburgh area. Just before it took place, a military convoy passed through Hudson Falls and Kingsbury on Route 4 en route to Plattsburgh. The exercise included regular army, army reserves, and National Guard troops. In all, the solders numbered over 20,000. This is the same convoy, which on the return trip south on Route 9 through Glens Falls, reportedly took most of the day to pass through Hudson Falls.

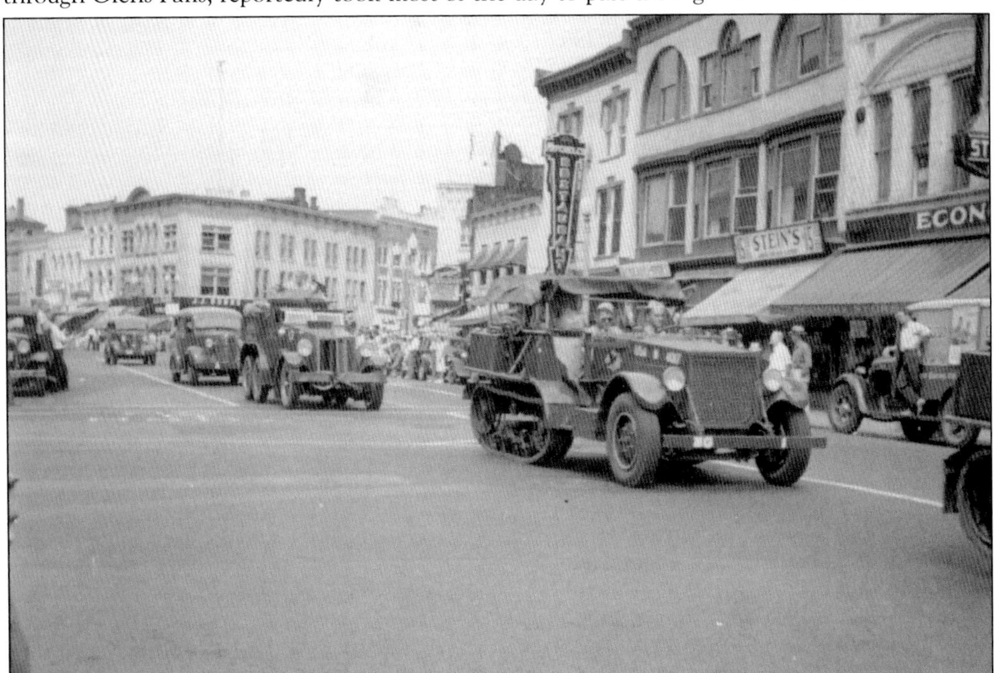

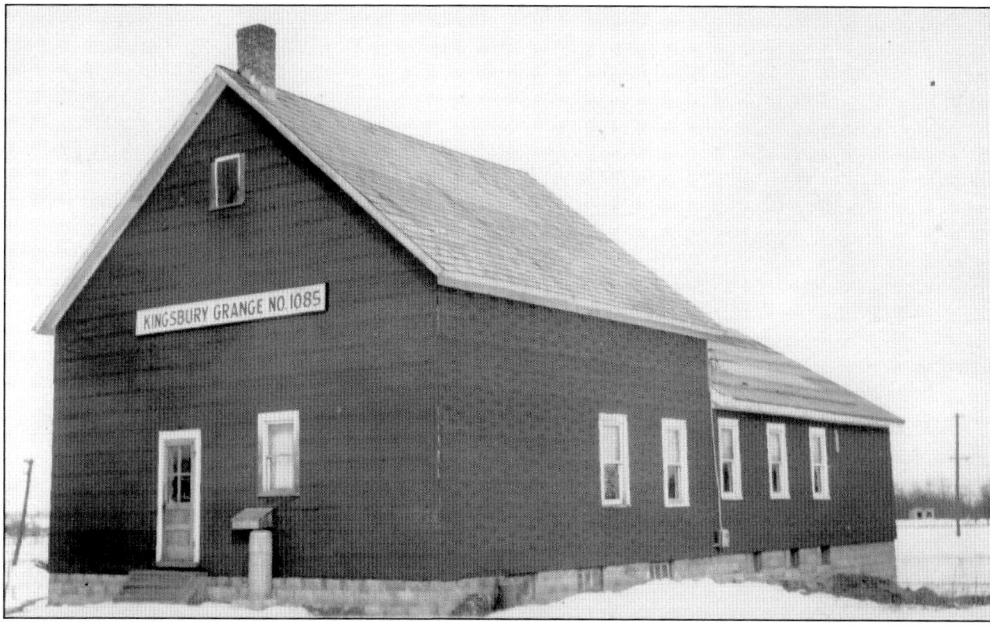

The Kingsbury Grange No. 1085 was located on Burgoyne Avenue just in from Moss Street. The Grange was chartered 1903 but did not have its own hall until this one was obtained in 1942. It took until 1945 for the work to be completed, and the Grange Hall was then dedicated. A short time after the dedication, the building burned to the ground. The Grange then bought another building on Broad Street in Hudson Falls. The Kingsbury Grange dissolved *c.* 1979.

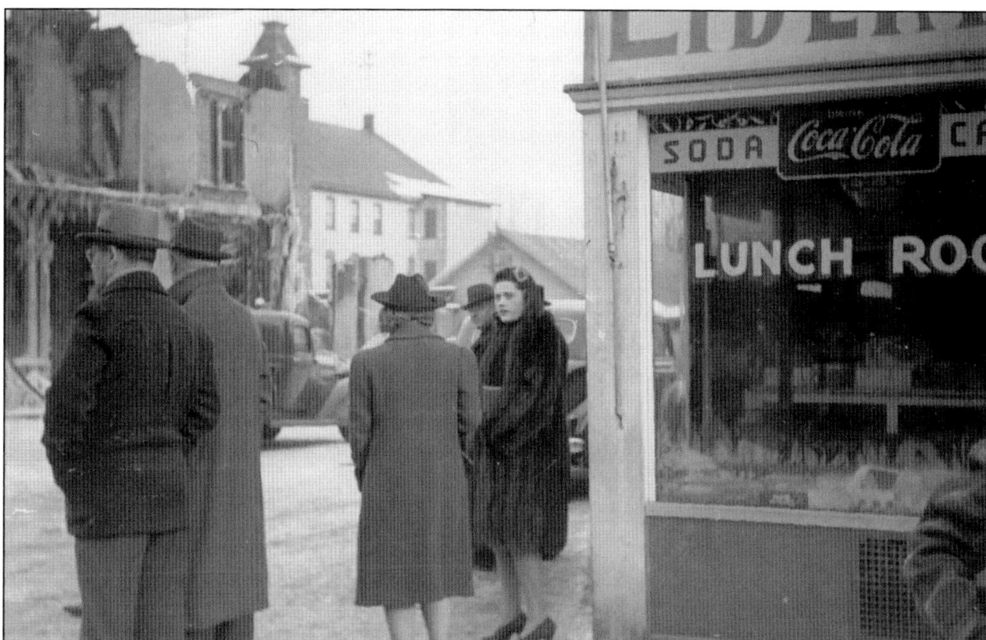

These women catch up on the morning news while participating in a long-standing village pastime, watching fires. They were out to see the early 1940s fire that struck the hotel building next door to the Strand Theatre.

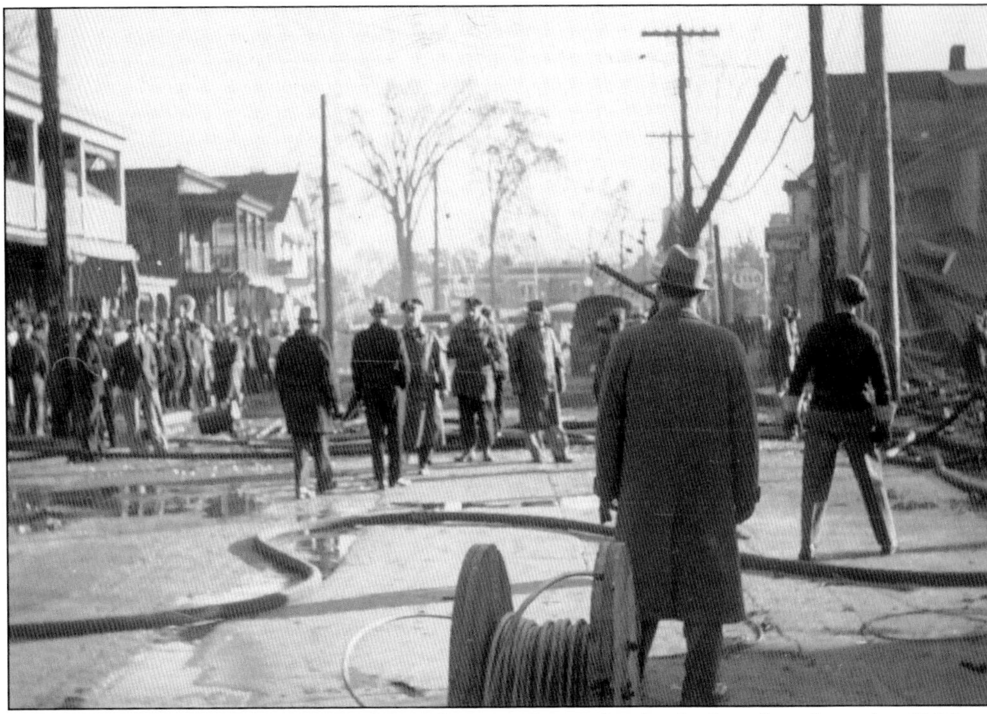

Paul Fisher, who took a number of the photographs in this book that date from the 1930s to the 1960s, took these two pictures. He worked for the *Glens Falls Times*, the afternoon paper, and was active in the fire department, as well. These photographs show the aftermath of the Riverside Hotel fire of October 1940. They show not only the destruction but also the number of people who came out to watch fires.

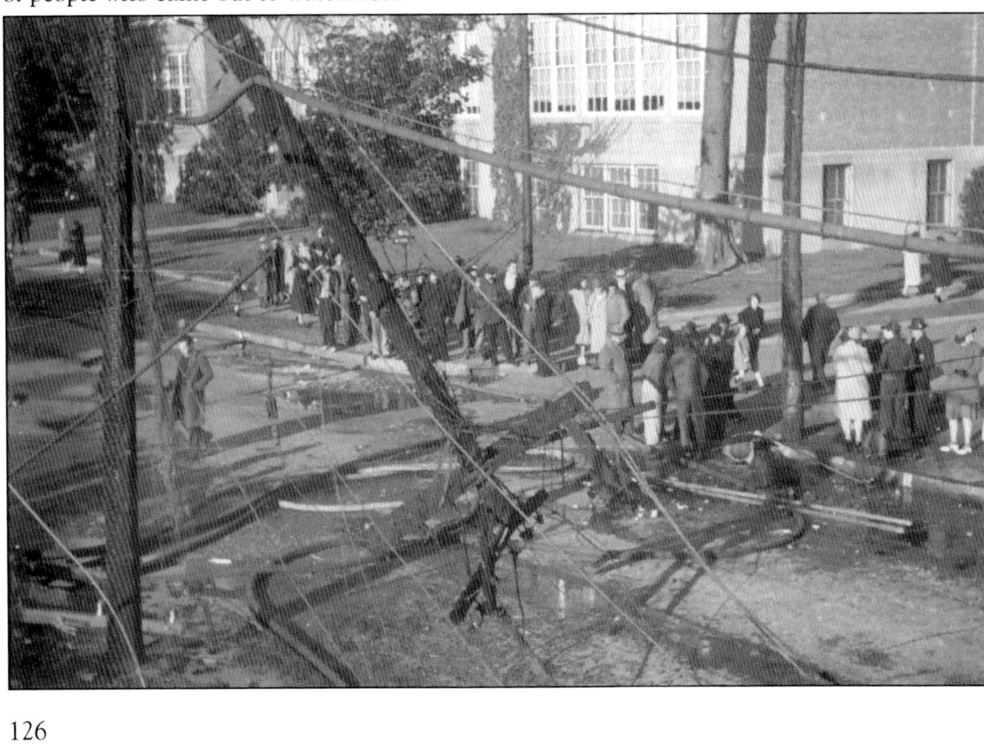

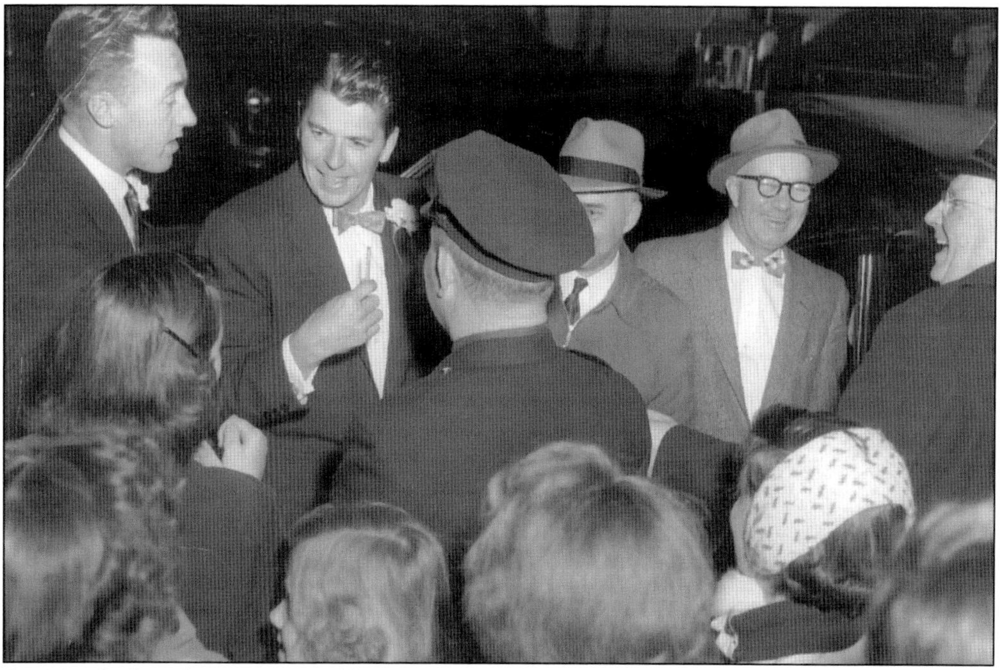

On March 5, 1957, actor Ronald Reagan visited Hudson Falls and met people in the Strand Theatre. This view shows him leaving his car. At the time who could have imagined what the future held in store for this movie star.

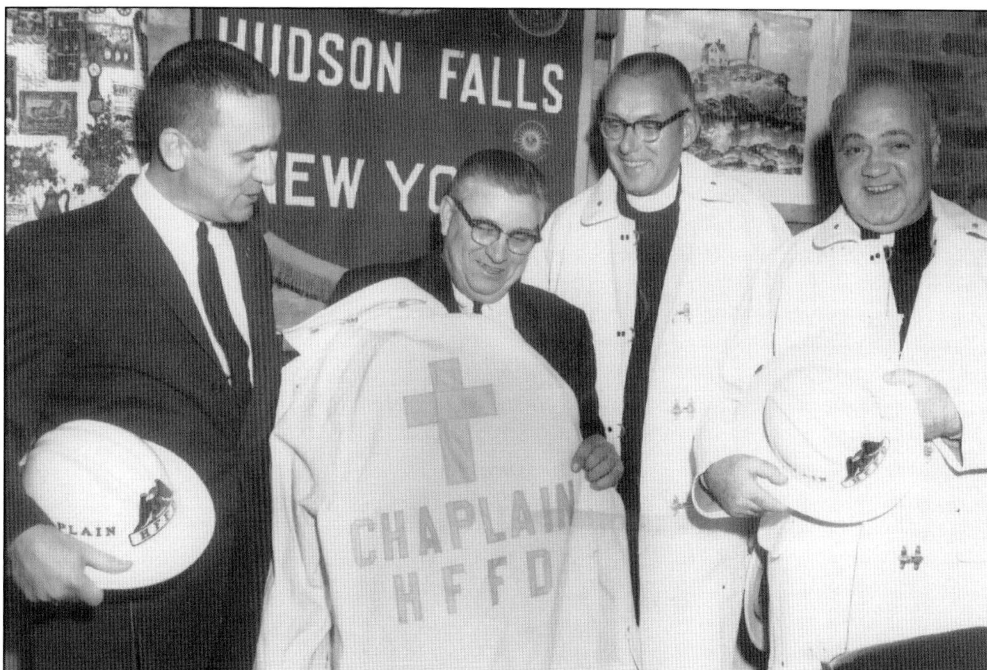

In the 1960s, the Hudson Falls Fire Department appointed three chaplains. Each was presented with white turnout gear. At the presentation are, from left to right, the Rev. George Bishop of the First Baptist Church, Fire Chief Leo J. La Belle, the Rev. Walter Lardner of Zion Episcopal Church, and the Rev. Leo Marcell of St. Paul's Church.

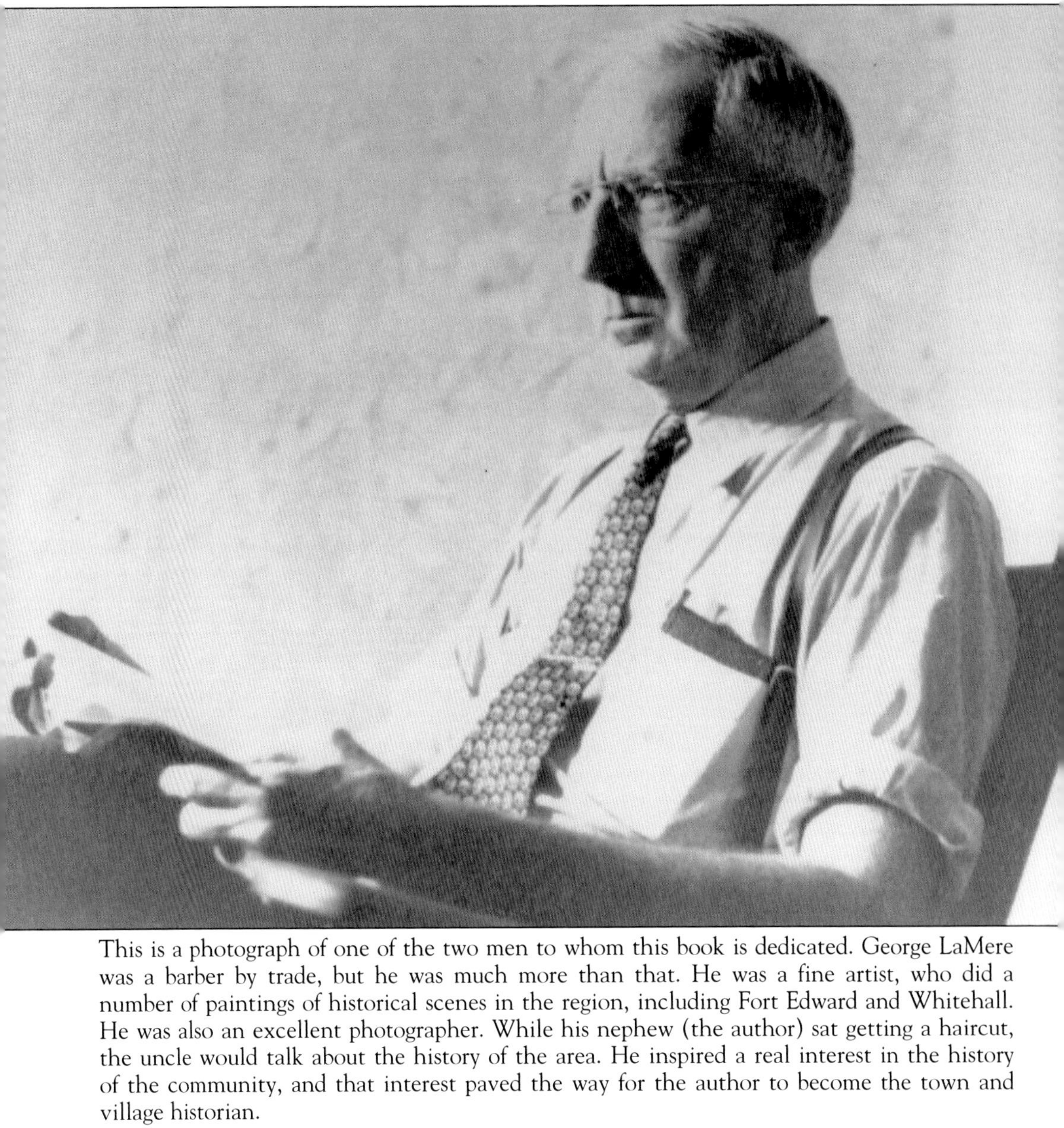

This is a photograph of one of the two men to whom this book is dedicated. George LaMere was a barber by trade, but he was much more than that. He was a fine artist, who did a number of paintings of historical scenes in the region, including Fort Edward and Whitehall. He was also an excellent photographer. While his nephew (the author) sat getting a haircut, the uncle would talk about the history of the area. He inspired a real interest in the history of the community, and that interest paved the way for the author to become the town and village historian.